The Chief Online Learning Officers' Guidebook

The Chief Online Learning Officers' Guidebook explores the essential competencies required of Chief Online Learning Officers (COLOs) using insights from real-world leadership and expert perspectives from higher education. Digital and online learning have become strategic priorities for higher education institutions working toward enrollment growth, learner engagement, revenue generation, brand diversification, and enhanced student flexibility following the initial COVID-19 lockdown. This book's unique framework substantiates and demonstrates key competencies that define the COLO role and enable advancements in the practice of online and digital higher education. Featuring over 50 contributions from COLOs, Chief Information Officers (CIOs), university presidents, and other higher education leaders, this UPCEA-endorsed guide offers practical strategies and comprehensive guidance for both current and aspiring COLOs.

Jocelyn Widmer, Ph.D., serves as the Dean for Weapons Learning Transformation at Los Alamos National Laboratory, USA. She has worked in digital and online education for more than 15 years in various faculty and leadership roles within academic colleges and as the Chief Online Learning Officer of Texas A&M University. Prior to her role at TAMU, Widmer held joint faculty appointments in the Colleges of Architecture and Public Health at both the University of Florida and Virginia Tech where she developed, administered, and taught in online and face-to-face undergraduate and graduate programs, including leading the first and only professionally accredited online master's of urban and regional planning (University of Florida) through the accreditation process.

Thomas B. Cavanagh, Ph.D., is the Vice Provost for Digital Learning at the University of Central Florida (UCF), USA. In this role, he oversees the distance learning strategy, policies, and practices of one of the nation's largest universities. Prior to UCF, he led online course design and production for Embry-Riddle Aeronautical University and has a long career in corporate e-learning and film/television. He has been recognized with a number of leading industry awards, including the Richard Jonsen Award (WCET's highest career recognition), USDLA's Leadership Award, and the 1EdTech Community Leadership Award. He has also been named a Fellow of the Online Learning Consortium.

The Chief Online Learning Officers' Guidebook

A Framework for Strategy and Practice in Higher Education

JOCELYN WIDMER AND THOMAS B. CAVANAGH

NEW YORK AND LONDON

Designed cover image: © Getty Images

First published 2025
by Routledge
605 Third Avenue, New York, NY 10158

and by Routledge
4 Park Square, Milton Park, Abingdon, Oxon, OX14 4RN

Routledge is an imprint of the Taylor & Francis Group, an informa business

ISBN: 978-1-032-81656-2 (hbk)
ISBN: 978-1-032-80143-8 (pbk)
ISBN: 978-1-003-50074-2 (ebk)

DOI: 10.4324/9781003500742

Typeset in Avenir & Dante
by SPi Technologies India Pvt Ltd (Straive)

For my parents, who invested in my education so I could commit my career to the education of others.

- Jocelyn

For Pam who has been sitting beside me, hands in the air, for all the ups and downs of our crazy roller coaster ride.

- Tom

And collectively:

For the leadership of UPCEA for leading the way in championing the work of COLOs.

Most of all, for all the "nontraditional" students pursuing higher education, balancing jobs and children, putting in the late nights and early mornings, so they can give themselves and their families a better life. You inspire us every day.

Contents

Acronym List

ACT	Academic Continuity with Technology
AI	Artificial Intelligence
AR	Augmented Reality
BYOD	Bring Your Own Device
CAO	Chief Academic Officer
CE	Continuing Education
CFO	Chief Financial Officer
CHLOE	Changing Landscape of Online Education
CIO	Chief Information Officer
COLO	Chief Online Learning Officers
EdTech	Educational Technologies
ERL	Emergency Remote Learning
ERT	Emergency Remote Instruction
F2F	Face to Face
FTE	Full Time Equivalent
HR	Human Resources
IPEDS	Integrated Postsecondary Education Data System
IR	Institutional Research
IT	Information Technology
LMS	Learning Management System
LTI	Learning Tools Interoperability
MOOC	Massive Open Online Course
OPM	Online Program Manager
OSS	Office for Student Success
QA	Quality Assurance

QEP	Quality Enhancement Plan
PCI	Payment Card Industry (also known as PCI DSS: Payment Card Industry Data Security Standard)
PCO	Professional, Continuing, and Online
R&D	Research and Development
RACI	Responsible, Accountable, Consulted, Informed model
RASCI	Responsible, Accountable, Support, Consulted, Informed model
RCM	Responsibility Center Management
ROI	Return on Investment
SCH	Student Credit Hour
SCNC	Some College No Credential
VR	Virtual Reality
XR	Extended Reality

Foreword

I vividly recall hearing about a new addition to the president's cabinet at my last institution. During a meeting of the academic council, our provost announced that a faculty member with a strong affinity for technology was slated to become the institution's first chief information officer. I was a bit surprised by this bold elevation of the role to a C-suite position, but in retrospect, I shouldn't have been. This was in the early 2000s, when the frenzied pace of technology had changed ... well ... everything. Institutions *needed* a CIO, both to signal the importance of the work of building the infrastructure of a modern university and to bring organizational coherence to this brave new world.

I also remember wondering (not out loud, but in time I would find my voice) why my division's mission of serving adult and nontraditional learners was not similarly elevated to a major institutional priority. After all, the median age at many tuition-dependent institutions like mine was in the mid-twenties. A strong case could have been made that serving this population successfully should have been paramount. Yet that mission was typically an afterthought for a legacy culture almost entirely organized around serving a shrinking number of residential students. If the future of the institution depended on effectively serving nontraditional learners, what role could be more important than accommodating their complicated lives?

I thought the answer to that question should be self-evident. But it took a long time for most institutions to recognize this strategic imperative, and longer still to elevate online leaders to the level required to drive transformative change. Some have still not done so, but they are now the outliers.

Indeed, we are now witnessing a parallel development to the rise of CIOs, as more and more institutions have created chief online learning officers (COLOs). They often have titles like vice provost for online and graduate education, dean of the school for professional studies, executive director of academic innovation, or chancellor of the global campus. This is their time, their decade, just as it was for CIOs a generation ago.

A reflection on how we got here helps us to understand the special DNA of today's COLOs. Apart from a few notable but lonely pioneers in the 1990s, the evolution of today's COLO occurred in three distinct phases that more or less correspond to the three decades of the 2000s.

The first major cohort of online leaders came in the first decade of the new century. Few would have thought of them as COLOs in the sense that we know them today. Like me, they were mostly leaders of professional continuing education looking for new and better ways to reach their core audience – adult and nontraditional learners who were unable to make it to campus for degree completion or professional master's programs.

While those newer to online learning may not recognize the family resemblance to professional continuing education, both career orientations should be situated historically within what I call "the great tradition of expanding access to higher education." Their common genes can be traced back more than a century to the novel idea that the benefits of the university should extend beyond the walls of campus to serve the needs of the state and nation. It was this revolutionary vision, often called the Wisconsin Idea, that fueled the founding of UPCEA in 1915. As Charles Van Hise, president of the University of Wisconsin and host of the first UPCEA conference, wrote: "This then is the purpose of University Extension – to carry light and opportunity to every human being in all parts of the nation; this is the only adequate ideal of service for the university."

The skillset required for building online learning units was a natural fit for those working in professional continuing education. These leaders collaborated with faculty and other academic deans to bring these programs online, and with IT on enterprise solutions. They developed online student services, marketing and enrollment management strategies tailored for the adult market, and new business models that were intentionally different from the rest of the institution.

In other words, they brought the same entrepreneurial mindset to the complicated business of online learning that had long defined their mission of expanding access to higher education. In fact, a common critique of online learning was that it was a misguided attempt to generate revenue and therefore suspect when compared to the core of the institution. The reality is that online was, and remains so today, primarily a means of stabilizing overall enrollments by expanding access for underserved learners.

The next major phase of online leadership took place last decade, from roughly the end of the Great Recession in 2010 to the onset of the pandemic in 2020. This is when the elevation of online learning to a major institutional priority often led to new organizational structures designed to facilitate growth and acceptance from faculty.

While many online operations remained under schools or divisions managed by senior leaders of professional and continuing education, many others were repositioned as separate, standalone online units. Still, others moved to decentralized models, in which each college or school had its own online learning staff. Apart from some variations of this last model, the common denominator was the elevation of senior leaders to champion academic innovation.

The third and most dramatic phase of development began in this decade, when exposure to emergency remote instruction during the pandemic evolved into a standard expectation for learners of all kinds. This introduced a new dynamic that would forever alter the landscape of higher education. All faculty and students experienced online education for an extended period of time, and it was impossible to un-ring that bell.

This current "decade of the COLO" could not have come at a better time for higher education. We face strong headwinds: the enrollment cliff, declining financial assistance from the states, and the devaluation of a college degree in public surveys. Now the question is not whether online learning should be a major institutional priority, but how best to fulfill its potential for strategic transformation.

This expansive vision of online learning and leadership is what excited me most about my role at UPCEA. I wanted to help elevate positions like mine to where I thought they belonged: vital partners in shaping the future of their institutions. During this inflection point for higher education and its evolving place within our society, I believe an effective COLO has more potential to transform an institution than any position apart from the president.

However unorthodox this viewpoint may appear to the academic establishment, the ability to attract and retain non-residential students is the single most important differentiator between success and failure among tuition-dependent institutions. If they are not able to attract online learners, they are likely to preside over a declining number of learners with the interest and wherewithal to become full-time residential students. Even elite private and flagship public institutions, which are far less tuition-dependent, have recognized two inescapable truths: academic innovation is essential to remain competitive, and most innovation is likely to be digital.

I'm honored to have been asked to write this Foreword to *The Chief Online Learning Officers' Guidebook*. The contributors to this volume include many of the greatest architects of the modern online learning enterprise. I leave you now in their very capable hands.

Robert Hansen, Ph.D.
CEO, UPCEA

Section 1

The COLO Context

This section provides an overview of the advent of the COLO in the U.S. higher education context over the past two decades. It also includes a discussion of how the role has evolved among universities that have gone through iterative cycles of centralization and decentralization of the functions that fall under the purview of the COLO. Included in this section are key socioeconomic moments that have served as inflection points along the evolutionary trajectory of online and digital education in the U.S.

DOI: 10.4324/9781003500742-1

The COLO Profile 1

Introduction

For everyone on a college or university campus with responsibility for online learning, whether they had the title of Chief Online Learning Officer (COLO) or something else (Dean, Vice Provost, Director, Assistant Vice President, etc.), there came a moment in March 2020 when they were summoned to a meeting with institutional leadership to implement a plan to immediately convert all instruction to remote delivery. The nature of the COVID-19 pandemic, with its accompanying societal lockdowns, meant the temporary closing of physical campuses and the inability to conduct face-to-face instruction. Virtual learning became a metaphorical lifeboat for all of higher education, enabling institutions to continue delivering instruction, faculty and staff to continue employment, and, most importantly, students to continue their education without falling behind.

Although the nature of emergency remote instruction (ERT), with its reliance on a rapidly developed, synchronous delivery of learning, differed significantly from the more established, intentionally designed, asynchronous model of online learning, the pandemic put a bright spotlight on the criticality of online learning for all institutions. Even after the acute emergency response was no longer necessary and institutions returned to pre-pandemic models of instruction, many colleges and universities came to realize (perhaps for the first time, or with a new focus) the strategic importance of online learning in serving the 21st-century student.

What had previously only been the concern of fully online institutions or those with large, established online initiatives, was now an imperative for all types of institutions, small and large, private and public, serving both traditional and adult learners. Online learning was no longer relegated to an

DOI: 10.4324/9781003500742-2

extension campus or considered an ancillary activity exclusively for students at a distance. Pandemic-era high school graduates were now arriving on campus expecting robust, quality digital options. These changing expectations bring the need for qualified, competent leadership to not just help articulate a digital learning strategy but to execute that strategy and ensure the institution's continued relevance to an increasingly online student population. As we move past the first quarter of the 21st century, higher education is arguably entering a new age of the COLO.

Defining the COLO

In many ways, the role of the COLO is following a similar trajectory to the evolution and ascent of the Chief Information Officer (CIO) within higher education. Although there were cases prior to the 1990s and early 2000s, it was around that time that colleges and universities really began to recognize the strategic value of information technology (IT) in achieving institutional goals. With the widespread ubiquity of personal computers, IT took on a new importance for serving students, employees, and other stakeholders.

Self-service class registration, online tuition and fee payments, research computing capabilities, employee payroll, benefits management, procurement and accounting, and numerous other activities became actualized and scaled through technology. It became clear to campus leadership that IT was more than simple "plumbing" infrastructure; it was a strategic institutional asset. Colleges and universities needed an executive leader to oversee IT strategy, planning, and infrastructure. While titles for this role varied, such as Director of IT or Vice President of Technology Services, they began to coalesce around the CIO label, even if the person inhabiting the role also carried another executive-level title (VP, AVP, Vice Provost, etc.).

Even before the COVID-19 pandemic, online learning had been growing steadily for many years. Today, it remains more relevant than ever. As cited in the 2024 CHLOE Report:

> online learning continues to scale, fueled by broadening student demand and met with an increasingly robust and strategic institutional response. While different sectors may focus on specific populations and offerings, online learning is now integral to nearly all institutions.
>
> (Simunich et al., 2024)

ERT during the pandemic further expanded the adoption of virtual learning and accelerated its acceptance as a legitimate learning modality capable of the same quality and outcomes as traditional, classroom-based instruction. Similar to the evolution of IT, online learning has become an essential tool in the academic enterprise and requires both institutional strategy and competent leadership.

While the title of COLO has not been adopted as universally as CIO, the COLO role has emerged as a discrete function at most institutions (Fredericksen, 2017). Embodied in a variety of titles, the role is generally consistent: to oversee the online learning initiative of a college or university. This may involve leading a team of internal staff such as instructional designers, media producers, or even faculty. Or it may revolve around stewarding one or more partnerships with outside enablers such as online program management companies (OPMs).

UPCEA updated the definition of a COLO in 2023 (from the original 2017 definition). This definition was the work of UPCEA's Council of COLOs and was intended to be general enough to account for the variability of the role while still being specific enough to define expectations. UPCEA's new definition is:

> A Chief Online Learning Officer (COLO) is the primary leader for an online, digital, or other technology-enhanced postsecondary enterprise and can have responsibilities inclusive of, but not limited to, digital and hybrid learning, instructional design, student experience, and faculty development (whether at the unit, college, or institutional level). They influence and/or make critical path decisions in strategic collaboration with other institutional leaders (e.g. outsourcing operational aspects vs. building internal teams, etc.)
>
> COLOs advocate for and with stakeholders to advance the strategy, leadership, and vision of postsecondary online education in keeping with an institution's mission and values. COLOs often bring business acumen and an entrepreneurial approach, and serve as conveners for innovation within higher education institutions. UPCEA recognizes there is diversity in the title of such roles, depending on institutional type, culture, and maturity of the online enterprise.
>
> (UPCEA, 2023a)

The reporting line for an individual COLO will vary greatly between institutions, ranging from reporting to the president as a cabinet-level position, to a Senior Vice Provost, to even the CIO. However, the most common reporting line for a COLO is to the institution's Chief Academic Officer (CAO)/Provost. This seems wholly appropriate given that the role is core to a college/university's academic mission. (After all, the word "learning" is in the COLO label.)

According to research from Fredericksen et al. (2024), currently, more than two-third of sitting COLOs report to a Provost or other senior academic leader, and their titles are most commonly Director/Executive Director or VP/AVP. Most of these COLOs have responsibility for the full gamut of digital learning at their institutions, including fully online, hybrid online, and web-enhanced online delivery modalities. Further, functions most likely to be unified with the COLO include instructional design, the learning management system (LMS), online policy development, academic technology, and faculty development. Additional implications of the COLO's reporting structure will be addressed in Chapter Four.

Pathways to the COLO Role

Unlike the typical pathway to a role such as CAO, the pathway to become a COLO is as varied as the individuals occupying the role. There are well-established paths to becoming a CAO/Provost. These might include beginning a career as an assistant professor, earning tenure and becoming an associate professor, becoming a full professor, serving as a department chair, perhaps a stint as an associate dean or a Vice Provost, and serving as a dean. When someone occupies a CAO role, there are valid assumptions about that person's expected academic background and preparation. For someone who aspires to become a CAO, it is fairly straightforward to identify the kinds of experiences and milestone positions he/she needs. Earning these positions and succeeding at them may not be so straightforward, but identifying what steps are necessary to become a CAO is established and evident.

In contrast, there are not yet any well-worn pathways to follow for someone who aspires to become a COLO. Those currently in the role have a variety of backgrounds, including serving as a faculty member, having experience in corporate training/e-learning, advancing as an instructional designer or technologist, having related experience in government or non-profit organizations, serving in leadership roles in educational technology/publishing/professional services companies, and experience in other academic leadership positions, among others. Approximately three-fifth of current COLOs were promoted from within their institutions (Fredericksen et al., 2024). This variability is partially due to the emerging nature of the position. The COLO role is nascent as a recognized, strategic function and, as such, has not yet reached its equilibrium in finding both the expected pathways for becoming a COLO, as well as its position within an institution's reporting structure.

Attributes of Successful COLOs

UPCEA has identified a set of competencies and attributes for successful leaders of Professional, Continuing, and Online (PCO) learning enterprises. These statements are aligned with UPCEA's Hallmarks of Excellence in Online Leadership. To better understand the competencies and attributes, it is useful to first begin with the context established by the Hallmarks of Excellence.

UPCEA's Hallmarks of Excellence in Online Leadership (UPCEA, 2017)

- Advocacy and Leadership within the University
- Entrepreneurial Initiatives
- Faculty Support
- Student Support
- Digital Technology
- External Advocacy and Leadership Beyond the University
- Professionalism

The competencies and attributes statements are complementary to the Hallmarks of Excellence and provide a compendium of concrete skills that COLOs should cultivate in order to be successful. While the specific institutional context in which a COLO is working might require more facility with one particular competency over another, they are all important to position the COLO for success. Any aspiring COLO, or COLO who aspires to be effective, should embrace and intentionally develop these competencies and attributes.

UPCEA's Competency and Attribute Statements for Professional, Continuing, and Online Practitioners (UPCEA, 2023b)

Entrepreneurship, Partnerships, and Relationship Building

1. Builds internal and external relationships
2. Employs an entrepreneurial mindset and business acumen

Resource Management

3. Manages overall operational resources (people, space, and money)
4. Manages facilities
5. Manages human resources
6. Motivates and develops team members
7. Understands the laws, regulations, policies, governance, and institutional contexts

8. Understands the implications of financial models, revenue sources, and higher education budgeting processes

Supporting and Advocating for Faculty and Students

9. Marshals and supports requirements to recruit, retain, and develop faculty
10. Identifies, recruits, and retains students

Program Planning

11. Plans, executes, and evaluates programs
12. Understands curriculum design, sourcing, and revisions inclusive of learning strategies and theories

Marketing, Research, and Evaluation

13. Employs market research
14. Possesses an understanding of marketing strategies and principles

Information and Digital Technology

15. Possesses functional and operational knowledge of information management and digital technology

Critical Thinking and Decision-Making

16. Engages in analytical and critical thinking
17. Engages in inductive and deductive reasoning
18. Engages in evidence-based decision-making
19. Navigates and/or resolves complex and sensitive situations
20. Thinks strategically

Integrity, Ethics, and Professionalism

21. Adheres to professional and personal standards and/or demonstrates conduct reflective of the ethics and theories
22. Models effective leadership and demonstrates a willingness to provide direction
23. Possesses social perceptiveness and orientation
24. Demonstrates broadly-accepted personal and professional attributes
25. Engages in active learning to stay current

The source materials for both the Competencies and Attributes statements and the Hallmarks of Excellence contain significantly more detail than can be included here, and anyone interested in understanding the expectations

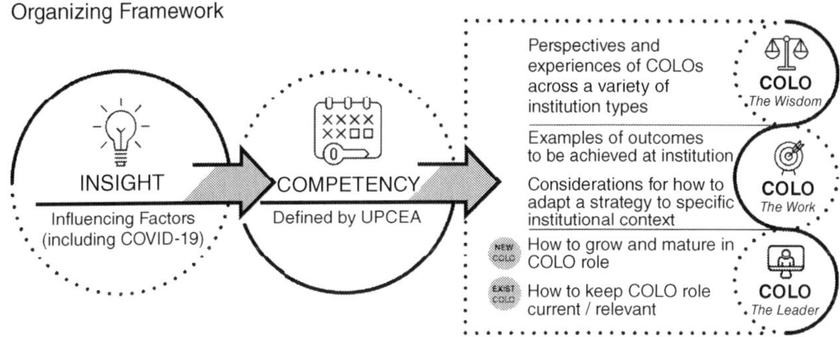

Figure 1.1 Competency Connections

associated with acquiring a COLO position and succeeding in it would be wise to familiarize him/herself with them. They are rich resources that can assist aspiring COLO to identify gaps in their preparation and implement a strategic professional development and career plan to progress toward that professional goal.

In Chapters 2–9 of this guidebook, you will see a table labeled *Competency Connection*. These brief summaries link each UPCEA PCO competency to key insights, influencing factors (including those resulting from the COVID-19 pandemic), and related institutional risks (Figure 1.1). Each of these chapters explores a different competency and its importance for a COLO's success.

The remaining four chapters explore additional aspects of the COLO role, including related leadership roles outside of academia. In total, the competencies and additional topics provide a comprehensive overview of the responsibilities, expectations, and challenges associated with the modern COLO role. Additional key elements of this *Guidebook* are the Expert Perspectives that accompany each chapter. These essays offer real-world insights, observations, case studies, and practical experience from the nation's leading online learning experts.

References

Fredericksen, E., (2017). A National Study of Online Learning Leaders in U.S. Higher Education. *Online Learning, 21*(2). Retrieved from https://olj.onlinelearningconsortium.org/index.php/olj/article/view/1164/270

Fredericksen, E., Simunich, B. & Uranus, J. (2024) *COLO Profile Study 2024 – A National Research Project about Chief Online Learning Officers.* Presented at OLC Accelerate 2024, Orlando, FL. https://olc.secure-platform.com/accelerate/gallery/rounds/82030/schedule/items/17650

Simunich, B., Garrett, R., Fredericksen, E. E., McCormack, M., Robert, J., & Ubell, R. (2024). *CHLOE 9: Strategy Shift: Institutions Respond to Sustained Online Demand, The Changing Landscape of Online Education, 2024*. Retrieved from the Quality Matters website: https://qualitymatters.org/qa-resources/resource-center/articles-resources/CHLOE-9-report-2024

UPCEA. (2023a, February 17). *Definition Update: Chief Online Learning Officer (COLO)*. Retrieved from https://upcea.edu/definition-update-chief-online-learning-officer-colo/

UPCEA. (2023b). *Competency and Attribute Statements for Professional, Continuing, and Online Practitioners*. Retrieved from https://upcea.edu/competency-and-attribute-statements-for-professional-continuing-and-online-practitioners/

UPCEA. (2017). *UPCEA Hallmarks of Excellence in Online Leadership*. Retrieved from https://upcea.edu/wp-content/uploads/2017/03/UPCEA-Hallmarks-of-Excellence-in-Online-Leadership.pdf

Expert Perspectives

- Deborah Keyek-Fransen, University of Utah
- Todd Nicolet, University of North Carolina Chapel Hill
- Josh Steele, University of Tennessee, Knoxville
- Eric E. Fredericksen, University of Rochester

Deborah Keyek-Franssen, Ph.D.

Associate Vice President and Dean, University Connected Learning – University of Utah

The path to becoming a COLO will vary, especially during this period of emergence for the role. Because there is no pre-defined pathway to the role yet, deep experience in key areas matters. A COLO will benefit from a background and proficiency in a broad range of areas such as teaching and learning, including curricular and instructional design across multiple modalities; educational technology tools and platforms; and the higher education ecosystem broadly, including governance, high-level strategy and goals, and the business of online education.

The COLO title itself is a hint to the heart of the role: a commitment to effective teaching and learning – amplified with the judicious use of technology, platforms, and data – to enhance online learning and student success. A solid background in instructional and curricular design is paramount. A COLO might get this background through an advanced degree in education (for instance, in instructional or learning experience design) or, with intentionality, self-study, and consistent use of a campus' teaching excellence unit, might successfully gain transferable design and pedagogical skills in a specific academic domain as a graduate or adjunct instructor, or a faculty member. A COLO must have sufficient experience planning, implementing, and measuring learning (including in synchronous remote or asynchronous online modalities), in which objectives, pedagogical strategies such as active or problem-based learning, and assessments are aligned to foster student success. A COLO should also have experience in a broader curricular or programmatic design that privileges the specific needs of adult or returning online learners for flexible, accessible offerings that support their varied schedules and credential goals. A strong academic background is crucial for a COLO's ability to persuade faculty to use effective practices in the design and facilitation of online learning in the service of student success, and for the ability to support and measure student engagement, satisfaction, and performance.

Familiarity with (and maybe even excitement for!) a wide-range of educational technology tools and platforms will help a COLO support online learning and, more importantly, innovate across academic domains and pedagogical practices. Whether or not the COLO is responsible for all educational technology services on campus, an understanding of how IT services are provisioned and run at a desired level of usability and stability will allow a COLO to choose and integrate tools and platforms for online learning. While being a power user of educational technology tools and platforms will help prepare a future COLO, there is nothing like the experience of working in an IT services unit that could help a COLO ensure that online tools and platforms are not just effective and aligned with student learning outcomes but also accessible, secure, stable, and appropriately integrated with enterprise systems. Experience in IT services would also enable a COLO to adequately address both practice-based and technical training needs for faculty and students, from self-help resources to workshops, one-on-one coaching, and help desk support.

Experience that gives a deep understanding of postsecondary education as an ecosystem, an ecosystem with a long history, with distinct ways of doing business, and with often beloved quirks, is also a critical requirement for the role. A successful COLO will have familiarity with and an appreciation for governance structures that guide decision-making, as well as the mission and strategic goals that drive institutional priorities. A COLO must be able to navigate these structures to ensure that online programs meet the same rigorous standards as their on-campus counterparts and also meet the university's goals for revenue generation, ROI, and workforce development. A COLO can acquire these skills in a variety of roles, including as faculty or staff. Observing or participating in academic governance meetings can provide empathy for faculty and instructors and be an excellent primer for how work gets done on campus. Though still fairly rare in higher education, experience in assessing market demand for online degrees or microcredentials and in the development of supporting materials such as pro formas and profit and loss statements would round out a successful COLO's background.

The role of a COLO requires the ability to integrate diverse experiences and translate them into actionable strategies that support online learning. Whether a COLO's background is in teaching, technology, or administration, the key is to develop a holistic understanding of how these areas intersect to create effective online programs. A COLO must be a leader who advocates for the necessary resources, builds relationships across the institution, and fosters an environment where online learning can thrive. That there are as many pathways to that leadership role as there are current COLOs ensures that the role will remain flexible and innovative for some time to come.

Todd Nicolet, Ph.D.

Vice Provost for Digital and Lifelong Learning, The University of North Carolina at Chapel Hill

The competencies UPCEA identifies provide a useful set of areas to explore as one considers roles and responsibilities for career progression. A challenge, however, is the sheer breadth of skills to develop. One solution is to seek responsibility for leading or administering a single, online program as that will require developing strategies and making decisions across most of the competency areas. For example, a program director often represents the program, hires and manages instructors and support staff, informs marketing and recruitment efforts, coordinates student support, and more. Being responsible for determining and implementing strategy for a single program provides deep experience in putting effective strategy into practice that can be adapted across the various program contexts you will experience as a COLO.

Another approach would be to seek administrative roles that focus on operations and management of services within or across units. These experiences not only increase exposure to multiple contexts but also highlight how working with different stakeholders and across programmatic needs can change opportunities and challenges. Most COLO roles are ultimately service providers for an institution, identifying and often supporting solutions that need to work efficiently and effectively across fields, programs, and academic units. Building experience leading service teams provides a strong foundation for this key function.

While I regularly inform my work as a COLO through experiences both from leading a specific online program and from broader administrative responsibilities, one of the most important skills to hone and continue developing has been influencing the decisions and actions of others. If the COLO role includes a portfolio of programs managed within their unit, they can take full accountability for those strategies, teams, and programs. Often, however, some or even the majority of programs reside in other units, meaning some other leader is ultimately responsible for the key decisions that will determine whether a program succeeds. For these programs, implementing the diverse set of competencies actually means getting others to reach a similar conclusion, to implement based on that guidance, and to build their own competencies to most effectively support their programs.

As the COLO role becomes established, clearer domains of authority and decision-making may become more consistent, but until then a key responsibility will be influencing others to make decisions that align with institutional priorities and industry best practices. The successful COLO must listen carefully to stakeholders, assessing needs and restating goals to make them explicit. The resulting framework provides an opportunity to share expertise and recommendations, focusing on the most effective approaches to help units achieve expressed goals. To build these skills, seek opportunities to manage in all directions: up to a supervisor, down to direct reports, and, in particular, sidewise to peers. The work a COLO does with deans and program directors depends on demonstrating expertise and support without wielding authority, or campus leaders will just work around you.

To further complicate efforts, at most institutions, the COLO role is relatively new and often poorly understood. Campus leaders may be unsure what responsibilities are included and may forget to include the COLO on key committees or in strategic discussions. Deans and academic leaders are often used to making independent decisions and may see a new central role as losing control or limiting options. In other words, the role is often not positioned well for influence, and the successful COLO must persist through these challenges to help programs achieve stated goals within the larger institutional framework.

The successful COLO looks for opportunities to shine and demonstrate their expertise, guidance, and leadership but also pays attention to when staying behind the scenes will be more effective. You can often move the needle farther and faster when providing consultation for others who will lead an effort rather than being the visible agent of change. While that may seem counterintuitive to establishing a new leadership role, the accumulation of successful changes and interactions across an institution, both visible and indirect, will establish a COLO's expertise to help them become the "go to" resource for leaders and programs, which is at the heart of the role.

Josh Steele, Ph.D.

Associate Vice Dean of Digital Learning, University of Tennessee, Knoxville

As indicated in the opening few paragraphs of this chapter, the COVID-19 pandemic was a critical moment in the fashioning of COLO roles at many institutions, mine included. It was with the pandemic that the University of Tennessee, Knoxville, created a brand-new AVP position within the Office of the Provost to develop and guide a centralized support structure for developing online programs and online courses. While online courses and even programs existed within the university, they were operated out of the decentralized academic units, developed, managed, and (maybe) marketed by their own blood, sweat, and (numerous) tears. The creation of the COLO position marked a definitive course change for the university.

In assessing my experience with respect to the "Pathways to the COLO Role" section above, I would squarely be defined as "experience in other academic positions, among others." My start in higher education was as an academic advisor for fully online students, and I worked in student services-type roles for more than a decade. I was not sure that a COLO-type position would be in my future, because it seemed as though my experience was an outlier to many of those in these senior leadership positions. However, I have come to believe that advising is an excellent pathway to COLO positions. Advisors thrive on deep, meaningful relationships with students and are frequently shifting between strategies to support the progression of individual students, or broad interventions that aid larger cohorts. Advisors also are acutely aware of the ways students navigate all components of the university, including student-facing portals, registration systems, and degree audit software. Relationship building, big-picture strategizing, managing technologies, and the willingness to get one's hands dirty are all key components of the COLO role.

At each institution where I've worked, there has been a reality of "flying the plane while we build it," specifically in retrofitting an infrastructure into existing university systems. This typically has meant bringing together IT, Institutional Research (IR), Registrar's Offices, and others to create standardized coding structures for online programs and students within the Student Information System (SIS). While not the most exciting meetings I've ever participated in, they were critical to our successes in building a culture around supporting the post-traditional student population. The joy comes from the future opportunities that came from this work – the ability to develop accurate data dashboards, craft customized online student experiences or journeys, develop outreach campaigns and experience surveys that provide deeper insights, or even just to bill a student appropriately. I have found that the ability to ask and answer, "what would make it easier for an advisor to support an online learner," has been helpful for these types of projects.

The types of projects I experience as a COLO regularly oscillate between the sexy and the unsexy. For every conversation about generative AI's impact on learning, there is a three-year project to negotiate revised intellectual property and course ownership practices; for every idea about AR or VR for learning, there is an 18-month project to add a new field to the SIS; for every engaging faculty-development workshop, there is building a coalition to manage the institution's response to changing state and federal regulations related to online education; for every exciting new program launch, there are (likely several) proposed revisions of student policies to be more inclusive of online learners that no one has looked at in 30 years. The student experience is central to all of these concerns, though in dramatically different ways. This is not to suggest that other backgrounds are any less viable for COLO roles. The fact that my background is in advising/student experience means that I've had a learning curve with other parts of the portfolio, including instructional design and course production. My argument here is that, with respect to COLO positions, student experience professionals are at least of equal stature to faculty or instructional design backgrounds. No matter where one is coming from, there will be areas in which one has more pronounced strengths than in other areas. Developing a network that can provide support and mentorship within those areas is a great way to establish one's vision for leadership in these broad roles. For those of us who come from a background of servicing students, the COLO role gives us a chance to continue to design a student experience at scale, for a population that historically has been left out of many of our institutions.

Eric E. Fredericksen, Ed.D.

Associate Vice President & Professor, University of Rochester

Several years ago, a national study of online leaders at universities (Fredericksen, 2017) and a national study of online learning leaders at community colleges (Fredericksen, 2018) provided a baseline understanding of the individuals providing leadership to this vital academic activity in U.S. Higher Education.

Those complementary studies helped shape a composite of the leaders guiding institutions in this important and innovative area. In general, this research painted a picture of a very seasoned leader with significant background in higher education, as well as a blend of relevant experiences including teaching (online and classroom), IT, management, instructional design and curriculum development, and educational research. It was clear that presidents and provosts have selected proven and established individuals to be on point for their colleges and universities.

In addition to the individual characteristics of the online learning leaders, the studies also explored information about the role of the leader, scope of their position, organizational structure and dynamics, and other institutional contextual elements. It was identified that most online learning leaders have responsibility for all modalities of courses, not just distance education. The vast majority of online learning leaders report to the Provost/CAO, emphasizing that online learning is an academic activity. And most institutions have used their online learning efforts and initiatives as a catalyst for organizational changes. This often includes the unification of several units/functions under the online learning leader. The goals and top priorities of the institution regarding online learning were also collected and ranked in these studies.

A benefit of conducting these two studies was the opportunity to learn what online learning leaders at universities have in common with their counterparts at community colleges, and where they differ. A summary of both is presented in Table 1.1.

Table 1.1 Similarities and Differences

Similarities and Differences	
What do they have in common?	*Where do they differ?*
Scope includes all courses for majority of institutions	University leaders more likely to have a faculty appointment
Online learning as a catalyst for organizational change	University leaders more likely to hold doctoral degree

(*Continued*)

Table 1.1 (Continued)

Similarities and Differences	
What do they have in common?	*Where do they differ?*
The same six units/activities are unified in organization	Two-year college leaders more likely to have online student experience
Reporting line through Provost or Chief Academic Officer	Two-year college leader positions have been in place longer
Faculty development and training are the top priority	Top goal of two-year college leaders is student retention and top goal for university leaders is growing enrollment
Associate with OLC, QM, and ELI	Two-year colleges more likely to use service providers
Years the individual has held this position and years of higher education experience	Two-year college leaders connected to state organizations
Professional experience (some)	University leaders more likely to stay informed through conferences and associations
Stay informed through Peers and Research	Gender – 61% female leaders in two-year institutions vs 50% in universities

Source: Fredericksen, 2018.

References

Fredericksen, E. E. (2017). A national study of online learning leaders in US higher education. *Online Learning*, 21(2). doi:10.24059/olj.v21i2.1164

Fredericksen, E.E. (2018). A national study of online learning leaders in U.S. community colleges. *Online Learning*, 22(4), 383–405. doi:10.24059/olj.v22i4.1458

The First 90 Days 2

Introduction

The hiring of a COLO is an exciting time for the life of a college or university. It typically represents collective momentum from Provost- and/or President-level endorsement and signals that the university strategically will invest its priorities in online and digital learning. A COLO today should expect that there are some activities related to online and digital learning already occurring. With that, the interview process likely revealed many of the legacy activities around online and digital learning that may be past their prime or problematic regarding quality of revenue flow/share, or do not meet their potential in terms of how peers stack up.

There are several different scenarios that one steps into when assuming a COLO role today and that will define the COLO role. No scenario is perfect and certainly no scenario is immune to the fluctuations in leadership that will inevitably occur above the role. How you navigate these scenarios will be a function of: your team (the talent you have and the talent you will need to recruit), your strategy (that which the leadership of the university has already shaped through larger strategic plans), your area of responsibility (defined as what is yours, what should be yours, and what is yours but should not be), and ultimately your ability to craft the narrative around your impact. A key consideration is how all of these elements will map to your success in the role. Nevertheless, as you hear individuals communicate their excitement for the institution's new or continued investment in the COLO role, harness this momentum. The newness of the role will only last so long.

DOI: 10.4324/9781003500742-3

Assessment of Existing Conditions

COLOs need to dedicate much time and energy to the interview process. The materials assembled for that process will be a key resource to leverage as COLOs get to know the institution through the lens of the new role, now that you are in the COLO seat. Provided below are several areas to focus on in your first 90 days that you can use to build upon the information and knowledge you accumulated during the interview process. One recommendation as you review this list is to make note of what has changed in the time since you interviewed, and consider how these changes may be leveraged for your success in the first 90 days.

- **Organizational Structure**: You studied organizational charts for the President's cabinet and Provost's Office in preparing for your interview. Now that you're the COLO you will want to understand several layers deeper than the leads of units and teams. Additionally, you will likely be part of a leadership team. Seek to establish relationships with these individuals. Particularly understand their portfolios and areas of responsibility. Often these conversations are the most formative in revealing what is distinctly your lane and where you will need to collaborate and partner (see Chapter 6) for greater success.
- **Academic Leadership**: You likely interviewed with many if not all of the academic deans responsible for the schools and/or colleges. Deans today generally have an interest in online and digital learning and can point to peer institutions that they know are successful in this space. Leverage this discipline-specific knowledge in your first 90 days to fast-track some of the market research you and your team will need to undertake.
- **Decentralized versus Centralized**: Many new COLO roles are created in an effort to centralize what has historically been ad hoc or decentralized online and digital learning efforts. In some cases, COLO roles are created to layer on top of robust efforts happening at the school or college level, where there also may be COLOs. Whatever the structure, in your first 90 days it is important to understand both the organization and the key players, seek out the advantages (e.g. are there early partnerships that can be formed between decentralized activities as a way to kickstart centralized efforts; and if so, what incentives will need to be explored), and attempt to assuage fear and anxiety that accompanies such transitions (e.g. get to know the history to the extent that you can be respectful of it as you go about your new role and implementing inevitable changes).

2

- **Vision and Strategy**: You likely presented a vision and strategy during your interview. Chances are you received feedback during the interview process. Circle back to this, as it was a valuable opportunity to test-drive your strategic ideas. Reflect on what generated excitement versus what raised questions and concerns. You will want to integrate this into your future visioning and strategic planning efforts, as it will engender trust and buy-in of your actual plans and provide tangible examples for you to reference as you present these plans to various stakeholders.
- **Staff**: You may have spent a great deal of time with your new staff during the interview process; or with staff who previously reported to a COLO-like role who may have been dissolved in favor or a clean slate; or perhaps you did not meet the team(s) at all. However the introduction to staff unfolded during the interview process, once you assume the COLO role, staff are among the most important groups to which you must commit time in the first 90 days. Much as with other stakeholders, staff offers key insights into where the opportunities lie, as well as the trepidation that will need to be carefully navigated.

You will not be able to do everything in your "honeymoon" period, yet you can make significant progress if you place some structure on this unique time. It will be a balance of wanting to hit the ground running while also learning the role and, for many, a new institution. An emerging trend in academic leadership is to engage with an executive coach as you begin your new role (Slater and Hancock, 2024). In fact, some of the experts contributing to this book have done just that. Consider how mentoring and/or coaching can ensure you get the most out of your first 90 days and position you toward success in your role.

Considerations for Insiders and Outsiders

There are many paths by which a COLO steps into the role, as explored in Chapter 1. In fact, one objective of this book is to showcase the unique competencies of those who aspire toward the role. No two COLOs will likely have the same path. We all come from various backgrounds: some have studied higher education leadership and online and digital education; others have stepped into online and digital learning from specific disciplines that were part of a university's growth plan; whereas others have had adjacent professional experiences that segue well into leadership of online and digital learning in a higher education context; and even others have found themselves as the last one standing during lean moments in an academic department, school, or college, and have assumed these responsibilities informally as other duties as assigned and then eventually formally. The formal credentials and experiences of COLOs vary as well and often determine if the COLO will assume a staff or faculty role. There are advantages and disadvantages for either classification (see Table 2.1). The majority of sitting COLOs possess a terminal degree and more than 40% have a faculty appointment (Fredericksen et al., 2024).

As mentioned in Chapter 1, approximately three-fifths of current COLOs were promoted from within their existing institutions (Fredericksen et al., 2024). Such a promotion might come with an existing faculty appointment or other internal affiliation. All of these scenarios are consistent whether

Table 2.1 Advantages and Disadvantages of Faculty versus Staff Appointment for COLO

	Advantages	*Disadvantages*
COLO as Faculty Appointment	• Peer among faculty • Experience with teaching and learning • Understanding of shared governance processes • Experience with end-user perspective in the digital learning environment • Likely has deep knowledge of digital learning from own disciplinary perspective • Likely has extensive experience with higher education culture, structures, traditions, and expectations	• Less % of time available to dedicate to position • Potentially fewer years of experience in digital/online learning • Often less exposure to disciplinary needs related to digital learning beyond own • May not have experience managing staff • May not have experience managing non-human resources/operations • May not have experience with both digital and online learning and learners • May not have exposure to the compliance side of online and digital learning (accessibility, student data, security)

(*Continued*)

Table 2.1 (Continued)

	Advantages	*Disadvantages*
COLO as Staff Appointment	• Should expect experience managing staff • Likely more years of experience and progression of related responsibilities • Likely more exposure to a broader range of disciplines for support • May have relevant adjacent experience in K-12/corporate that's advantageous • Should have experience with both digital and online learning and learners • Likely exposed to trends and best practices with digital and online learning from engagement with industry and professional organizations	• Challenge establishing peer relationships with faculty • May not have teaching experience • May not understand the academic mission and associated educational processes, structures, and culture • May not have had exposure or engagement with shared governance • May not have had exposure to key facets of academic affairs (e.g. student success, assessment) to contextualize online and digital learning within

ascending into the COLO role from within an institution or transitioning to a new college/university to assume the COLO role. Whether the COLO steps into the role as a promotion from within the institution or from another institution, the first 90 days present an opportunity to learn the role in the context of orienting oneself to his/her new place in the academic institution.

For those coming to their COLO role as insiders or outsiders to the institution, it will be advantageous to bring your prior experiences to the role. Consider how you position your experiences in the context of your new role as an opportunity to bring others along and see what is possible. You will also want to focus on building your network. This applies to those new to the university as well as those who have ascended into the COLO role. For the former, you established a network among the institution's leadership during the interview process. Seek to expand this network in your first 90 days as a way of identifying allies and also discovering where you will need to overcome obstacles. For the latter, you will want to expand your network beyond what is familiar to you from past roles. In both instances, your internal institutional network will be critical to you both in future successes and failures. Dedicate the time to getting to know individuals and teams during your first 90 days so that you can scaffold yourself with this enduring resource as you mature into your role as COLO.

Creating Alignment

A key finding of a COLO's assessment of existing conditions during the first 90 days should be understanding broader institutional priorities so that work may begin in aligning online and digital learning activities with these institutional-level priorities. This alignment will offer a vernacular to leverage in crafting strategic narratives (e.g. institutional efforts to elevate the brand will lend key words and phrases already at play to anchor your work as COLO); data to use as a baseline (e.g. strategic momentum toward enrollment growth will offer ways to organize conversations around segments of existing or potential student populations that online and digital learning can likely augment); and student success aspirations to advance (e.g. online and digital learning strategies that afford greater flexibility for all students are important to conversations around accessibility). Alignment with such institutional priorities will create a familiar framework which your leadership and stakeholders will recognize, and thus create efficiencies as you begin to lay out your vision and strategy unique to your institutional online and digital learning context.

These institutional priorities also create opportunities for quick wins within your first 90 days. Seek out avenues where institutional priorities have not leveraged or included online and digital learning and offer ideas and/or programmatic assistance where you have available resources. This will help reinforce the value of the COLO role early and create tangible examples that may be referenced either by your leadership or yourself in the first 90 days. These early wins will also make your efforts more resilient as you will inevitably make changes and shake things up as a result of all that you learn in your first three months.

Revisiting your first 90 days throughout the course of your time as COLO adds another important dimension to your success. It will offer you some empathy and strategy as the landscape at the top of your institution inevitably shifts during the unprecedented leadership changes we are experiencing in higher education today (Stephens, 2024). Onboarding a new President or Provost to the nuances of online and digital learning is a competency in its own right.

Competency Connection

UPCEA COLO Competency	*COLO Insight*	*Influencing Factors*	*Influencing Factor (COVID-Era)*	*Institutional Risk*
Integrity, Ethics, and Professionalism	Early failures often transform into a COLO's most significant wins	Unprecedented rate of change occurring in higher ed Comparative analysis of face-to-face instruction	Allowed forgiveness of earlier failures and/or greater tolerance for failures	Failure needs to be considered an essential duty of the COLO. Stability is a platform for success.

References

Fredericksen, E., Simunich, B. & Uranus, J. (2024) *COLO Profile Study 2024 – A National Research Project about Chief Online Learning Officers.* Presented at OLC Accelerate 2024, Orlando, FL. https://olc.secure-platform.com/accelerate/gallery/rounds/82030/schedule/items/17650

Slater, A., & Hancock, L. (2024, September 25). "Leadership coaching as a powerful tool for intentional leadership." *The Department Chair* 35 (2), p. 24–25.

Stephens, J. (2024, August 9). *How to help reduce higher ed's leadership deficit* [Opinion]. *Inside Higher Ed.* https://www.insidehighered.com/opinion/career-advice/2024/08/09/advice-how-help-reduce-higher-eds-leadership-deficit-opinion

Expert Perspectives

- Craig Wilson, University of Arizona
- Kelvin Thompson, University of Louisville
- Susan Seal, Mississippi State University
- Kim Siegenthaler, The City University of New York

Craig Wilson, J.D., Ph.D.

Vice Provost for Outreach, Distance and Continuing Education, University of Arizona

As you begin your first 90 days as a COLO at your institution, approaching your position with humility and humor will go a long way. If you are new to your university or college, understanding the culture and climate is very important. Starting with a "Listening and Learning" tour is a very useful way to gain insight into where the challenges lay (beyond the job description and interviews). You will find there are parts of the university that are supportive of online/distance education and some that are not (even post-COVID!). Regardless of the headwinds, stay confident about your path forward and circle back frequently to the "why" you were hired to be a COLO – to make the quality education at your institution more accessible to students who cannot attend classes on campus due to life circumstances (e.g. family, work).

If your unit does not have mission/vision/values (MVV) statements and philosophies, invest time in developing them (or deeply familiarize yourself with existing statements and philosophies). This not only helps establish buy-in from your team and external stakeholders but also provides a framework for problems and challenges that are unforeseen and those that may not have a clear-cut solution. The return on the MVV time investment cannot be overstated. Having MVV as a focal point when I first arrived at the University of Arizona (at the beginning of the pandemic when my team was working from home) proved to be useful and successful. While I was hired to lead the online unit, a few months after hire, I was asked if I could take on the distance education unit (hybrid education at multiple locations around the state of Arizona). Understanding the inherent synergies of asynchronous and synchronous learning, I agreed to do so. Just as I was getting the two teams settled (online and distance education), I was asked once more if I could add continuing education to my portfolio. Adding continuing education to my responsibilities was exciting and challenging due to the noncredit microcredential focus, differing enrollment terms and systems, and a budget model that was unlike the other two units. The exciting part was the nimbleness of continuing education to respond quickly to professional and workforce needs and more affordable enrollment costs compared to credit-based programs. Frankly, by being flexible and open-minded (great traits of a COLO), I was able to work with my team to develop our Lifelong Learning Loop that empowers students of all ages and stages of life to become learners at the University of Arizona.

To be clear, the reason this all worked out is the department teams were super high-performing, student-centered, able to see synergies, and collaborated across departments. I count myself blessed to have been a COLO during this wonderful, sometimes messy, process. Along the way, our online enrollment doubled and achieved U.S. News top-ten rankings for three straight years. And our continuing education department received outstanding non-credit program regional awards from UPCEA for two straight years. It was an honor being a COLO at the University of Arizona, and serving as a member of the Arizona State Authorization Reciprocity Agreement (AZ SARA) council throughout my time in the role greatly enhanced my professional experience. I am confident the fulfilling lessons I've learned will continue to serve me in the future.

Kelvin Thompson, Ed.D.

Vice Provost, Online Strategy and Teaching Innovation,
University of Louisville

Know Yourself

I came to the COLO role at a new institution after more than 20 years of deep involvement in online leadership at a single university and wide engagement with the broader online education community. While I had touched multiple facets of the online enterprise, I embraced my roots in instructional design, teaching, and faculty professional development. I had already learned that my strengths lay in relationships, communication, and strategy. I knew what it was to have far-reaching institutional contextual knowledge and a network of institutional trust. While those factors would not be traveling with me to my new institution, my valuing of them would. I would also be bringing a bag full of background experiences, knowledge of the field, a wide web of inter-institutional colleagues, and a fresh perspective on the new context.

Frame the Challenge

I did not have to start from a blank slate. That was not my challenge. Instead, my new institution had been engaged with online learning for decades in niche ways, accelerated by the emergency remote learning (ERL) pandemic response. An existing 80-person central unit was available to support 50+ online programs plus campus-based digital learning, albeit on something of an elective basis. The establishment of a new vice provost role, while not using the term "COLO" per se, was a concrete institutional commitment to doing something new. I recognized the institution's past successes and a potentially bright future via better alignment of institutional resources. I began to speak of "moving forward" together into new ways of doing things toward aspirational goals of educational access, scale, and social mobility. This included stating the need for sustainable growth-oriented funding from my time as a candidate and throughout my first 90 days on the job. (I would later leverage that need statement for a concrete proposal to do things differently.) Understanding the current state of the institution can be further informed by a more robust "environmental scan" (Casimiro et al., 2023, p. 480) as an in-coming COLO.

Lay a Foundation for the Long Term

During my first 90 days on the job, I sought to establish patterns of behavior and underlying structures that were aligned with the eventual results I wanted to see. At an institution with high administrative turnover and low institutional trust, I looked for ways to demonstrate trustworthiness and a commitment to the long-term. I followed through on a promised "90 conversations in 90 days," and I published a written report-out after that period. In conversations with faculty members, I asked how to elevate the view of online teaching, and I followed-up with scheduling semi-structured faculty "swap shop" sessions for online teaching practices. Even though my position was classed as "administrative," I pursued a secondary faculty appointment to have an academic home. Realizing that the work is bigger than one person, I undertook to reinvigorate and rebrand the leadership team I inherited. I looked for ways to engage, invest, and empower, and together we identified "big rock" strategic imperatives to focus the unit's time, effort, and energy. On the whole, consistent with my framing of the challenge, I attempted to shift the unit's and the university's attention to focus on quality online education at scale.[1]

Note

1 A version of the ideas in this expert perspective case study was first presented in a conference session (Thompson, 2023).

References

Casimiro, L., Wa-Mbaleka, S., and Thompson, K. (2023). Leadership in online higher education. In S. Wa-Mbaleka, K. Thompson, and L. Casimiro (Eds.). *The SAGE handbook of online higher education*. SAGE Publishing.

Thompson, K. (2023, October 26). *From the first 90 days and into the first year: Strategizing as a new COLO. Presentation at Online Learning Consortium Accelerate Conference*, Washington, DC. Available online https://bit.ly/thompson_2023accelerate

Susan D. Seal, Ph.D.

Dean, College of Professional and Continuing Studies,
Mississippi State University

There are two points from the chapter that I would like to relate to my experience. The first is getting to know your team, and the second is building your institutional network. You likely have broad goals in mind but achieving them requires the support of your team and the expertise of others outside your immediate circle. Listening and learning from these interactions might also prompt you to adjust your goals or the methods to achieve them.

When I became the Executive Director of Mississippi State University's Center for Distance Education, one of my first actions was to meet individually with each staff member. With over 20 people on the team, this took time, and initially, there was some skepticism and trepidation about these one-on-one meetings. However, as the meetings progressed, staff members began to request time on my calendar, eager to share their thoughts. This was a time for me to learn more about the operations of the unit, connect with the staff, and allow them to get to know me and my leadership style.

During our conversations, we discussed personal topics such as families, backgrounds, hobbies, and passions. We also delved into professional matters including the positive aspects of their role and the unit, challenges to their success or that of the organization, and their career aspirations. These discussions provided me with valuable insights into what was working well and what needed improvement. Some staff members felt their skills were underutilized or that they (or others) were not in the best roles. It helped me adjust my initial priorities to be more effective.

There were a number of positives, not the least of which was to begin building a relationship with each team member and to set a foundation of open communication. The conversations also allowed me to identify areas of programmatic development and opportunities for professional growth for some of the staff. Culture has a great impact on an organization, and these conversations gave me immediate insight into the current culture and how it has been shaped. One thing to keep in mind is that in this early stage, in particular, people may tell you what they think you want to hear. For the most part, people were very open and honest, though I later discovered that some information had been presented in a somewhat more favorable light.

The second point is to begin meeting with key individuals across campus. Share your goals with them and ask how they could be a part of the success. I was fortunate to have been at the university for over ten years and had strong relationships already, but those now needed to be strengthened in light of my new role. I also needed new partners on campus. I welcomed opportunities to serve on committees, councils, and task forces that gave me the opportunity to meet people as well as share our vision.

Relationships are key to your success. There were many people that I had known for years, and in some ways, we have grown together into administrative roles. Those strong relationships developed over the years and served me well as I began to expand into new areas and push against traditional models. Even if individuals didn't fully understand or even agree with some of the innovations that we were pushing for, they trusted me, which allowed for productive conversations and collaborations.

Although those first 90 days may be a whirlwind, taking the time to get to know your staff and to begin identifying key partners will be time well spent. In retrospect, after more than eight years, those initial meetings stand out as some of the most pivotal actions I undertook.

Kim L. Siegenthaler, Ph.D.

Associate Vice Chancellor for Academic Innovation, The City University of New York

I have found information gathering and relationship building to be the most important things I can do as a new COLO. This holds true when moving into the COLO role as an insider or as someone new to the institution. As an insider, I have the benefit of understanding institutional and unit culture; however, when moving into the COLO role, many things will change including scope of responsibilities, reporting lines, interactions with other units, and information access. As an outsider, whether taking over an established PCO unit or building one, it is essential to understand the President's and Provost's vision and priorities for my work and for the unit. While you hope that what you heard in the interview process and read in the job description is accurate, getting confirmation of that at the start can help you avoid early missteps that might derail your long-term success.

When beginning work with an established team, I find it helpful to ask each team member questions such as: What are we doing well that we should continue? Where do we need to improve? What are your recommendations for improvement? What are we doing that we should stop doing? What are we not doing that we should be doing? How I gather this information is influenced by unit size and functional health, my insider/outsider status, and unit or institutional characteristics. Responses enable me to quickly identify bright spots and pain points and get a sense of morale across the unit.

I begin relationship building with academic leaders and service units on day one to understand points of intersection, identify areas of concern, learn how they view online education and what they hope I will (or will not) do. I often ask what they think is important for me to know about the institution. These conversations are important to the insider COLO as well as the outsider. As an insider moving into the COLO role, I am likely to interact with higher level leadership in each of these areas who may have very different perspectives and greater influence than those I interacted with in a number two position, or from outside the PCO unit. As an outsider, these conversations can reveal where I can find eager partners, expect resistance, or build on strong foundations. They are invaluable in situations where I have been charged with building a new PCO unit, merging multiple autonomous units, or restructuring the PCO unit. Conversations with IR/effectiveness leadership are essential in identifying what data are available about online programs and students.

We recognize that each higher education institution has a unique culture that shapes policy and practice and influences where the online education enterprise is positioned. Having served as a COLO at large public institutions in three different states, I have learned the importance of understanding the funding model for the university, procurement rules and state laws, and HR policies. Each may differ dramatically from state to state with significant implications for how I can purchase technology, outsource work, or restructure my team. Doing this discovery work early enables me to identify potential roadblocks and establish more realistic timelines to advance initiatives.

3 Designated Survivor – COVID-19

Introduction

Every COLO remembers what they were doing when they got *The Call* on some seemingly ordinary day in late February or early March 2020. That was the day that forever changed the role of the COLO for all those who occupied the position at the time. Among the first resources to circulate and grow in direct relationship to the outbreak map originally created by Johns Hopkins University (https://coronavirus.jhu.edu/map.html) was the spreadsheet of *Keep Teaching* (Keep Teaching n.d.) websites that emerged, with each listing becoming an iteration of those who were generous enough to share before (see the References list for a link to an archive of this resource). In fact, the co-authors got acquainted with each other for the first time in the early days of the pandemic, as they were COLOs of two of the largest higher education institutions by student headcount in the U.S. (National Center for Education Statistics, 2022). Our exchanges were rarely about anything that did not include the word "scale."

For many institutions and for some long-standing COLOs, the 2009 outbreak of the H1N1 virus, otherwise known as Swine Flu, was a pivotal moment when many universities particularly in the southern part of the United States prepared for academic continuity in the face of an acute public health disruption. Activities such as provisioning a course shell to every course section were part of the preparedness measures that were mainstreamed during the most recent COVID-19 pandemic and today is considered a best practice. As with several of the emergency actions that COLOs took during the COVID-19 pandemic, higher education has since adopted these as best practices.

DOI: 10.4324/9781003500742-4

Institutional Vulnerabilities Revealed

The early days of planning for the shift to remote instruction and then the implementation of this shift revealed vulnerabilities to colleges and universities at every turn. Many of these vulnerabilities became more pronounced as the pandemic shifted horizons from necessitating solutions in order to conclude the final weeks of a spring semester, to completely reconceptualizing the academic calendar and all associated activities – from new student conferences to commencements and everything in between – for the start of a fall semester. While COLOs and their teams found themselves to be frontline workers for the education sector during March 2020, August 2020 was the real moment of reckoning, as most higher education institutions supported at best single digits of course sections delivering face-to-face instruction, with the remainder having a significant digital component. It is important to note that ERT as the dominant form of instruction lasted different time periods for different universities across different states.

The units supporting the lion's share of course sections for many universities evolved, merged, and in some cases were created during the pandemic. While there may have been talent in place at universities, it was often housed in units focused on supporting online programs for a subset of universities' faculty and student populations. When these units, their resources, and their leadership were forced to scale to support the entire university in Spring 2020, many vulnerabilities surfaced that varied in impact and revealed where critical decision points were necessary (and in many cases without all of the available information). This thrust the COLO role and responsibilities into the spotlight perhaps as never before.

Early in the COVID-19 pandemic, we discovered how much our students relied upon the infrastructure, services, and community fostered by bricks and mortar institutions. Among a COLO's first round of calls in preparing for remote instruction was to the online proctoring vendors, where an ensuing cascade of vulnerabilities was revealed: from the capacity of these companies to provision their products and services at the scale a global pandemic necessitated; to prepare faculty to effectively implement and manage their use; to the speed by which university procurement offices could route contracts; to how ill-equipped our academic integrity offices were in the face of digital assessments. From there we discovered the limits of the reach of campus WiFi, as many students drove to campus to tether onto what connections they could find in parking lots and garages. The list goes on and on, as does the myriad of innovations that were put in place, with many now becoming best practices. Underpinning so many of these vulnerabilities were the vignettes of student, faculty, and staff daily life that played out in the background of video calls, as the lines blurred between "home" and "university." COLOs particularly carried the burden of reconciling exclusionary and inclusionary practices across so many domains where there needed to be a digital solution. Among the pervasive words that the pandemic surfaced specific to the many transformations we experienced in higher education is *flexibility*. The impacts of a new-found embrace of flexibility will be further explored in Chapter 9.

Decision Points

COLOs had to quickly learn the nuances of compliance requirements around accessibility, security, and FERPA, which typically Chief Compliance Officers, CIOs, and the university Registrar, respectively, have distinct jurisdiction over. Not only did COLOs have to learn these spaces, but they were often translating the compliance requirements into the realities of the digital learning environment. Many of the decision points that COLOs influenced are at the heart of best practices universities follow today. These include:

- Describing instructional modalities so that the expectations are transparent and clear to students
- Requiring all faculty to be trained to teach across online and hybrid modalities
- Provisioning a learning management system (LMS) course "shell" for every course section, no matter the assigned mode of instruction
- Ensuring lecture capture content remains available as a learning asset for subsequent use, irrespective of whether or not a student attended that class session
- Sustaining BYOD policies so that students have the necessary hardware, software, and network capabilities that align with course requirements so that students are set up for success
- Upholding policies that specific fees for technologies are not passed on to students
- Supporting virtual options for academic success services that in many cases transitioned online for the first time to serve all learners during the pandemic, and subsequently saw their highest usage once virtual
- Considering how to administer exams as close as possible to the Thanksgiving holiday, so as to maximize student breaks by reducing extraneous reading days

- Where not feasible, integrating mental health breaks into what were traditionally reading days and designating them as such on the official university calendar
- Implementing robust accessibility technologies made available to all learners as a recognition of the tenets of universal design for learning
- Maintaining good relationships with educational technology vendors so that they know what makes one university's academic culture distinct and unique so that they may best support that culture with their products and services

Many of these best practices are now being developed by UPCEA as imperatives for Presidents and Provosts. Academic Continuity with Technology (ACT) is a series of actionable recommendations for university administration, teaching and learning, communication, and engagement with campus stakeholders that draws on the many lessons learned among COLOs during the COVID-19 pandemic to be applied to future scenarios where academic continuity is necessary.

Evolution of Instruction Beyond Emergency Remote Instruction

The COVID-19 pandemic brought to the surface the nuances of instructional modes of delivery and the power dynamics of choice that tipped in favor of learner preference perhaps for the first time en masse (Robert, 2022). COLOs found themselves best positioned to advocate for the tradeoffs for learners, faculty, and institutions as academic leaders began to flex course offerings beyond what had been bifurcated online and face-to-face instruction. With the COLO role largely focused on the online offerings of a college / university prior to COVID-19, the pandemic cast the COLO into a role where he / she was supporting all forms of instructional delivery, which included digital components. Organizationally, as a result of a greater range of instructional modalities being supported by universities today, COLO roles are increasingly charged with prioritizing digital learning strategy for the university as a larger umbrella under which online learning strategy now nests. This broadening of scope creates more opportunities for domains of specialization among COLO portfolios, as well as career pipelines for aspiring COLOs as the portfolios broaden. The result is that digital learning is woven into the academic fabric of the learner experience, which is at the heart of the flexibility imperative our learners demand today.

From Designated Survivor to Newfound Seat at the Table

While the COVID-19 pandemic was not the first time that universities found themselves preparing for academic continuity in the face of an acute disruption, it stands as a turning point in higher education for how instructional delivery fundamentally changed (Cavanagh, 2023). Given that the COVID-19 virus persists, and there is a range of other acute and chronic disruptions that will necessitate a shift in instructional delivery in the future, UPCEA is leading the conversation nationally to standardize ACT as a series of enduring best practices should the need arise to shift in the future. The responsibilities that COLOs had to assume during the COVID-19 pandemic offered a rare glimpse into the breadth of activities that occur at a college campus on a daily basis; and for many COLOs, they were called into action to support many of these activities that reached far beyond what any COLO could imagine prior to early 2020.

COLOs served as higher education's designated survivor during the COVID-19 pandemic and were forced to wield decision-making prowess as academic instruction experienced a dramatic and sustained transformation. COLOs were also among the first groups in higher education to experience a subsequent wave of change that swept through and transformed norms of the higher education workforce: Burnout, the Great Resignation, Quiet Quitting, and Quiet Hiring (Klotz & Bolino, 2022). These were memorable employment eras defined by the pressures to which the workforce, who at the beginning of the pandemic performed heroically, eventually started to succumb. COLOs thus became an experienced voice affecting institutional change not only with relentless staff attrition data but also with the very solutions that carried universities through the pandemic and are at many institutions today transforming the work culture and ameliorating space constraints by way of remote and hybrid work arrangements.

The instructional, workforce, and cultural changes which amalgamated into pervasive digital transformation for higher education would have never had the positive impacts on teaching and learning without COLOs having a seat at the table, which is the title of the next chapter. It goes without saying among COLOs: the collective power of COLOs across the U.S. networked problem after problem into solutions that arguably every college/university in the U.S. has adopted in some capacity as a best practice today.

Competency Connection

UPCEA COLO Competency	*COLO Insight*	*Influencing Factors*	*Influencing Factor (COVID-Era)*	*Institutional Risk*
Critical Thinking and Decision-Making	Ability of COLO to influence and autonomously make decisions for online learning depends on reporting structure and reporting adjacencies	Reporting line + structure of COLO Alignment with divisions of Academic Affairs and IT Vendor engagement (partner with the CIO)	Leadership turnover	Championing of contemporary learners across all teaching modalities is lost if COLO is absent from decision-making.

References

Cavanagh, Thomas B. "Leadership Lessons from the Pandemic." in *From Grassroots to the Highly Orchestrated: Online Leaders Share Their Stories of the Evolving Online Landscape in Higher Ed.* Eds. Bettyjo Bouchey, Erin Gatz, & Shelley Kurland. Online Learning Consortium. (2023): 9–23.

Keep Teaching website collection (n.d.) https://docs.google.com/spreadsheets/d/1VT9oiNYPyiEsGHBoDKlwLlWAsWP58sGV7A3oIuEUG3k/edit?gid=1552188977#gid=1552188977

Klotz, A. C., & Bolino, M. C. (2022, September 15). When quiet quitting is worse than the real thing. *Harvard Business Review*. https://hbr.org/2022/09/when-quiet-quitting-is-worse-than-the-real-thing

National Center for Education Statistics. (2022). *Digest of education statistics 2020 (NCES 2022-105)*. U.S. Department of Education. Table 312.10.

Robert, Janay. (2022, October 3). *2022 students and technology report: Rebalancing the student experience. EDUCAUSE*. https://www.educause.edu/ecar/research-publications/2022/students-and-technology-report-rebalancing-the-student-experience/modality-preferences

Expert Perspectives

- Joseph Riquelme, GrowthEco Partners
- Deb Miller, University of North Florida
- Karen Pedersen, Consultant
- Kevin Shriner, University of Nebraska-Lincoln
- Amy Collier, Middlebury College

Joseph Riquelme

Founder and Managing Partner GrowthEco Partners

The first week of March 2020 was my first week as Vice Provost and Chief Online Officer. There were discussions taking place before the pandemic of possibly moving to a new LMS, faculty were not happy with the current platform, and only 30% of all courses were using the LMS as a course shell. As talks of a possible closure began because of the pandemic, I commenced working on outlining what the cost would be of a migration. I needed to capture both the short, one-time cost and the long-term recurring cost. I mapped out two migration models: an aggressive one and a slower rollout. I developed slides that had pros and cons of both and why my choice was to be aggressive in our migration. Since we had low LMS adoption and only 3% of undergraduate courses were offered online, we had to train faculty regardless of what system they used. Understanding how hard it sometimes can be to get funding, I did not want to invest resources into training faculty on an LMS that we needed to migrate from, as it was nearing the end of support by the vendor in addition to functional issues.

I presented the migration plan, explaining the costs and the long-term benefits. The discussions were tense with some folks on the leadership team expressing concerns about completing a migration in the middle of a pandemic when faculty and students were dealing with a lot of change already. Others understood the need and the benefit it would have for all parties. Some had seen demos or taught on the new LMS at other schools and understood the benefits. Luckily, the Provost at the time gave us the support and funding needed to move forward. In my 17 years in higher education, I had never seen a contract process move faster. We had both Zoom and Canvas contracts approved within a week of submission. We soft-launched Canvas for the Summer 2020 session and began large efforts of weekly professional development sessions, bringing together resources from three different departments. We also began hiring contract remote instructional designers to help scale our support for faculty.

There were many that thought introducing another change would be overwhelming and others who felt it would be too much change for students, but what we found was that the new system was easier for faculty and students to use. The resources and support provided by the vendors were extremely helpful in the transition. The LMS allowed for new ways of engagement and ways for students to communicate outside of the classroom. By no means was it easy, but it was the right decision to make for students, faculty, and the university long term. There is an old saying by Renaissance philosopher Niccolo Machiavelli, who reportedly said, "Never waste an opportunity offered by a good crisis." The pandemic rallied everyone to work together to accomplish an extremely fast migration and bring courses online.

As I reflect, I think about how important it is to develop well-rounded leadership. Future COLOs need to have a deep understanding of data analysis, forecasting, and financial modeling among many other skill sets. Without those traits, it would be hard to forecast financial impact and the resources needed for different initiatives. That experience taught me that you must push forward with your conviction and experience and find partners who are willing to work collaboratively for the overall success of the institution and students. It's not possible to have 100% buy-in, but the rest will come around when they see the momentum and success.

Deb Miller, Ed.D.

Associate Vice President for Digital Learning and Chief Online Learning Officer, University of North Florida

Building Connectivity through Crisis

In February 2020, I was pulled into a working group monitoring the outbreak of COVID-19 and updating the academic continuity plans previously developed for the H1N1 virus. Those plans primarily focused on short-term continuity of instruction and did not consider continuity of support services in any meaningful way. Tasked with wrangling a subgroup of folks who provided services, I pulled together representatives from IT, Library, Registrar, and others to begin working out how we could extend support services for students and faculty and move to a virtual support model for an extended period. A few weeks later, the day before spring break was to begin, we got word that the university would be pivoting to remote instruction for at least two weeks after spring break. We remained in that mode until Fall 2020.

Through some lucky alignment of the stars, three decisions placed the university in a favorable position for the pivot. A few years back, we shifted from creating course shells upon request to auto-provisioning a shell for every course section during an LMS migration. Just a few weeks earlier, I was convinced by an eager staff member to make the Zoom LTI available in every course shell as a replacement for the Big Blue Button option that came with the LMS. The university had also recently rolled out Microsoft Teams, and we set up a channel for CIRT, the faculty support unit housing instructional designers, LMS support, and media production to experiment with it for departmental communication and file collaboration. That last piece was key in not just surviving but also thriving during the remote period. From keeping up staff morale with a virtual retreat and scavenger hunts to keeping groups connected and working across silos, Teams kept us connected and humming along.

I say thriving, because with some major infrastructure pieces in place, while the onset of the COVID-19 pandemic brought many challenges, it also presented opportunities to strengthen connections and deepen understanding across campus. As the "online person," I was part of the executive leadership team making decisions and had the opportunity to work closely and develop relationships with colleagues in areas such as public safety, HR, and student health that I previously knew only superficially. Those relationships provided the ties to develop other projects post-pandemic.

Regarding the extension of student and faculty support services, we made great strides in expanding services in ways that were more convenient and flexible, and many of those services remain available through nontraditional channels. That work also led to a deeper understanding of our true student profile and the support students needed to remain engaged. The same is true for our instructors, both those on tenure lines and our contingent faculty. We should never again assume that everyone has a reliable device and strong Internet connectivity readily available in their home.

My faculty support unit had a good reputation and relationship with faculty prior to the pandemic, but there was always a pocket of outliers who avoided anything related to online as if it might be contagious. Through necessity, those folks came into contact with our support folks and developed positive relationships during the pandemic that persist today. More importantly, many faculty deepened their understanding of what is possible online, which led to teaching innovations and strategies that continue in their on-campus courses. Several of those are cataloged at teachinginnovations.domains.unf.edu/.

As crises often do, the COVID-19 pandemic experience presented opportunities to work together to solve common problems, leaving us stronger and more connected.

Karen Pedersen, Ph.D.

Consultant

In 2003, while serving as a vice president of professional studies, I pitched a proposal to the President where I would move two states away from the campus. At the time, I considered it a long shot as I would be the only remote employee at the institution. But as a dual-career spouse, I thought I had a compelling plan. I was fortunate the President agreed. I remained at the institution for another eight years building and growing an even larger online presence for the institution.

I knew working from home with some limited telecommuting worked for me, so I was intrigued when I read *Nine Shift – Work, Life and Education in the 21st Century* in 2007 (Draves and Coates, 2007). The authors highlighted nine shifts that were already occurring, which they postulated would become commonplace by 2020. I took note of "Shift One – People Work at Home" (pg. 85).

Ironically, in 2020, I pitched to the Provost that the shift to remote operations, which we all adopted due to the global pandemic, could become permanent for our entire online learning operation. It just so happened that the lease on our current 20,000 sq ft building was up for renewal at the same time, so making this pitch with clear benefits to the university (e.g., reduced operating costs, increased productivity, greater employee satisfaction and retention, larger talent recruitment geography) made sense at that moment.

Every day COLOs are asked to serve, lead, and manage a plethora of stakeholders including learners, faculty, staff, administrators, board members, employer partners, and vendors. We do so within various organizational configurations and institutional contexts. Each of us does this while the world around us is also changing, quite rapidly.

The pandemic of 2020 changed how we do our work and institutions can now pivot to remote as other situations arise. But what is next? How can you future-proof your organization ensuring it is agile, responsive, and able to facilitate making decisions and moving quickly, while at the same time future-proofing yourself?

As a COLO, it is essential that you hone your "seeing around corners" abilities. I appreciated Rita McGrath's book focusing on how to spot inflection points before they happen. According to McGrath, "Inflection points have the power to change the very assumptions on which organizations were founded" (2019, pg. 7). I believe we are in a time of enormous change and the competencies COLOs need today are very different from the competencies I needed when I began my administrative career years ago.

To prepare you…I offer these five future-proofing capabilities:

- Remain Curious – read, attend, engage, and learn
- Think Broadly and Critically – solutions may be transdisciplinary, very amorphous, or straightforward and elegantly simple
- Be Strategic and Differentiate – remain adaptable, resilient, and relevant
- Collaborate to Create – use your maker instinct and design thinking mindset every day
- Understand Value and Impact – know this for yourself and your organization; showcase ROI

In my mind, seeing around corners is now part of the role of today's COLO. Use your seat at the table to position your institution to successfully navigate higher education's coming inflection points.

References

Draves, W.A. & Coates, J. (2007). *Nine shift – Work, life and education in the 21st century*. LERN Books.

McGrath, R.G. (2019). *Seeing around corners – How to spot inflection points in business before they happen*. Houghton Mifflin Harcourt.

Kevin Shriner, Ed.D.

Assistant Vice Chancellor for Digital and Online Learning, University of Nebraska-Lincoln

My experience during the COVID-19 pandemic differed significantly from many of my COLO peers. During this period, I worked outside higher education for an education company that provided marketing insights and best practices to our higher education partners, helping them navigate and communicate effectively with prospective students during a very challenging and unpredictable time. Contrary to expectations that the pandemic-induced recession would drive an influx of enrollments, similar to what occurred in 2008, we observed the opposite trend. Undergraduate enrollments declined by 3.8% from 2019 to 2020 and further declined by 3.2% from 2020 to 2021, marking the largest decline since 2011 (Lederman, 2024).

As anticipated, the shift to remote instruction led to a surge in students enrolling in at least one online course, with a 92% increase from Fall 2019 to 2020. The undergraduate level saw a 97% increase, while the graduate level grew by 71%. It's crucial to understand this shift, as some higher education pundits have used the post-COVID declines in 2021 and 2022 to devalue the role of online education. However, it's important to note that, prior to the pandemic, student enrollments in at least one online course across undergraduate and graduate levels had been growing at an annual rate of 5% from 2013 to 2019. As Joshua Kim (2021) succinctly put it in his October 2020 blog for Inside Higher Ed, "Residential education will come back, but online education will never again be a fringe activity of the institution."

When I arrived at the University of Nebraska-Lincoln in February 2023 as the inaugural Assistant Vice Chancellor for Digital and Online Learning, the shift away from remote instruction had already occurred. My primary focus in this new role was to establish a comprehensive, transformative, and inclusive strategy for online and digital education that would increase enrollments, enhance program offerings, and broaden access to a diverse student population at UNL. The outcome of UNL's COVID-19 remote instruction was a renewed emphasis on providing quality online education, enhanced support services for online students, and affordable nondegree and degree online programs.

This is not to say that these emphasis areas did not exist before. UNL has an excellent Center for Teaching and Learning where professional instructional designers and faculty collaborate on hybrid and fully online course design. A more robust faculty development program, which includes an orientation to the LMS, student engagement expectations, and instructional design best practices, has been implemented to ensure that more faculty are engaging with online instruction than in pre-pandemic times. Further utilization of customer relationship management systems and the student information system to uniquely identify online students has been critical for assessing and providing action-oriented insights into student engagement and progress.

An unintended consequence of the pandemic has been the shift of the COLO's role to include engagement in noncredit and for-credit microcredential offerings. At UNL, this shift has strategically led to the creation of certificates and badges that meet workforce-ready skills. The current skepticism regarding the value of higher education, along with many organizations seeking to hire individuals with less than a baccalaureate degree, underscores the need to engage in this educational space. This shift presents a unique opportunity for COLOs to be more entrepreneurial and engaged across various educational levels while also aligning costs and affordability to these models.

In summary, the COVID-19 pandemic catalyzed a profound transformation in higher education, shifting the landscape toward an increased reliance on online learning. While the initial response was a surge in online course enrollments, the long-term effects have positioned COLOs as pivotal leaders in the academic C-suite. At the University of Nebraska-Lincoln, these changes have underscored the importance of a robust digital education strategy, encompassing quality online programs, enhanced faculty support, and student engagement. The pandemic has also expanded the scope of COLOs to include the development of noncredit and microcredential offerings, addressing the growing demand for workforce-ready skills. As higher education continues to navigate these changes, the unique professional experiences and strategic insights of COLOs will be crucial in shaping the future of academic institutions, ensuring they remain relevant and responsive in an evolving educational landscape.

References

Kim, J. (2021, October 20). *9 reasons why your next provost should be a CTL director. Inside Higher Ed.* https://www.insidehighered.com/blogs/learning-innovation/9-reasons-why-your-next-provost-should-be-ctl-director

Lederman, D. (2024, January 30). *Online college enrollment continues post-pandemic growth. Inside Higher Ed.* https://www.insidehighered.com/news/tech-innovation/teaching-learning/2024/01/30/online-college-enrollment-continues-post-pandemic

Amy Collier, Ph.D.

Associate Provost for Digital Learning, Middlebury College

As the leader of a digital learning organization for a residential undergraduate college in New England and a mostly residential graduate school in California, I felt ill-suited to be called a COLO prior to the COVID-19 pandemic. Online learning was not part of our institutional DNA, and it was only a small part of the portfolio of our digital learning organization. Our focus was primarily on the intersections of digital tools with the engaged and deeply interpersonal teaching and learning experiences our faculty provided in their classrooms.

The sudden transition to Emergency Remote Learning (ERL) caused by the pandemic disruptions of March 2020 ushered in new expectations. The instructional design support we had provided to a handful of online programs at our graduate institute was now expected for all undergraduate and graduate classes. It was an all-hands-on-deck moment, with our small team conscripting student workers, librarians, and IT staff to provide both technical and pedagogical support to our faculty. The challenge wasn't only in dealing with the disruptions to our academic and student support offerings but also in addressing disruptions to core and long-held beliefs about our institutional, professional, and learner identities and responsibilities.

As our digital learning team consulted with faculty about transitioning to ERL, we emphasized the importance of maximum flexibility and accessibility for students. We knew that students had dispersed around the globe, some struggling with basic needs such as housing and food. These students often had difficulty with Zoom class sessions and needed more options for accessing and participating in their classes. We recommended centering asynchronous learning options, such as pre-recorded videos and discussion boards, to help our more vulnerable students stay engaged. For some faculty, our recommendations were at odds with their core teaching values that emphasized immediacy, interpersonal connection, dialogue, and mentorship.

Fortunately, in a wise move, the Provost created a task force of faculty, staff, and administrators – including me, in the role of Associate Provost for Digital Learning – to make necessary academic decisions, address issues, and provide guidance to the community on academic matters. This task force represented the tightest integration we'd had between the digital learning organization and college faculty. It demonstrated what was possible when we combined the expertise of undergraduate teaching/learning experience of the faculty with the expertise of digital learning professionals. Through conversations on this task force, we grappled with the tensions around online learning best practices and ultimately issued guidance suggesting that faculty offer more flexible learning options to students.

Some faculty who embraced unfamiliar modes of learning expressed interest in continuing to explore and refine those approaches, even as they returned to in-person or hybrid learning. Our digital learning organization responded to this interest by creating a Faculty Fellows program to provide funding, support, and community for further developing digital learning approaches. Over the last two years, the program has supported 11 faculty, with an additional 6 joining the program in the following academic year.

After all that has happened since 2020, would I now consider myself the COLO of our residential institution? Today, our graduate school is significantly expanding its online program offerings. More programs across our institution are exploring a variety of modalities for credit-bearing, noncredit bearing, and auxiliary/support offerings (e.g., student orientations). With the arrival of generative AI, our digital learning organization has added yet another realm of work to its portfolio.

Our work feels more necessary than ever. We can continue building on the lessons learned from the last few years, integrating digital tools and pedagogies into our traditional residential programs and expanding our portfolio of multimodal learning opportunities. To deliver on these goals, it is key to continue supporting digital learning leadership at our institution – whether or not we have an official COLO position – and giving them a seat at the table with other institutional leadership and faculty. As we navigate this evolving landscape, our challenge will be to harness the power of digital innovation while preserving the essence of our institution's educational mission. By doing so, we can create a more resilient, flexible, and inclusive learning environment that prepares our students for the complexities of a rapidly changing world.

Section 2

Strategy Overlays for COLOs

This section takes a deep dive into six strategy overlays for COLOs to consider as their roles evolve within their unique institutional contexts. Chapters 4 through 9 each highlight one of the remaining six of UPCEA's eight professional Competencies for COLOs (Professional and Continuing Education leaders).

DOI: 10.4324/9781003500742-5

4 The COLO's Seat at the Table

Introduction

A common question that a COLO might receive is "how many online students are enrolled in your institution?" It's a deceptively complex question. The mental model behind such a question typically assumes 100% online students who are studying at a distance from the institution. However, the reality of the modern digital student is varied and multi-layered, especially in light of the changes wrought by the COVID-19 pandemic.

Sometimes, the answer is framed by definitions provided by accrediting bodies or state agencies. The COLO needs to thoroughly understand these parameters and ensure that the institution is properly interpreting them and accurately reporting required data.

However, depending upon the context, and where not otherwise defined, the question of "how many students" could be answered in any number of ways. "Online-ness" as a concept can be idiosyncratic and highly contingent upon institutional context. Does it refer to headcount? To enrollments? FTE? Programs alone or also courses? Is blended learning included, where a portion of a course is taught online? What about HyFlex? The following are just a few of the various permutations of how this question could be answered.

- Unduplicated headcount (unique students) enrolled in fully online *programs* in any given term (e.g., fall census date)
- Unduplicated headcount enrolled in fully online *programs* throughout a complete academic year
- Unduplicated headcount only enrolled in fully online *courses* in any given term (e.g., fall census date)

DOI: 10.4324/9781003500742-6

- Unduplicated headcount only enrolled in fully online *courses* throughout a complete academic year
- Unduplicated headcount enrolled in online courses as part of a course load that also includes other modalities (e.g., face-to-face) in any given term (e.g., fall census date)
- Unduplicated headcount enrolled in online courses as part of a course load that also includes other modalities (e.g., face-to-face) throughout a complete academic year
- Unduplicated headcount of students enrolled in either fully online or blended/HyFlex courses as part of a course load that also includes other modalities (e.g., face-to-face) in any given term (e.g., fall census date)
- Unduplicated headcount of students enrolled in either fully online or blended/HyFlex courses as part of a course load that also includes other modalities (e.g., face-to-face) throughout a complete academic year
- Full-time students in any of the above scenarios
- Part-time students in any of the above scenarios
- Full-time equivalent students in any of the above scenarios
- Enrollments (duplicated headcount) in any of the above scenarios
- The number or percentage of online/blended sections in any given term or throughout an academic year
- The number or percentage of online/blended student credit hours (SCH) in any given term or throughout an academic year

Like any executive leader, COLOs must understand the context and intent of a question in order to properly frame an answer. The complexity of an apparently simple question such as "how many online students" points to the criticality of the COLO's expertise in not just interpreting critical data but also helping to shape strategy and bring that expertise to bear in the service of the institution. However, the only way to ensure that the COLO's knowledge and experience are properly leveraged is – to quote the musical *Hamilton* – to be in the room where it happens.

The Evolving COLO Portfolio

Although the role of the COLO has been appearing on campuses more and more over the last decade, the actual title of COLO has not. In some cases, the title is a legacy of existing hierarchical structures at an institution, in other cases the title is a reflection of the expanding expectations for the senior online leader. The terms Digital Learning and Innovation are being increasingly used to describe the responsibilities and portfolios of the college/university COLO.

In addition to distance learning, activities under such a COLO could include blended learning, AR/VR/XR, simulation development, adaptive learning, artificial intelligence, and any number of other primarily campus-based digital strategies. Some COLOs also have responsibility for their campus centers for teaching and learning. There is a recognition – especially post-pandemic – that digital technologies and techniques cannot exist exclusively on the online campus. Digital innovation is a critical element for all parts of the academic enterprise.

As articulated by the Education Advisory Board (EAB), the COLO (or PCO) leader is being tasked with an increasingly diverse portfolio. Various stakeholders have growing expectations for what the COLO's unit can do – from students to the institution, to employers, to the general public, and more (Figure 4.1). As responsibilities and expectations grow, so does the complexity of the COLO role.

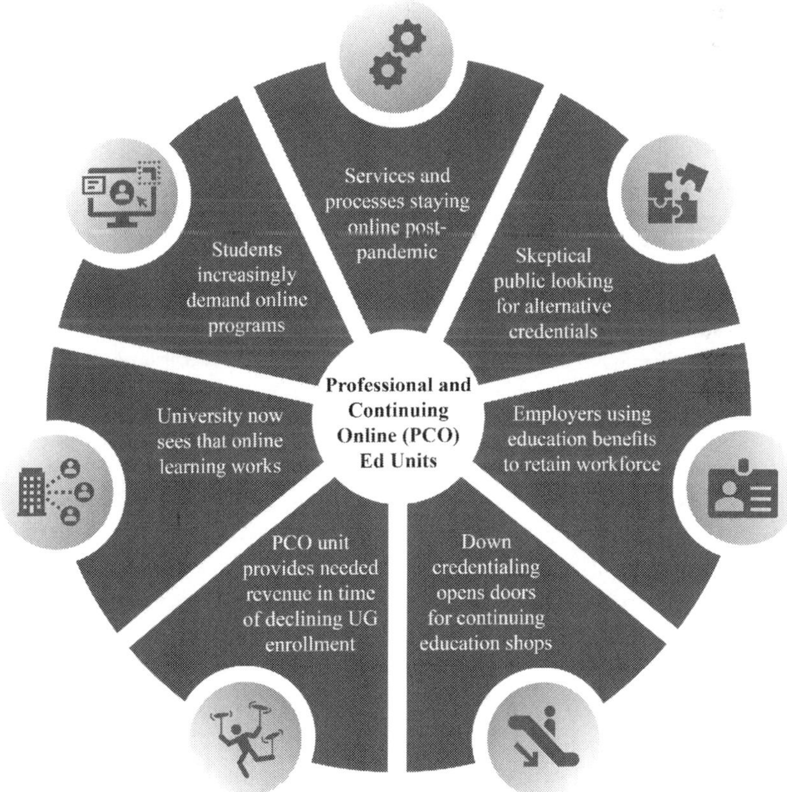

Figure 4.1 The Newly Central PCO Unit.
Used with permission from EAB.

Reporting lines often signify how an institution prioritizes online learning. The majority of COLOs report within their institution's academic affairs organization, often specifically to the college / university chief academic officer, while others report to a Senior Vice Provost, depending upon the institution. According to a UPCEA research study (Uranis et al., 2024), 41% of online education units reside in the Provost's office, while 25% are contained within multiple academic units, and 17% are standalone units. Example COLO titles within the academic affairs reporting structure could include: Vice Provost for Digital Learning, Associate Provost of Online Learning, Vice Provost for Online Strategy and Teaching Innovation, Dean of the Global Campus, and even COLO. These positions typically sit on their respective Provost's councils, sometimes deans' councils if the title warrants, but they rarely sit on the President's / Chancellor's cabinet.

Those few COLOs who do sit on the President's cabinet have a unique voice within the institution to position the online and digital operation as a strategic lever to accomplish key institutional objectives such as increased enrollment, reduced time to graduation, greater student success, and new revenue for reinvestment elsewhere. Yet, whether they sit in the President's cabinet or not, it is critical that *all* COLOs position their portfolios as solutions to institutional problems and assets for achieving strategic goals.

Align with Institutional Priorities

It is important for a COLO's success that his / her work leading online and digital learning is perceived as an investment with a measurable return for the institution and not merely as an expense. Online learning and digital innovation should be core to the academic enterprise, not a utility.

An apt comparison might be with an honors college. Many universities have an honors college that is created to attract and serve a particular type of high-achieving student. Honors students are offered special classes with fewer enrollments, honors-only facilities, dedicated dormitories, guest lectures, and other custom programming catered to their unique needs. In many cases, an honors college does not offer any of its own courses; rather, it offers honors sections from other academic colleges. In essence, they offer specially designed versions of courses from other academic units to a targeted student population.

Many online learning operations could say the same. Unless an online unit has its own faculty and programs, it is offering online sections that belong to academic colleges and programs. Like the honors college, the online program offers specially designed versions of courses from other academic units to a targeted student population. This may be a nontraditional student, a student on campus who needs schedule flexibility, or some combination.

A wise university would never consider an honors college an expense. It is an investment to attract the highest achieving students, raise its academic profile, and attract other students. Likewise, a sensible university would realize the strategic value of a supported online learning unit. Ensuring that this perception is understood not just by the President and Provost of an institution but also by the other key leaders (vice presidents, deans, and vice provosts) should be a continual effort by the COLO.

Therefore, it is imperative that the COLO become not merely familiar with the institution's strategic plan but internalize it into his/her own operation. The online learning unit's goals, activities, and measures should be directly aligned with the broader strategic plan. By executing against an online operational plan that supports the objectives in the institutional strategic plan, the COLO can help to ensure that online learning is positioned as an asset – an investment with a measurable return – and not simply an expense.

The COLO should read board minutes, attend (or watch) board meetings, and seek to understand key goals that both the President/Chancellor and the board are pursuing. The COLO should proactively meet with colleagues on campus, such as deans, vice presidents, and vice provosts, in order to better understand each of their challenges and seek ways that online learning can assist them in solving their problems and accomplishing their unit goals.

Advisory boards are also extremely useful. A COLO would be well-served to establish bodies of faculty, students, and internal staff to provide critical stakeholder feedback. Depending upon the COLO's portfolio, an external/industry advisory board may also be appropriate.

Strategically, the COLO's orientation should be pointed outward to determine how online learning can support the institution at all levels. Tactically, the COLO will need to shape his/her organization internally to align personnel, activities, and measures with broader institutional objectives.

Even without a formal seat on the President/Chancellor's cabinet, the COLO can still arrange ad hoc meetings with university leadership when warranted to seek authorization for projects or to provide briefings. The importance of communication cannot be overstated. A COLO must not only align his/her organization to the institutional mission and effectively execute against that strategy, he/she must also ensure that institutional leadership is aware of these efforts. Regular briefings, annual reports, newsletters, updated websites, and other strategies that leverage diverse communication channels should be regularly employed to ensure that others across the campus community – especially leadership – know of the online learning unit's contribution toward accomplishing the institutional strategic plan.

If the COLO truly wants a seat at the leadership table, he/she must align his/her unit's activities to the strategic plan, execute effectively, and then ensure that leadership is aware of online learning's broader impact. In so doing, the COLO will be best positioned to be "in the room where it happens."

The Importance of Data

An essential component to a COLO's ability to align strategy, successfully execute, and effectively communicate is access to data. Only by understanding key metrics and tracking performance against those metrics can the COLO effectively coordinate tactics with strategy. Without data the COLO cannot know what is working (or is not working), make proactive course corrections when necessary, and compellingly communicate impact to others at the institution.

Few COLOs have robust data collection and analytical capabilities within their own units. Not every COLO even has access to institutional LMS data (especially where the LMS is procured and managed by central IT). However, most institutions have established IR offices. COLOs should make use of their IR office's expertise and services, especially for data that support the institutional strategic plan.

One challenge a COLO could face when requesting data and reports from an IR office is the IR department's own limited resources balanced against too much institutional demand. The COLO's needs can end up at the bottom of a priority list below those of the President, Provost, and various legal and compliance requirements. Some COLOs have mitigated this by electing to fund a position (full or partial salary) within the IR office dedicated to their own data needs. Such an investment in a COLO's budget should be seriously considered. Without data, a COLO will be unable to effectively manage his/her operation, akin to a ship captain without a compass.

Given the criticality of data in making informed decisions and data's importance in demonstrating impact to institutional stakeholders, the decision to fund dedicated IR personnel (or data analysts within the online learning unit itself) should be driven by the COLO's ability to collect, analyze, and report critical data. Strategic use of data is a necessary ingredient for the success of today's COLO.

Competency Connection

UPCEA COLO Competency	*COLO Insight*	*Influencing Factors*	*Influencing Factor (COVID-Era)*	*Institutional Risk*
Program Planning	Domain of COLO responsibilities is ever-evolving and the organizational structure of the reporting unit needs to evolve in sync (or before). COLO priorities must align with institutional strategic priorities.	Maturity of online learning enterprise Institutional prioritization of online learning Access to data Resources to execute strategy	Scope creep: expanded definition from online to digital	Priorities of role/unit will shift as the domain evolves and the institution evolves (e.g., leadership transitions). Identity of the role/unit needs to be able to evolve.

References

Uranis, J., Ives, K., Etter, B., & Sullberg, D. (2024). *Benchmarking Online Enterprises: Insights into Structures, Strategies, and Financial Models in Higher Education* (N. Mack, Ed.) [Review of *Benchmarking Online Enterprises: Insights into Structures, Strategies, and Financial Models in Higher Education*]. UPCEA.

Expert Perspectives

- John O'Brien, EDUCAUSE
- Asim Ali, Auburn University
- Robert Bruce, Rice University
- Carmin Chan, Northern Arizona University

John O'Brien, Ph.D.

President/Chief Executive Officer, EDUCAUSE

It is no surprise to me that COLOs consider having a seat at the table a key measure of success and an overdue indicator that the profession and role of a COLO is no longer just *emerging*. When COLOs earn and take a seat at the table, it likely means that the importance of their role is settled science, and they no longer have to keep making the case, a desirable destination to be sure.

CIOs (or whatever title they have) know this table story quite well, and yet another advantage of CIOs and COLOs working closely together is that there's something to be learned from each other. EDUCAUSE has tracked two "seat at the table" sorts of measures over the years: whether CIOs report to the President and whether CIOs are part of the President's cabinet. COLOs should note that these numbers don't move quickly or easily. For example, from 2003 to 2016, the percentage of CIOs reporting to the President started at 30% and ended at 32%. More seats were pulled out for CIOs on the cabinet, with this percentage going from 44% to 55%, a better showing. A 2020 EDUCAUSE QuickPoll during the pandemic sees this cabinet number jump up to 60% and, more encouragingly, also finds the CIO role holding more operational and strategic influence connected (Brooks, 2020).

Over time, I've come to focus primarily on the cabinet seat, figuring that CIOs reporting lines are less critical than being in the room where it happens. Our workforce research shows that serving on the cabinet makes it significantly more likely that CIOs discuss IT implications of institutional decisions, help shape institutional directions, and even help shape academic directions (Pomerantz and Brooks, 2016). Being at the table matters.

What EDUCAUSE has learned about the seat and the table over the years is likely relevant to COLOs, especially those who may be at an early phase of this journey.

- You're not alone. It's a small table and a tough path for new entrants, but it's been navigated before, most recently perhaps by CIOs and chief diversity officers. Talking to them might be time well spent.
- The path was faster due to the pandemic, and that's a phenomenon worth paying attention to. No one wants another pandemic, but elements of the pandemic that made a difference may not require a global health crisis. What are the topics that create urgency for senior campus leaders now? Certainly, the ongoing crisis of student success comes to mind, and the flurry of hype and appropriate enthusiasm/interest in AI

shimmer with energy these days. Finding a way into topics like this will accentuate the indispensability of the COLO role.

- At EDUCAUSE, we supported CIOs aspiring to be at the table in a number of ways. For example, we have focused on connecting CIOs to institutional "grand challenges," an initiative that goes as far back as 2006 (Hawkins, 2006). CIOs who focus on institutional challenges make themselves indispensable and more relevant to senior leaders. CIOs or COLOs who are identified exclusively or mostly with tactical execution and problem solving won't be on the speed dial of a President struggling with grand challenges at a strategic altitude. In support of our community we have published articles and elevated the conversation about what a CIO could and should do in this regard, for example, in the 2020 Top 10 and in a series of podcast episodes (EDUCAUSE, 2023) on the idea of the "integrative CIO" (Wulff, 2022). As former EDUCAUSE board member Elias Eldaire has said, "CIOs need to be the CIO of the entire campus, not CIO of the IT department!" Integrative COLO? Why not?
- I talked to an extraordinary CIO who has been systematically and maddeningly blocked from a seat at the table, and I reassured her that in her case "it's not about you." And I meant it. And yet, sometimes it actually *is* about you. It's perhaps easy to get mad at the table when you're not invited, but CIOs who have navigated the path will usually say that it was as much about changing themselves as it was changing the minds of others. They talk about changing how they presented themselves, reconsidering what kinds of things they said and didn't say, connecting the dots to grand challenges, and reflecting on their strategic presence.

These reflections may be helpful, and it may also be true that the path for COLOs is and will be markedly different. Either way, my personal hope is that once we're all at the table together we can begin the more interesting and vital work of re-imaging the table itself. As higher education is buffeted by unprecedented attacks and financial exigencies, I think we need to explore how leaders approach strategic and existential challenges, and it could be that the traditional table – whose defining feature is that it *excludes* – may no longer best serve our needs.

References

Brooks, D.C. (2020, October 9). *EDUCAUSE QuickPoll Results: Senior IT Leadership*. EDUCAUSE Review. https://er.educause.edu/blogs/2020/10/educause-quickpoll-results-senior-it-leadership

Pomerantz, J. and Brooks, D.C. (2016). *The Higher Education IT Workforce Landscape: 2016*. EDUCAUSE. https://library.educause.edu/~/media/files/library/2016/4/ers1603.pdf

Hawkins, B. (2006). *The EDUCAUSE Grand Challenges Initiative*. In EDUCAUSE 2006 Annual Conference Proceedings. EDUCAUSE. https://events.educause.edu/annual-conference/2006/proceedings/the-educause-grand-challenges-initiative

EDUCAUSE. (2023). *EDUCAUSE and the Integrative CIO*. EDUCAUSE Review. https://er.educause.edu/channels/educause-and-the-integrative-cio

Wulff, M. (2022, August 25). *The Evolving Role of CIOs in Higher Education*. EDUCAUSE Review. https://er.educause.edu/articles/2022/8/the-evolving-role-of-cios-in-higher.education

Asim Ali, Ph.D.

Executive Director, Biggio Center, Auburn University

When Auburn University's 2013 Strategic Plan called for enhancing the institutional e-Learning culture and establishing online undergraduate programs, it set the stage for my role as the Founding Director of Auburn Online. From the outset, my focus has been on aligning our initiatives with the broader goals of the institution, ensuring that the work we do contributes meaningfully to Auburn's mission. Success in this role has required a commitment to collaboration and engagement with key stakeholders. A key to this approach is understanding that credit for major accomplishments does not need to be individually claimed. An engaged manager already recognizes your contributions; celebrating others for their work fosters a positive and productive environment.

My Evolving Role

Over the years, my role has evolved significantly. At Auburn, online teaching is not a siloed entity. It is integrated into the broader academic enterprise. In January 2020, we expanded the Biggio Center for the Enhancement of Teaching and Learning to include Auburn Online and meet the needs of faculty and students across all teaching modalities. This expansion has invited faculty to approach teaching more holistically, engaging in the development of in-person, hybrid, and online courses with a focus on student-centric learning.

The expanded role of Auburn Online, and now the larger Biggio Center, has fostered a culture where faculty actively seek partnerships to achieve strategic goals. This collaborative spirit has allowed us to contribute to key initiatives such as the Auburn First dual enrollment program, AUX virtual and augmented reality, and AI literacy. Recognizing the need to continually adapt, we have taken the lead in emerging conversations around microcredentials and often take on external projects to leverage our expertise and elevate Auburn's brand.

An entrepreneurial mindset has been essential in this evolving role. As the landscape of online learning continues to change, I am mindful of the need to explore new strategic priorities that can benefit the institution. While online teaching remains a core focus, we are constantly seeking opportunities to apply our team's talents to new initiatives that align with Auburn's goals and enhance outcomes across the university.

The Strategic Use of Data

At a university primarily focused on the on-campus student experience, it's crucial to select projects that elevate the overall student experience and contribute to the larger campus narrative. Data play a role in these efforts. For example, the Biggio Center offers market analysis for all proposed programs at Auburn. These reports don't dictate programmatic decisions, but they provide insights that support faculty and administrators in designing innovative and impactful programs.

We also regularly review data on students' enrollment and success in online courses and programs. Tracking metrics such as the average number of SCHs completed in online courses by graduating classes allows us to understand the growing role of online offerings in helping students' timely completion. This approach ensures that online courses are not only aligned with student demand but also contribute positively to Auburn's broader objectives.

Institutional Integration and Alignment

Auburn University's Quality Enhancement Plan (QEP), AuburnAchieve, focuses on improving first-destination outcomes and quality, and helping students articulate the relevance of their academic and co-curricular experiences. The Biggio Center supports various units in their QEP-related projects. Auburn Online has taken a proactive role by modeling an effort to identify key professional skills gained in undergraduate online programs. We are collecting and reporting data on students' ability to explain how their coursework relates to their career goals. This initiative supports the QEP's goals and evaluates a potential model for online programs contributing to major institutional priorities.

Continued and Consistent Leadership

Communicating major accomplishments with senior leadership, for example, via occasional emails, is not just warranted but is a responsibility for those leading innovative work. Additionally, a genuine desire to collaborate keeps us connected with the most innovative and hard-working colleagues on campus. By maintaining a focus on institutional success over personal recognition, we build positive relationships that allow for engagement with important initiatives. Our communications team highlights these accomplishments through stories that align with the campus narrative. When you consistently support and enable innovative projects on campus, even detractors find it difficult to overlook your expertise and contributions.

Advice for Aspiring COLOs

For those aspiring to leadership, it's important to define success by your ability to enable others to succeed. Bringing a genuine desire to collaborate and support others in their success drives institutional success and allows you to be part of impactful initiatives on campus. Moreover, it connects your talented team members to projects that build and highlight their expertise, ensuring that achievements are recognized and celebrated.

Looking Ahead

The role of the COLO at traditional institutions continues to evolve, requiring adaptability and a forward-looking approach. As online and hybrid learning become more intertwined with all students' success, the COLO's role in driving innovation and aligning with institutional goals will remain critical. By staying mission-driven, collaborative, and data-informed, COLOs can ensure their impact elevates units across the institution, securing their place in the future of higher education leadership.

Robert Bruce, Ph.D.

Dean, Susanne M. Glasscock School of Continuing Studies and Adjunct Professor of Humanities, Rice University

I might be making a mistake with this early confession, but I am not the COLO at Rice University. Should you choose to read on, however, I think you will find that my career history walks in lockstep with the evolution of online learning and, thus, the COLO role and responsibilities.

Before the advent of the COLO moniker, I served as Associate Dean for the Division of Instructional Innovation and Assessment (DIIA) at the University of Texas at Austin (UT Austin). We focused on technology-enhanced learning and innovation with a portfolio including three centers: teaching effectiveness, instructional technologies, and assessment. Some of the results of our work led to recommendations for investment and scale of flipped classroom models, which eventually gave way to fully online classes. Three characteristics were key to DIIA's success: a faculty-driven innovation model, an assessment team proving (or disproving) the efficacy of our pilot models, and the division's position as a fully-funded central unit reporting to the Provost.

In 2011, I joined the University of North Carolina at Chapel Hill (UNC) as Director of Continuing Education. UNC did not have a COLO when I arrived, but Continuing Education served both matriculated and non-matriculated students with a large portfolio of online classes. In 2016, I became the founding Director of the Carolina Office for Online Learning (COOL) when we expanded our existing Continuing Education marketing and instructional design team. Combining the two units (Continuing Education and Online Learning) under one leadership position was a sound strategy, but the funding model was not ideal, the interaction with deans was intermittent, and a lack of resources hampered overall growth and service to the university. Progress was certainly made, however, and UNC has since improved its organizational model and outcomes by creating the Vice Provost for Digital and Lifelong Learning position and restructuring Continuing Education and COOL into UNC Digital and Lifelong Learning.

At Rice, I serve as Dean of the Susanne M. Glasscock School of Continuing Studies. Like many of our peers, our mission-driven portfolio includes personal and professional development programs, with an ever-growing amount of those delivered online, especially in the wake of COVID-19. The Continuing Studies dean works closely with other school deans by serving on the Provost Deans Council and participating in all academic and strategic gatherings, even if the gatherings are focused on the residential student experience.

Covering university mission-critical activities such as strategic planning, budget transformation, general education reform, executive search committees, capital campaign planning, and board of trustees meetings, it is vital that the Continuing Studies dean have a seat at the table and a voice for innovation and access. Unlike several peer institutions that treat continuing and professional studies schools as standalone fiscal and academic units, Rice Continuing Studies operates in the exact same credit and noncredit expense / revenue model shared by all of the traditional academic schools.

Although Rice is known for its face to face, undergraduate residential college system, the university has put forward plans for strategic growth in graduate programs, summer sessions, and alternative and nondegree credentials. I am admittedly biased, but I believe Continuing Studies has the greatest potential for online growth and our school's strategic plan reflects this in its emphasis on the university's ambitious goals. Online growth, however, for any of Rice's schools, can only come through strong collaboration and strategic partnership with Rice's COLO, the Associate Provost for Digital Learning and Strategy. A key distinction worth noting is that "online" is not part of the Rice COLO title. We have found at Rice, as many other universities have, that digital innovation has strong applications in a traditional classroom setting as well. It is not lost on me that the evolution of online learning has come full circle to the technology-enhanced learning and innovation work where my journey began back at UT Austin. I suppose at the end of the day, whether a professor, Provost, dean, or COLO, we are all seeking the same outcome: transformational learning experiences for our students.

In all three university settings, the success of online initiatives, or lack thereof, whether led by a centralized online learning department or a school of Continuing Sstudies, can be traced back to four fundamental components:

- A direct reporting line to the Provost
- Strong collaboration with academic deans
- A funding model that is easily understood and fully endorsed by university partners
- An uncompromising goal of transformational education experiences

I believe these same indicators of success can and should be applied to COLO positions.

Carmin Chan, Ph.D.

Vice Provost of Northern Arizona University Online, Northern Arizona University

Online leaders have an opportunity to modernize our stoic higher education institutions from within, making them more responsive to the needs of modern students across all modalities. Historically, college students were expected to adapt themselves to the expectations of a traditional college-going experience, especially within four-year residential college campus settings. However, in recent years a "marginalized majority" of college students have increasingly enrolled in higher education institutions while balancing other life demands (Deil-Amen, 2015). Unfortunately, marginalized groups are often presumed deficient, rather than re-examining educational systems that fail to meet the needs of post-traditional learners. This is where online leaders have a critical role to play. COLOs have the opportunity to be "at the table" among campus senior leadership and can help reframe misunderstandings or deficit-laden narratives about post-traditional learner populations.

That said, COLOs must understand that many of our campus colleagues personally experienced higher education in a traditional, even elite, college environment. They are accustomed to relying on metrics (such as IPEDS) that were built upon assumptions of a traditional, residential college experience. These metrics govern almost everything we do – from gauging student success outcomes to financial modeling and resource forecasting, faculty workload analysis, and much more. Further complicating matters, these same traditional metrics are also often used to inform institutional goals and the benchmarks given to our senior leaders by external entities such as elected or appointed boards, regulatory bodies, and governmental agencies. However, these metrics heavily emphasize first-time-in-college cohorts. They have significant limitations when evaluating online learners and other populations who deviate from "traditional." Our online students are more likely to have experiences at numerous colleges (transfer-in) or are pursuing graduate credentials, typically enroll less than full-time, often self-pay or rely upon employer tuition benefits rather than parents, and balance school alongside caregiving commitments. Contextualizing the dynamic journey of post-traditional learners for our colleagues is a keystone to successfully transforming their (potentially) antiquated view of modern college students, identifying what these learners need to be successful, and understanding how online education can help achieve institutional goals.

COLOs operating within traditional institutions have a dual obligation to align their efforts to the traditional metrics while also offering colleagues additional information that better aligns with the operations of an online enterprise. For example, while IPEDS reporting may be used for census snapshots, we can also capture enrollment snapshots and funnel reporting at other key dates within a term (particularly if your online enterprise uses rolling, year-round admissions, and enrollment). Critiquing and updating institutional reporting systems to be inclusive of online operations is critical because these are the same reporting tools used by other senior campus leaders. Online needs to be present and reflected with valid and reliable data, so that it can be positioned more visibly with these senior leaders. Furthermore, if your institutional goals are centered around first-time-in-college learners (who are typically a small portion of online enrollments), view that as an opportunity. COLOs can forge campus partnerships focused on ways online education can bolster first-year retention–especially among lucrative non-resident students. I've used this partnership approach to execute numerous new online success programs such as virtual peer mentorship, microgrants, and revised catalog policies that mutually benefited my institution's residential and fully online learners alike. Ultimately, COLOs must carefully consider how to align their efforts to institutional priorities and ensure that these efforts are accurately captured and visible.

Understanding the goals and metrics used to assess your institution's senior leadership is a critical tool for COLOs. Aligning your team's efforts and measured impacts on institutional strategic goals helps demonstrate the value of online education within traditional college campuses. Integrating the online unit's efforts into the minds of other campus leaders helps make your online unit's goals become a part of the institutional goals, as well.

References

Deil-Amen, R. (2015). The "Traditional" College Student: A Smaller and Smaller Minority and Its Implications for Diversity and Access Institutions. In M. Stevens & M. Kirst (Ed.), *Remaking College: The Changing Ecology of Higher Education* (pp. 134–166). Redwood City: Stanford University Press. https://doi.org/10.1515/9780804793551-009

5 Without a Strategy, Your Budget Becomes Your Strategy

Introduction

As has already been stated, to be successful, COLOs must act purposefully and in alignment with their institution's strategic plan. With planning and intentionality, a COLO can direct his/her unit in a manner that ensures, as much as possible, that it is contributing to the college/university's goals. That means that COLOs cannot be passive and simply wait for specific guidance on *how* they should develop and prioritize activities; they must be proactive and initiate new programs, practices, technologies, and partnerships in the service of institutional objectives. This may include making hard decisions about ending certain ongoing initiatives to free up resources to pursue new opportunities. Discerning these strategic opportunities and then navigating the internal mechanisms to bring them into reality is one of the most important skills that a COLO can develop.

Strategy vs. Tactics

How can a COLO effectively execute in support of an institutional strategy? The first step is to clearly understand the difference between strategy and tactics. Each is critical and dependent upon the other for success.

The conventional wisdom is that strategy refers to the overarching objectives for an organization, sometimes spanning a long-term time horizon. It can include high-level commitments such as deadlines, resource commitments,

DOI: 10.4324/9781003500742-7

and responsible parties. Tactics, on the other hand, are the day-to-day efforts that are pursued to actually achieve the goals identified by the strategy. These might include budget allocations, staff tasking, prioritized activities, specific investments, and other quotidian activities on a more short-term basis.

Both are necessary. Strategy sets the destination and the deadline. Tactics travel the route required to arrive. What sets a leader apart from a manager is that a leader understands the value of both strategy and tactics and can effectively navigate them both.

Strategic Budgeting

Understanding financial management and overseeing a budget are critical skills that a typical COLO will need to master. While this book won't delve into the details of budget management, we strongly recommend that anyone either currently occupying or planning to pursue a COLO role who does not have experience managing a higher education budget seek out appropriate educational resources. Understanding revenue source concepts such as Education and General (E&G), Auxiliary, Contracts and Grants (C&G), and foundation funds would be of great value for any COLO, whether working in a public or private institution. Other budget-related topics include Incremental Budgeting, Zero-Based Budgeting, RCM budget models (including hybrid RCM), Activity-based Budgeting, Centralized Budgeting, Performance-based budgeting, carry forward funding, and state-dictated performance-based funding models. A COLO is not expected to be a CPA-certified accountant; however, to effectively marshal resources in support of an overarching strategy, COLOs need to deeply understand their own institutional budget model and the broader financial context in which they work.

Against this backdrop, a COLO must determine the tactical priorities that will support his/her overarching strategy, which should, in turn, support the institution's strategic plan. This can be accomplished through the judicial application of strategic budgeting, which ensures that strategic goals drive tactical decisions. Because tactical activities will dictate whether or not strategic goals are achieved, the funding dedicated to specific tactics is an investment in success.

There is a saying: without a strategy, your budget is your strategy. This encapsulates the importance of priority-driven resource allocation. If your annual budget is passive, merely a repeat of previous years' funding decisions, then you are trapped in the priorities of the past. Although the overall funding a COLO may receive annually may be a fixed total – or even a reduction, depending upon the wider financial context – the COLO likely has considerable autonomy to make decisions about how to distribute that total sum within his/her own operation. How can those funds be most strategically assigned to accomplish the institutional mission?

Should a vendor license be renewed? Should another tool be acquired? Should you hire an instructional designer or a media producer? Should you fund a partial position in the IR office? Should you increase your media spend for marketing? There are innumerable questions that a COLO will face when building a strategic budget and the circumstances of each institution will be unique.

One challenge a COLO will face in building a strategic budget is the fact that, in most higher education institutions, the single largest budget expense is personnel. Higher education is a people-oriented enterprise. It may be difficult to free up new financial resources for the innovation of new initiatives when the majority of the budget is already allocated to salary and benefits.

However, this does not necessarily mean that in order to free up the budget to pursue new initiatives staff must be eliminated. A more fundamental question would be: Are staff being directed toward the strategic priorities of the unit or institution? Can they be reassigned to other activities or projects? Can they be retrained through professional development to focus on new areas (such as artificial intelligence or microcredentials)? Can you strategically leverage natural attrition to reshape the composition and skill set of the workforce over time?

Like in any enterprise, staff layoffs should be a last resort. While always difficult for both those directly affected and those who remain employed, layoffs are especially hard in non-profit higher education where they are fairly uncommon. Personnel reductions are not part of the culture. As such, they are typically reserved for financial exigency, not strategic prioritization. Because they are rare, when implemented layoffs can lead to reduced morale and increased attrition. They should be very carefully considered and only after all other options have been explored.

Overcoming Obstacles and Leveraging Momentum

It is easy to say in the abstract that a COLO should set a strategy, align budget resources, and execute operations to achieve goals. However, the real-world experience is more complicated and nuanced. There are always finite resources, competing opinions, and inevitable setbacks. The types of obstacles and priorities a COLO will encounter will vary depending upon the context in which he / she works.

In some cases, a COLO will need to act within a start-up context. This might mean a focus on internal and external partnerships, shared staff positions, and bootstrapped initiatives. The start-up COLO should be focused on establishing infrastructure, policies, and process, looking for early wins and validating investments.

In other cases, the COLO is operating in an emerging or established context, where the online enterprise is somewhat mature and basic infrastructure, policies, and practices are in place. However, the online operation may be limited in scope, local / regional, or reliant on external partners such as an OPM. In this context, the COLO will be focused on ensuring that quality, service, and revenue are maintained for the core stakeholder populations (students, faculty, and administration).

Sometimes a COLO will be overseeing an online enterprise that has achieved scale. These COLOs will need to ensure that systems and processes are in place that support volume and that efficiency is maintained even within a large operation. Multiple vendor relationships will likely be integral to the portfolio. Communications become more challenging the larger the organization and a COLO in such a context will discover that the axiom "one cannot over-communicate" is quite true.

A COLO may exist in any of these contexts or elsewhere along this spectrum. Or they may move between them as an organization grows. Yet a theme that runs through all contexts is the need for the COLO to sustain an entrepreneurial mindset. Being creative, agile, and fiscally responsible – while maintaining a high risk tolerance – is applicable in both start-up and scaled contexts, and everywhere in between.

How can a COLO overcome objections, competing priorities, and other internal obstacles to accomplish strategic goals? In some cases, objections will come as a result of program success. As an online enterprise grows, it can put pressure on other parts of the administrative capabilities of the institution, such as the financial aid office, admissions, IR, advising, and elsewhere. A tactic that was previously discussed was using strategic budgeting to fund staff in key areas to mitigate that pressure and address objections.

Another effective tactic is to align activities with the objectives of other units, particularly academic schools / colleges. For example, if a business program has ambitions to grow but is limited by classroom space and a saturated local market, prioritizing online business program development and marketing can serve as a win-win for both the program and the online unit. The institution itself may have identified strategic priorities and goals. As previously discussed, the COLO should "follow the energy" (Cavanagh and Thompson, 2018) of institutional momentum and position his/her operation as an asset for achieving those priorities and goals. This orients the online enterprise as a key solution worthy of investment and will significantly reduce internal obstacles. Dexterity between a college/university's administrative and academic units is a unique opportunity for COLOs to scaffold their strategy across critical domains of the institution.

In almost all cases it will be critical to an online operation's success to ensure that the unit's funding model is effective and establishes enough financial incentive for internal participation while still providing adequate revenue to cover the online operation. These funding models can take many forms including an internal OPM, a student fee, an allocation based on an RCM budget, or some combination of these (or other) models. An important maxim is that the level of investment/risk should determine the level of participation/return and that return can be shared between academic units and online support units. As much as possible, a COLO should frame finances as a *partnership*, not a transaction.

Maintaining Alignment

A COLO should regularly confirm that his/her operational orientation is aligned with the institutional leadership's priorities. Strategic plans evolve, unforeseen opportunities arise, leadership changes, and external forces impose new realities. The COLO must periodically calibrate his/her operation against the in situ conditions of the day to ensure that the institution's strategy and the online strategy have not drifted out of alignment.

A lack of alignment could result in resources being wasted on non-critical endeavors, a reduction in funding, reputational damage, staff morale impact, employee attrition, or other negative outcomes. A proactive COLO will continually monitor the broader institutional context, meet with peers and others, review materials and minutes from leadership and board meetings, and consistently interrogate assumptions. Using these various data inputs, as well as others, the COLO can make regular course corrections and strategy adjustments that will help ensure ongoing alignment and continued value-added contributions toward achieving institutional objectives.

Competency Connection

UPCEA COLO Competency	*COLO Insight*	*Influencing Factors*	*Influencing Factor (COVID-Era)*	*Institutional Risk*
Resource Management	Strategic budgeting ensures relevance and alignment Personnel is the largest expense and evolving talent needs are top of mind for COLOs	Resource limitations Changing institutional priorities Various budget models Remote work as a business proposition for online learning Total experience (employee + learner experience)	Evolving institutional prioritization of online strategy Burnout, Bore-out, Great Resignation, Quiet Quitting, Quiet Hiring, Quiet Firing, shared experience online for 5+ years	Leadership transitions Funding challenges Misaligned budget model incentives HR should lean on COLOs for data, best practices, skills trends, and success stories to inform contemporary talent strategies (how can blended learning inform blended/remote work?)

References

Cavanagh, T.B., Thompson, K. (2018). Keeping FIRRST Things First: The Delicate Dance of Leading Online Innovation at Your Institution. In: Piña, A., Lowell, V., Harris, B. (eds) *Leading and Managing e-Learning. Educational Communications and Technology: Issues and Innovations*. Springer, Cham. https://doi.org/10.1007/978-3-319-61780-0_1

Expert Perspectives

- Sasha Thackaberry Voinovich, SkillsWave
- Julie J. Thalman, University of Cincinnati
- Joshua Kim, Dartmouth College

Sasha Thackaberry-Voinovich, Ph.D.

President, SkillsWave

Resource allocation and budgeting are one of the most important dependencies for success in building and growing high-quality online programs. If your available resources are insufficient to meet institutional goals, you need to get more resources or adjust your goals.

All good COLOs know that funding allocations within an institution are all about politics. While aligning to the strategic plan is important, it is only the beginning of the goal setting that the COLO must navigate in order to be appropriately resourced. Oftentimes what the highest level executives care about on "the daily" may not be the same goals articulated in the institution's strategic plan.

Regardless of how well you align your goals to the institution's "published goals," as well as their less published daily priorities, you will still need to allocate your departmental budget in order to achieve your goals. As the co-authors mention, while ending work streams, committees, initiatives, or grant projects that do not have a demonstrable impact on your goals may be difficult, it is also necessary.

Yet institutions love initiatives, committees, and grant projects. The mechanisms that most institutions operate under are highly collaborative, from decision-making to actioning on objectives. There can be good side effects of this, but often there are also negative side effects of zombie projects with little to no impact. You need to be an effective zombie hunter, but with a twist. In killing ineffective work sets, you cannot simply send an arrow into the heart of a zombie. You must "transition" out of that set of work in a classy, communicative, and data-driven way.

In any effort regarding a change in resourcing or personnel, change management is critical. Keeping the messaging forward-facing, rather than articulating what didn't work, is a better approach.

Because what we do as COLOs lives in a space of continual innovation and change, it's more important that specific "hard" technical skill sets are the dispositions of the individuals on your team. Though it may be difficult to engage in layoffs, it also presents a unique opportunity to build a team that is proactive and problem-solving, rather than spending significant time doing performance management to attempt to get entrenched individuals on board.

The truth of employment at educational institutions is that, even though staff are not typically protected by tenure, the approach to employment typically mirrors tenure: unless an individual does something beyond the pale, there is an expectation of continual employment. Yet you need to build an effective team to meet your goals.

Also, in all cases, how you layoff or transition staff will make or break your reputation at the institution. Be classy, offer employment placement support whenever possible, extend additional weeks of severance where possible, and potentially even delay a layoff so that a longer-term employee can make it to their retirement service requirements. Be deeply respectful to the service of those who have left after they are gone.

Each activity you engage in to create and manage an effective budget will require you to be adept at change management. You can help folks adjust to change with continual communication. Communication is tricky though: not enough, and it seems like you're withholding information. Too much, and people ignore it.

Consider the following techniques:

- Use short videos instead of long missives
- Use direct emails with a handful of bullets rather than well-produced newsletters that are infrequently read
- End out the communications with a slightly unpredictable cadence so that they are paid attention to
- Never send such an update on a Monday or a Friday, when it is most likely to be overlooked

As you communicate, you will need to articulate how the infrastructure that you are building will provide the necessary foundation for achieving your goals. Your goals will likely include enrollment growth, but they may not. Your communication methods should include "call backs" to the institution's key strengths and differentiators.

Through all the infrastructure building, resource alignment, and innovation, remember that your financial model must always incentivize the behavior that you need to see to grow your program. Depending upon your institution, faculty might be teaching online courses as an overload, they might be taught by instructors instead of professors, or even exclusively by adjuncts.

Funding might flow to your department centrally. You might receive funding from student fees, or you might receive a revenue share of the tuition. Regardless of structure, tie the funding to the outcomes that you are going for with a clear, bright line. This will be your greatest change effort, and you need executive support to accomplish it.

Finally, to achieve your goals, you have to be an effective salesperson. If you don't have an elevator pitch, make one. At Louisiana State University, when I created an internal OPM and significantly grew enrollments and revenue, I repeated one thing at every opportunity. What we did was: create high-quality online programs, with world-class student support, in a fiscally sustainable model.

Write your "three things" and repeat them until you hear other people echoing your verbiage. Then you'll know that your change is starting to stick, your resourcing will be coming, and your goals will be realized.

Julie J. Thalman, Ed.D.

Vice Provost, University of Cincinnati Online

At my former institution, a public land-grant R1 university, the budget faced relentless cuts year after year. Despite these challenges, the online unit, which housed over 60 programs and certificates, survived and thrived for many years under an entrepreneurial budget model tailored specifically for online education. This model, a beacon of innovation and flexibility, fostered a culture of growth and success, inspiring the deans to focus on the online landscape and reach nontraditional learners. Our unit was built to serve the underserved – the responsibility of a public institution – and was one in which all team members took pride.

However, this prosperity took a sharp turn following the long-standing dean's departure. In a sweeping decision, the provost's office dismantled the entrepreneurial budget model and replaced it with a traditional one. This change proved to be a precursor of decline for the once-flourishing online unit. The new budget allocation was a mere $2 million, encompassing everything from marketing and salaries to recruitment, summer terms, noncredit courses, and special sessions. Such a constrained budget left little room for meaningful investment in any area, let alone the critical marketing efforts instrumental in driving enrollment growth.

The entrepreneurial spirit that once fueled innovation was stifled, forcing the department to focus solely on maintenance. This shift had profound consequences. Without the robust marketing campaigns that had previously attracted new students, the unit experienced a noticeable decline in enrollment growth. The former forward funding model used to spark new programmatic growth was no longer available, resulting in limited market-driven programs and a portfolio no longer relevant to today's employer needs. The once thriving unit became a team that was slowly dismantled, intertwined with paranoia, job confusion, and fears. How could we have gone from once being seen as the go-to unit to now as an area that was overlooked and often forgotten? The answer is straightforward: managing a budget simply to survive became our campus identity.

Reflecting on this experience, it became evident that the true cost of budget cuts is both financial and strategic. When managing a unit's budget becomes its strategy, the focus shifts from growth and innovation to survival. The strategic vision, the guiding light of any institution, gets lost in the scramble to allocate limited funds across too many needs. This approach ultimately undermines the long-term goals and adaptability of the institution, a cause for concern and heightened awareness.

The story of my former institution serves as a cautionary tale about the perils of short-sighted financial decisions. It underscores the indispensable value of strategic innovation and the importance of maintaining a vision that looks beyond immediate fiscal constraints. Institutions with online units risk compromising their ability to thrive in an increasingly competitive educational landscape by undervaluing online units' needs and allowing the budget to dictate strategy. It's a call to action for all of us to uphold and protect our strategic vision, even when managing the budget seems to become our full-time job.

Joshua Kim, Ph.D.

Assistant Provost for Online Learning Strategy, Dartmouth College

We COLOs tend to see ourselves as the protagonists in a higher education hero's journey. And why not? Many, if not most, are the first to hold our institution's online learning leadership title. We have likely moved up following an untraditional and uncharted academic career path. We possess unwavering evidence-based and data-driven confidence in the knowledge that there is "no significant difference" in the quality of student outcomes between online and F2F learning (Bernard et al., 2004).

The self-regard that we COLOs have for ourselves is, perhaps, understandable. After all, haven't we had a central hand in catalyzing the growth of online education at our traditional (and non-profit) residential institutions? Aren't we part of a profession that has served to dramatically increase educational and credentialing options for full-time workers, parents, and other nontraditional learners? Haven't we, through our leadership in developing the institutional infrastructure for the expansion of online programs, served to support the educational and knowledge production goals of our colleges and universities by helping to develop much-needed new sources of revenue? By hiring learning designers to collaborate with instructors to build all these online programs, haven't we played a role in elevating the role of learning science across the teaching enterprise at our institutions?

The last thing I want to do is diminish the pride that we COLOs feel about our work. Yes, we have much to be proud of. However, I sometimes worry that our COLO self-image might be too congratulatory. Is it possible that, in some areas, we early institutional online learning leaders have done as much harm as good? Might it be that in some places, those of us leading online learning initiatives and units might be exacerbating rather than ameliorating some of the structural inequalities and long-term risks colleges and universities face?

Let me give you two examples of COLO as an anti-hero. You can judge our culpability. The first indictment that might be made is our complicity (at best) or significant blame (at worst) for the adjunctification and contingification (is that a word?) of the higher education instructional workforce. Today, two-thirds of postsecondary instruction is provided by non-tenure-track educators (American Association of University Professors, 2024). What is the causal linkage between the growth of online education and the increasing percentage of courses taught by adjunct and contingent faculty?

If we COLOs are being honest with ourselves and others, we might admit to seeing many advantages in recruiting non-tenure-track educators to teach our online programs. Contingent and adjunct instructors are almost always cheaper than their tenure-track counterparts. As the growth of our online programs – and to an extent our professional success and compensation – are tied to financial performance, doesn't it make sense that we would want to reduce instructional costs by hiring adjunct and contingent faculty?

We COLOs know that adjunct and contingent educators are often the most effective online instructors. As our COLO mission is to create sustainable revenue streams while offering high-quality educational programs, pairing a (less expensive) contingent/adjunct instructor with an instructional design team is appealing. I'm arguing here that a logical strategy to expand the impact of online learning (a good outcome) may be contributing to the adjunctification of teaching (a bad outcome). How often do we see COLOs out in front of the fight to shift college and university hiring practices toward less contingent and more full-time tenure-track positions?

A second domain of possible critical COLO self-reflection is our role in bringing about a new centrality of university/company partnerships. How many of us have been co-conspirators in outsourcing the work of funding, developing, marketing, and supporting some portion of an online program? I know that I'm guilty of these activities. Sure, in the moment of working with an OPM (online program management) or online platform company, our motives are pure. We think we need these company partnerships to address the scarcity of our universities in terms of capital, expertise, or bandwidth to launch new online degree and nondegree programs. And maybe we are right. But do we understand what the long-term consequences of these actions might be?

The area that I worry most about in university/company partnerships is not OPMs. At this point, there is little debate that we should not enter into contracts with online learning companies defined by long (10 years!) terms and revenue share agreements that give the companies two-thirds of tuition dollars. If anything, the COLO community is actively working to get out of these terrible contracts, usually negotiated before our time as COLO by some dean or another. Instead, my concern is with non-profit higher education's increasing dependency on for-profit online learning platform providers to enable our nondegree and alternative credential portfolios. Are universities trading the ability to relatively inexpensively reach tens of millions of potential lifetime learners on these platforms by too cheaply renting our brands to these companies? What will happen when the platform providers, having built their brand equity on ours, pivot to getting their content away from universities and toward other for-profit companies?

Again, I'm not trying to use the opportunity to contribute some words to a book about COLOs to be overly critical of this important (and still relatively new) role in higher education. I am suggesting that an essential marker in the maturity of our identity as COLOs is the confidence to bring a critical perspective to our work. We should be out front in asking uncomfortable questions about the impact (both positive and negative) of our roles in expanding online learning on the broader story of higher education.

References

Bernard, R. M., Abrami, P. C., Lou, Y., Borokhovski, E., Wade, A., Wozney, L., Wallet, P. A., Fiset, M., & Huang, B. (2004). How does distance education compare with classroom instruction? A meta-analysis of the empirical literature. *Review of Educational Research, 74*(3), 379–439. https://doi.org/10.3102/00346543074003379

American Association of University Professors. (2024). *The annual report on the economic status of the profession, 2023–24*. Retrieved from https://www.aaup.org/report/annual-report-economic-status-profession-2023-24

Internal and External Relationships 6

Introduction

Relationships are at the heart of any successful COLO. Ask any seasoned COLO and he/she will likely share stories of difficult relationships turned successful and/or strategies for how to manage perennially prickly relationships that are necessary for day-to-day operations. This chapter is not necessarily about managing interpersonal conflict; rather, it is about leveraging the inherent characteristics that many COLOs share to be a magnetic force for garnering a following in the tough work that COLOs lead. The work of COLOs and their teams cannot be done in isolation. This chapter charts many of the important relationships that should be prioritized. Depending upon a COLO's background and professional trajectory, some of these relationships will come more naturally than others. Fostering and managing relationships takes time out of the day. When COLOs deem this as among the most important investments of their time, the results yield dividends. Conversely, when not enough time is committed to stewarding relationships, the investments in time required to remediate compromised relationships can take their toll with impacts that extend beyond losses in productivity.

This chapter will characterize relationships as those that are internal and those that are external to the university. This characterization is not intended to be mutually exclusive nor exhaustive of the types of relationships that COLOs typically foster. While the constellation of relationships may resemble what others manage in the academic C-Suite, COLOs occupy a unique role in that they are continuously juggling the totality of these internal and external relationships. Central to COLOs' relationships are those that are

DOI: 10.4324/9781003500742-8

made with other COLOs. Often this network serves as a trusted body for new and unsuspecting alliances to move online and digital learning forward, as well as a source of timeless wisdom for those relationships that teeter upon unsteady footing.

Internal Responsibilities and Associated Relationships

Each institution's organizational structure will determine the relative positioning of the units listed below in relation to the unit led by the COLO. While organizational alignment may be a mechanism to promote and/or suppress relationships, it is suggested that organizational structure not be the only predictor of the allegiances COLOs form. Recognizing the importance of all of the relationships and prioritizing those that are necessary for the success of online and digital learning is a core competency of any COLO today. The list below is not meant to be exhaustive; and depending on a university's size, some of these functions may either be combined and/or further expanded. Furthermore, depending on a COLO's purview and associated portfolio, there may either be redundancy in the central university units listed below and those under the purview of the COLO, and/or matrixed lines from the COLO's unit to these central units. Those relationships can prove even more complex to manage. Many of the nuances of these relationships are explored in other chapters in this *Guidebook*, which are referenced below.

Academic Partners – COLOs steward the academic mission of a college or university by expanding access and adding a level of flexibility to an institution's academic offerings. The leadership of the units listed below are among the COLO's regular collaborators. While a COLO may rely on the expertise of each of the units below to execute the online and digital learning strategy, these units have also become more inclusive of online learners and conscious of the complexities of offering more diverse instructional modalities thanks to the relationships established with COLOs and their associated organizations.

- University Registrar
- Enrollment Services
- Office for Student Success
- Office for Assessment and Evaluation
- Disability Resources
- Student Affairs

Operational Partners – Much as with the academic partners, there has been mutual gain among COLOs and operational partners as a result of these relationships. We explore the nuances of these partnerships in further detail in the *Guidebook's* other chapters (e.g., the relationship with the CIO in Chapter 7 and connections to the CFO in Chapter 5). The COVID-19 pandemic necessitated closer relationships among COLOs and the leadership of the units below as a result of the regulatory and compliance-related challenges that emerged when universities were largely serving students online.

- Office of CIO
- Office of the CFO
- Offices responsible for contracts and procurement
- Export Control
- Office responsible for risk management and compliance
- Office of Marketing and Communication
- Human Resources (HR)

Academic Leadership – In addition to the Cabinet-level and academic affairs leadership of colleges/universities, leadership in academic units are key collaborators with COLOs. Academic deans typically have experience in, and some have a vision for, online and digital learning within the context of their disciplines. COLOs frequently liaise with this group of leaders, as well as those assistant and associate-level deans who operationalize their leadership's vision around online and digital learning. It is important to note that COLOs may work alongside academic leadership in a school or college-level engagement, as well as with a university's cohort of academic leaders, such as the Council of Deans. Establishing individual relationships facilitates better relationships with the full group, particularly when concurrence is sought by the COLO.

- Academic Deans
- Academic Assistant/Associate Deans with purview over the curriculum at the undergraduate and graduate levels
- Academic Assistant/Associate Deans with purview over online and digital learning
- Department and Program Chairs

Faculty Governance – The Faculty Senate and derivative committees and task forces are all governance channels that any successful COLO should be regularly engaging. It is best to circulate among these groups proactively so that the relationships are established ahead of any issues that inevitably arise from time to time where a COLO is summoned before the group. These groups have formal convenings and less formal gatherings. Engaging with both and maintaining an open-door policy with faculty is not only a marker of a COLO's success but also an avenue by which COLOs more deeply learn about their roles.

Student Governance – COLOs occupy a unique position often mediating between faculty and students in the dynamic that is teaching and learning. Bringing students along in the academic governance process reveals an important and often under-engaged voice. When you consider that students engage with the digital learning environment and online support services at a ratio that far exceeds that of faculty, it is important to ensure their experiences and perspectives are part of the decision-making process for key decisions. Much as with faculty, integrating into formal student governance processes, as well as maintaining a visible and accessible presence for students, is central to a COLO's ability to broker dialogue between student and faculty experiences with respect to online and digital learning.

The Relationships In-Between

How a university is structured will also largely determine the composition of relationships that a COLO establishes with those individuals and entities external to the university, yet that have some affiliation to the university. The groups below may not all be applicable to every COLO, and likely there are others unique to each institution not listed below.

Governing Bodies – College / University and foundation boards have become increasingly interested in online and digital learning following the COVID-19 pandemic. These governing bodies afford a forum for COLOs to advocate for the institutional benefits of online and digital learning.

Alumni – As online and digital learning continues to grow, evolve, and become mainstream across U.S. higher education, alumni are important touchpoints to communicate the value-add to the institution, as well as can be lucrative connections for additional external relationships explored in the next section. It is important to note that when online and digital learning is perceived as a threat to a college / university, the alumni groups can present a challenge to COLOs.

System Universities – COLOs at the flagship campus in a university system are often called upon to be a thought leader for COLOs at the regional campuses. Conversely, some of the innovations in online and digital learning often originate in the regional campuses given the learner populations served. Relationships across system-level COLOs often have mutual gain.

System Offices – System policies that guide the academic mission of individual colleges or universities may impact the work of COLOs. System offices can also be a source of funding for pilot programs and initiatives relevant to online and digital learning. In some cases, centralized systems have established aggregated units that are distributed across campuses at the system level for cost savings or other efficiencies. There are myriad ways that a COLO may engage with a postsecondary system office, thereby emphasizing the importance of relationships at this level.

Community Colleges and Other Two-Year Institutions – Articulation agreements and pathway programs often have a connection to a COLO's portfolio, given that online and digital learning contributes to learner flexibility that these agreements and programs rely on. COLOs often have great influence on a learner's journey into, through, and from one institution to another as a result of these relationships between universities and community colleges and other two-year institutions.

Regulatory Bodies – COLOs may intersect with state and federal regulatory bodies for approval for new online degrees. An emerging area where COLOs are increasingly intersecting with these same groups is in aligning state workforce needs with online degree, certificate, and nondegree offerings. This is another space where funding may be available for pilot programs and initiatives. COLOs stewarding these relationships ensures institutions are well positioned when an opportunity arises. In addition, there are an increasing number of federal regulations and regional accreditation requirements specifically related to online learning. These compliance tasks call for careful oversight and internal campus collaboration, and fall under the purview of the COLO.

External Responsibilities and Associated Relationships

Like the previous two sections, the list of relationships that COLOs forge with partners external to the university is unique to each university. Captured below are broad domains that a COLO intersects with as part of his/her role and where external relationships are critical to the success of the COLO. COLOs often find these relationships to be a source of energy and new ideas from which universities benefit.

Education Technology Vendors – EdTech vendors are an important set of relationships COLOs manage. While they may be transactional in nature, at their best, these institutional relationships become true partnerships. The most successful vendor relationships are forged when the COLO can communicate the unique facets of a university's academic mission so that the EdTech vendors know how best to steward this mission and associated culture of teaching and learning with their specific product. Many EdTech companies now have chief learning officers, some of whom have come from COLO roles. Leaders in EdTech companies who commit to having healthy relationships with COLOs are often the ones with their fingers on the pulse of online and digital learning needs. In some cases, COLOs may find themselves engaging with venture capitalists given that EdTech is now a global industry estimated to be worth $142B (Grand View Research, 2023). We encourage you to speak with your university's General Counsel before engaging in any conversations with venture capitalists.

Online Program Managers (OPMs) – University relationships with OPMs have evolved over the past two decades. In many cases, the COLO role has emerged as a university sunsets its relationship with an OPM. Even in such cases, some individual schools and colleges at universities may still maintain these relationships, adding to the complexity that a COLO must manage. The OPM space is currently in a period of transition, impacted by a variety of factors such as evolving federal regulations, institutions electing to "in-source" online capacity, evolving student demographics, demand for different types of offerings (such as non credit microcredentials), and tuition revenue sharing (the dominant business model) coming under fire – it is now literally outlawed in Minnesota (Swaak, 2024).

State and National Professional Organizations – State and national professional organizations provide a rigorous peer-review process for the work of COLOs, while also being a testing ground for new and emerging COLO-led initiatives that benefit from feedback among a community of practice. COLOs typically serve in ad hoc leadership roles for these organizations, whereas membership among aspiring COLOs can be an effective way to enhance marketability for future COLO roles. Chapter 10 explores the relationship between COLOs and the national professional organizations relevant to online and digital learning.

Donors – COLOs may intersect with donors who have a particular interest in funding a facet of online and digital learning (particularly those motivated by educational access). COLOs are also called upon by university leadership to highlight to donors innovations in the academic mission by way of online and digital learning.

Public and Private-Sector Employers – A COLO's relationship with employers creates opportunities to glean emerging workforce trends, ensure academic and industry alignment, and foster a pipeline for career-ready learners. There are also economic gains to be had with specific program-level and employee partnerships that many COLOs contributing to this *Guidebook* have successfully established.

COLOs Outside of Higher Education – Being a COLO is not a role unique to academia (see Chapter 13). Organizations are increasingly recruiting COLOs (Attri, 2023), particularly as more and more organizations quantify the economic impact of employee attrition as a result of lack of career mobility (Brafford and Loble, 2024). As more and more institutions commit to digital transformation, learning and an associated culture of learning become leading drivers of that transformation.

The Invisible Work of the COLO

Much of the invisible work of COLOs is not only consumed by forging relationships among these often disparate groups, but it is also in doing the work that often falls between the COLO's unit and a partnering unit. Given that many units led by COLOs can be much newer within a university's organizational structure than say the Office of the Registrar or an Office of the CIO, these partnering units have well-established processes and workflows. The COLO may introduce new policies, procedures, and/or practices in unique support of online and digital learning. The new and invisible work necessary to scaffold these activities is often assumed by the COLO and/or his/her units. Not only is there risk of burnout among staff, but there is also a fundamental risk to students who are uniquely served through online and digital learning. Ensuring elasticity in the partnering units, even those with more long-standing tenure within the organizational structure of the university, will ensure that all students are served equitably and that the policies, procedures, and practices in support of online and digital learning scale to impact the university in its entirety. We know from precedent that there are times when this is necessary (see Chapter 3); and we also know it is COLOs' unique propensity to navigate the myriad internal and external relationships that sets them up for growth opportunities beyond the confines of their specific position descriptions (see Chapter 12).

Competency Connection

UPCEA COLO Competency	*COLO Insight*	*Influencing Factors*	*Influencing Factor (COVID-Era)*	*Institutional Risk*
Marketing, Research, and Evaluation	Understanding the unique insights necessary in managing both internal and external relationships Pressures from "invisible work" are essential to the efficacy of the COLO role and need to be accounted for beyond 5% of other duties as assigned	Compliance and reporting requirements Governance and advocacy within/external to the institution Shifts in revenue models	Cultural legacies	Failure to understand the "invisible work" of the COLO will lead to succession issues with institutional-wide impacts

References

Attri, Raman K. (2023). *Chief e-Learning Officer: In the Era of Speed*. Speed To Proficiency Research: S2Pro©

Brafford, C., & Loble, M. (2024, April 16). *Following in FedEx's footsteps: A successful approach to staff upskilling*. *The EvoLLLution*. https://evolllution.com/following-in-fedexs-footsteps-a-successful-approach-to-staff-upskilling

Grand View Research. (2023). *Education Technology Market Size & Share Report, 2030*. Grand View Research.

Swaak, T. (2024, July 9) Why One State Is Cracking Down on Online-Program Managers. *Chronicle of Higher Education* retrieved from: https://www.chronicle.com/article/why-one-state-is-cracking-down-on-online-program-managers

Expert Perspectives

- Cheryl Murphy, Unilversity of Arkansas
- M.J. Bishop, University of Maryland Global Campus
- Christopher P. Steele, University of Maryland Baltimore County
- Asher Haines, University of North Carolina at Charlotte

Cheryl Murphy, Ed.D.

Vice Provost for Distance Education, University of Arkansas

As a COLO of a service-oriented unit, relationships are at the heart of every initiative, project, and activity my team pursues; and the success of my unit relies on my ability to forge and maintain strong relationships. Successful relationships exceed general transactional connections, which requires a COLO to give extra time and intentionality to the "invisible" work of relationship cultivation.

To build strong relationships you must establish a foundation of trust. Ultimately, you want to create relationships where your partners feel comfortable calling to give you a heads-up when new regulations, policies, or business directions are being proposed; connecting with you to brainstorm a best path forward in difficult situations; and reaching out when things are not going smoothly. It is this depth of trust in a relationship that will help you and your unit succeed, but how do you get there?

While there are distinct differences in the approaches between internal/external relationship-building and every situation is nuanced, there are a few basic steps I suggest you consider that have helped keep my relationships on "TRAC."

Train – Seek training in both mediation and negotiation. The skills learned in these areas will be invaluable in helping you identify the common ground and shared goals that often serve as the foundation for strong relationships and win-win partnerships.

Respect – Respect others' positions and acknowledge the parameters under which they must operate, particularly if they are under-resourced or their position is at odds with yours. This is especially important with external partners when we lack understanding of the regulations, constraints, and time frames that inform their decision-making. Taking others' perspectives into consideration and respecting limitations sets appropriate expectations and builds solid relationships.

Associate – Attend events, connect at conferences, hold informal gatherings, and actively associate with colleagues, peers, and would-be partners. The saying "showing up is half the battle" rings true when trying to forge strong relationships. What may be more important is associating with and supporting prospective partners well before you need to approach them for help. Relationships are give-and-take. They work better when you have given before you attempt to take.

Communicate – Intentionally communicate and regularly touch base, even if it is a simple "how's it going?" One misspoken phrase from a well-meaning uninformed constituent can sink a deal you have been working on for months. If you have been communicating regularly, chances are you will learn of missteps, issues, and dumpster fires immediately and can quickly take corrective action.

As a real-world example of the TRAC steps in action, my team worked for two-plus years to bring to fruition a large non credit to credit workforce project that involved an external employer and OPM, and internal governance, academic partners, academic leadership, and operational partners. During this process, I was continuously focusing all involved on our shared goals, which required extensive use of mediation tactics. Additionally, I had to respect and understand the ever-changing perspectives and constraints of each party, which guided negotiations. I also created multiple communication channels that helped me immediately identify when things started going off track, and because I had supported the academic and operational units in their work prior to this project, they were willing to do extra work to make this project successful.

While many issues arose during the two-year project, it was kept on "TRAC" thanks to the relationships I was able to build. As a COLO, it is important to recognize there are give-and-take moments in every relationship. TRAC steps will help you navigate these moments. As my grandmother used to say/warn, "Don't show up to the potluck without a dish, take the first spot in line to fill your plate, and then criticize my casserole." What she meant was we must all strive to be both a giver and a taker if we want to create and maintain relationships. To this point, my suggestion to you is to bring something to every table, always ask how you can help, and make sure others know you appreciate their contributions…especially if you plan to ask for something in return.

M.J. Bishop, Ed.D.

Vice President of Integrative Learning Design, University of Maryland Global Campus

Clarity in Roles and Responsibilities: A Key to Success in Online Learning

In the rapidly evolving landscape of online education, the role of a COLO is multifaceted and complex. At the University of Maryland Global Campus (UMGC), where we deliver high-quality, scalable online education, I've learned that clarity around roles and responsibilities is not just important – it is essential. As the Vice President of Integrative Learning Design (ILD), I've seen firsthand how a lack of clarity can lead to confusion, inefficiencies, and even conflict, both within the institution and in our partnerships with external providers.

The Challenge of Internal Role Clarity

Internally, one of the most persistent challenges has been navigating the division of labor between the ILD team and faculty, particularly when it comes to the balance between content (faculty purview) and design (ILD purview). Faculty members, understandably, feel a strong sense of ownership over the content they deliver. However, when that sense of ownership extends into areas of instructional design – where ILD has the expertise – there can be friction. It's crucial to establish clear boundaries and responsibilities early on, ensuring that faculty understand their role in content creation while ILD leads on the design and pedagogical structure.

Similarly, the boundaries between academic program support and the services provided by the Office of Student Success (OSS) – such as tutoring, library resources, and writing support – can sometimes blur. Without clear delineation, it can be difficult to determine where OSS's responsibilities end and where faculty or program-specific support should begin. This lack of clarity can lead to gaps in support for students or duplication of efforts, neither of which serves our learners well.

Instructional technology decisions present another area where role clarity is vital. Often, decisions about technology tools are made without full consideration of the instructional design implications. This can result in the selection of tools that don't align well with our pedagogical goals or that add unnecessary complexity to course design. Ensuring that the ILD team is involved in these decisions from the outset is critical to maintaining alignment between technology and design.

Managing External Relationships with Clarity

Externally, the challenges are similar. Our partnerships with instructional design firms and technology providers are essential to scaling our online learning offerings, but these relationships can become strained when roles and responsibilities are not clearly defined. We've experienced instances where instructional design providers overstep, attempting to dictate design decisions or adhere too rigidly to their guidelines, rather than collaborating with us to meet our specific needs. Without clear boundaries and expectations, these partnerships can falter, leading to suboptimal outcomes.

We also face challenges with learning resource providers, including content vendors, educational technology providers, and our bookstore. Too often, these external partners engage directly with faculty or departments, striking deals or making decisions that ILD is not aware of. These actions can have significant design and cost implications, such as breaking links to content, causing discrepancies in the student-facing information about the course, and assigning additional costs to students.

The Importance of Discipline in Role Definition

To address these challenges, we've found that employing the RACI (Responsible, Accountable, Consulted, Informed) model – or its more detailed variant, the RASCI model, which includes support – has been invaluable. These frameworks help to clearly define who is responsible for each aspect of a project, who is accountable for ensuring the task is completed, who needs to be consulted, who should be informed, and who will provide support. This discipline in role definition has significantly improved our project management, both internally and externally.

For a COLO, the discipline of using tools like the RACI or RASCI models is not just a best practice – it is a necessity. These frameworks ensure that everyone involved in a project, from faculty to external partners, understands their role and the roles of others. This clarity prevents misunderstandings, reduces overlap, and ensures that all participants can focus on what they do best, leading to better outcomes for our students and our institutions.

At UMGC, we've learned that when roles and responsibilities are clearly defined and respected, collaboration flourishes. Whether we are working with faculty on course content, partnering with the OSS to support learners, or engaging with external instructional design firms or learning resource providers, having clear, well-communicated roles is the foundation for success. As COLOs, we must champion this clarity to navigate the complexities of online education effectively and to deliver the best possible learning experiences for our students.

Christopher P. Steele, Ph.D.

Vice Provost, Professional & Extended Studies, University of Maryland Baltimore County

Chapter 6 refers to the "invisible work" of the COLO. As with many "new" approaches and ideas in higher education, there is often a backstory that typically goes untold because it is the work of a set of networked relationships, rather than that of an individual person or unit. Since the emergence of online learning in the early 2000s (with the exception of the response to the COVID-19 lockdown) UMBC has not made online instruction a strategic institutional priority. The work to develop, build, launch, teach/manage, and assess online courses and programs has – indeed – been invisible. As we do not have a formally designated COLO, relationships have been fundamentally important.

This is not to suggest that UMBC has not made important contributions to our region through online instruction, but that the modality has been framed more as an instructional location (like a campus) rather than a distinct modality. Since the early 2000s, those of us who have seen online programs as important and necessary have approached the work as a network of college-level and department-level colleagues (both academic and operational). The leaders and staff of the Division of Professional Studies (DPS) and the Division of Information Technology (DoIT) have worked together in a deep, decades-long partnership. Our approach has been to work with faculty who want to work with us to build online courses and programs. Rather than push a rope, we chose to push on open doors. Two examples illustrate our experience at UMBC.

The DPS/DoIT partnership is rooted in a faculty development program called the Alternative Delivery Program (ADP). In those early days (circa 2005) of online learning, our faculty were skeptical about online teaching and learning. The ADP partnership emerged as a way to engage interested faculty in online teaching through a cohort-based course design program. Quality Matters has been the guiding standard for course design. We directed the effort to courses taught in the summer semester. Over a decade, the program yielded more than 110 faculty who developed and taught courses online. The use of summer sessions as a testbed for online learning has served UMBC well. Seventy-six percent of our summer courses are now taught exclusively online. Our ADP faculty participants have become online instructional leaders across the university. Additionally, as a primarily residential campus during fall and spring, UMBC has been able to extend our reach to students during the summer months via online courses.

A second example of our "invisible work" in building online programs is our master's degree program in Teaching English to Speakers of Other Languages (TESOL). Our 40+ year-old program is internationally renowned. Faculty in the program were initially divided on the prospect of online teaching and learning. Yet, those in the opposition were not so opposed that they hindered willing colleagues from proceeding. The TESOL faculty took a "dip a toe in the water" approach and built the online expression of the program one course at a time. Faculty built a development schedule and worked with DPS/DoIT instructional designers and others to chip away at what seemed like a mountain of work. This iterative approach – while taking nearly five years to complete – allowed the department to gradually build experience and comfort with the online modality. Faculty realized that online instruction was effective, popular with students, and resulted in enrollment growth. Choosing both/and over either/or served the program well and has enhanced the overall robustness of the in-person and online versions of the program. The MA TESOL experience engendered credibility and confidence among other faculty. Several applied master's programs have since taken a very similar approach.

Academic traditionalism had served as a hurdle to our institutional embrace of online learning. Progressive faculty and staff, while honoring the past, saw opportunities to serve our students with an additional modality that enhanced student success and the overall student experience. UMBC now has a meaningful number of online applied master's degree programs and myriad undergraduate courses. The invisible work in which many have engaged paid off in dramatic fashion when UMBC was able to pivot to 100% online instruction during the COVID-19 pandemic of 2020–21. While that was no moment to claim success, those of us who have worked to build online capacity quietly pat ourselves on the back for the previous thousands of hours of work that went into building the foundation of online teaching and learning.

Asher Haines

Associate Provost, School of Professional Studies, University of North Carolina at Charlotte

As a COLO, one of the most pivotal aspects of my role is the cultivation and maintenance of relationships, both within and beyond the institution. Chapter 6 aptly highlights the multifaceted nature of these relationships, underscoring the importance of a strategic approach to relationship-building that prioritizes mutual problem-solving and collaboration.

Shifting the Mindset from Competition to Collaboration

When stepping into the role of a COLO, it is crucial to acknowledge that many of the individuals you will be working with might initially view you as a competitor. In a resource-constrained environment, this perception is understandable but counterproductive. The key to overcoming this challenge lies in shifting the mindset from competition to collaboration. This begins with active listening – understanding the needs, concerns, and goals of your colleagues. Once you have a clear understanding of their objectives, you can identify areas of overlap and work together to achieve shared goals.

In my experience, the most effective shared goals that can align the interests of various stakeholders are student success and enrollment growth. These are not only universal objectives across the institution but also the very essence of why we, as COLOs, exist. By rallying your team and partners around these goals, you create a unifying purpose that transcends individual agendas and fosters a spirit of collaboration.

Mutual Problem-Solving Builds Relationships

Building strong relationships hinges on the ability to solve problems together. Mutual problem-solving is not just a strategy; it is the cornerstone of relationship-building. When you engage with internal and external partners to tackle challenges collaboratively, you demonstrate your value not as a competitor but as a collaborator. This approach builds trust and establishes a foundation for long-term relationships that are resilient in the face of change.

For example, working closely with academic and operational partners to build new programs, streamline processes, enhance student services, or integrate new EdTech can lead to significant improvements in student outcomes and operational efficiency. These successes, born from collaborative efforts, reinforce the importance of working together toward common goals.

Agreements Keep Relationships

While mutual problem-solving initiates relationships, formal agreements and clear expectations are what sustain them. Whether it's a memorandum of understanding with an external vendor or an internal service-level agreement, having clear, documented agreements ensures that all parties are on the same page. These agreements serve as a reference point that can be revisited as relationships evolve, providing a framework for accountability and continuity.

Moreover, formal agreements are particularly important when navigating complex relationships with external partners such as EdTech vendors or OPMs. In these cases, having a well-defined agreement that outlines roles, responsibilities, and expectations can prevent misunderstandings and ensure that both parties are working toward the same objectives.

Empowering Your Team: The Heart of Internal Relationships

As a COLO, your ability to make a significant impact is inherently tied to the strength of your team. The relationships within your team are arguably the most important relationships you will cultivate. It is essential to develop a culture where team members feel empowered to build their own relationships across the institution and with external partners. By fostering an environment where your team is trusted, empowered, and encouraged to engage in mutual problem-solving with others, you multiply the impact of your efforts.

Empowering your team also means providing them with the tools, resources, and support they need to succeed. This could involve professional development opportunities, access to new technologies, or simply the autonomy to make decisions within their areas of expertise. When your team feels supported and valued, they are more likely to take initiative and build productive relationships that contribute to the overall success of your institution.

You Already Learned All This in Kindergarten

The role of a COLO is as much about relationships as it is about strategy and technology. The breadth of relationships we must manage – ranging from internal academic and operational partners to external vendors and regulatory bodies – requires a strategic approach centered on collaboration, problem-solving, and empowerment.

At the heart of all these interactions, remember the basic rules we learned in kindergarten:

- Be nice (collaborate, don't compete)
- Share (solve mutual problems, share in student success and enrollment growth)
- Treat others with respect (manage agreements and empower your team)

Finally, be sure to connect with peer COLOs (like me!). You may be the only COLO at your institution, but you are not alone. The COLO community is as supportive as it gets!

COLOs and IT: Strategies for Engaging the CIO 7

Introduction

The term distance learning has long since evolved beyond the concept of correspondence education, where materials were mailed to students who would complete coursework independently and then send it back for evaluation and grading. For the past quarter century, distance education has become synonymous with online education, where the instructional experience is completely facilitated via technological means.

The advent of the Internet brought about entirely new industries, such as social media and e-commerce, and disrupted traditional industries, such as newspapers and broadcast media. One of the industries that was disrupted by the Internet (and is still being disrupted to this day) is higher education. Online learning is a uniquely technological endeavor, one as dependent upon IT as it is on instructional design.

This dependency upon technology creates an interesting dynamic between an institution's COLO and its CIO. For a COLO to be successful he/she will need to avoid a transactional, utilitarian relationship with the CIO. Rather, the COLO should strive to cultivate a true partnership with the CIO – one based on mutual respect and shared mission.

Aligning Digital Learning and IT Strategies

While the COLO is typically positioned within the academic affairs leadership team, the CIO is often (although not always) situated at a higher level in the

DOI: 10.4324/9781003500742-9

institutional hierarchy, usually sitting on the president's/chancellor's cabinet. The CIO, therefore, holds a particularly influential position in determining IT policy and practice, which may include important aspects of digital learning.

Among the long list of deans, department chairs, vice provosts, faculty, and others with whom a COLO must forge a productive working relationship, the institution's CIO should be at the top. Digital learning strategies can only be effective if they are aligned with the broader institutional IT strategy. This alignment can include foundational considerations such as information security for EdTech vendors, procurement rules, integration and support, network strain and bandwidth, shared services, and others.

However, the truly effective alignment goes beyond these more compliance and infrastructure-oriented topics and seeks, rather, to drive impact. How can the COLO and the CIO best collaborate to help drive the institution toward meeting its strategic goals?

At many institutions, the CIO has ultimate responsibility for procurement and support of the LMS due to its nature as enterprise software. Yet, the proper functioning and use of the LMS is essential to the COLO's work. Within other institutions, the COLO may own responsibility for the LMS under a broader, decentralized IT model. In either scenario, if the CIO and the COLO are not aligned regarding LMS resourcing, support, and strategy, particularly with respect to integrated third-party tools that serve both business and academic needs across the enterprise, it will be extremely difficult for the institution to maximize any strategy related to online learning.

For example, the provisioning of online course shells within the LMS may vary greatly, depending upon the academic model. An institution that uses standard course templates may auto-create these sections within the LMS, complete with content, and assign them to instructors as turnkey offerings. However, an institution that prefers a more bespoke delivery model that allows each individual faculty member to construct his/her course may need to control the creation of unpopulated development shells on a per request basis. In either case, access may be contingent upon faculty training requirements. Both contexts will require the CIO and the COLO to have a shared vision of goals, affordances, and constraints.

But this alignment extends beyond the LMS. For instance, if an institution's online strategy is primarily focused on external, long-distance students who reside out of state, the associated IT strategy might emphasize cloud-based technologies and extended help desk hours to accommodate different time zones. In contrast, if an institution's online strategy is primarily focused on serving local students as a supplement to the F2F experience (either fully online or blended), then the associated IT strategy might instead emphasize device loans, campus WiFi, and walk-in support services. In all cases, the COLO and CIO must have a common understanding of the macro goals and necessary operational practices required to achieve them.

When it comes to third-party and vendor EdTech solutions, the COLO and the CIO will need to be in lockstep so that these solutions can be properly vetted, procured, and guaranteed to be in compliance with all institutional IT expectations, including FERPA, use of data, information security policies, and credit card/PCI compliance, as applicable. Another aspect of third-party solutions is integration into existing enterprise systems, especially the LMS. This will often take the form of ensuring that vendor solutions are standards compliant, such as 1EdTech's (2023) Learning Tools Interoperability (LTI) for application integration, Caliper for data analytics, Question and Test Interoperability (QTI) for assessments, Common Cartridge for course portability, Open Badges for alternative credentials, and state specific cloud-based computing requirements, among others. While the COLO might oversee the need for compliance with these (and other) standards, it may fall on the CIO to handle the technical implementation. Each executive must be aware of the other's requirements and ensure that specific roles are delineated and executed appropriately.

Interdependency: The Two ITs

Colleges and universities are complex organizations, serving many different stakeholders, bound by laws and regulations, and increasingly dependent upon technology for almost every aspect of the enterprise, including academics. This 21st-century reliance on technology can create a natural tension between information technology (traditional IT) and instructional technology, "the two ITs" (Hartman et al., 2007).

Broadly speaking, IT is the use of computer hardware and software to provide, manage, store, transmit, protect, manipulate, exchange, and display information and data. In that context, instructional technology would be a subset of IT, directed specifically at the use of hardware and software to impact teaching, learning, and assessment. Instructional technology often also assumes an embedded level of instructional design to ensure effective pedagogy/andragogy.

One area of tension that must be navigated is the ongoing need for innovation. Like any other aspect of IT, instructional technology is continually evolving, forcing rapid change into a higher education culture that can sometimes be change resistant. Artificial intelligence, personalized learning, virtual and augmented reality, holograms, and other emerging technologies each have the potential to cause sudden disruption in educational practice. Digital learning leaders are at the forefront of identifying and preparing for these new technologies.

Only in collaboration with the CIO can a COLO adequately prepare the academic enterprise to confront and leverage new instructional technologies. Jointly, the two ITs will need to discern the appropriate resources (funding, facility, personnel) required for R&D. How much can be dedicated toward experimentation when the day-to-day IT demands of the institution are likely already consumed by the available resources (or may even exceed the available resources)? Yet, the institution cannot be exclusively focused on today's issues. Refusing to allocate any resources toward R&D carries its own future institutional risk.

Another tension that can emerge between the two ITs is how to anticipate and support scale. Because it is not dependent upon the campus's physical plant, online learning can become a source of growth for an institution, expanding enrollment in a way that, theoretically, has no limits. However, online learning still requires its own infrastructure, and a large part of that is typically overseen by the IT department. As observed in the 2024 CHLOE 9 Report:

> Scale, however, invites tension as schools grapple with bottom-up versus top-down approaches, when to innovate and when to be conservative, and where to invest limited resources.
>
> (Simunich et al., 2024)

Is the CIO and his/her organization prepared for potentially rapid scale? Is the technical infrastructure in place to support the continued growth of these nontraditional, 21st-century digital learners? Considering scale in this way may be a true paradigm shift for an institution, especially for those who have historically privileged the in-person or residential student experience. Many of these institutions experienced rapid scaling of IT infrastructure at the onset of the COVID-19 pandemic. If such institutions invested in sustaining scale post-pandemic, they are better poised for subsequent scale of nontraditional digital learners. It behooves the prudent COLO to stay in communication with the CIO about scale before being confronted with issues.

Tension doesn't have to be a liability. In many ways, the tension may be a healthy way to test ideas and work toward the optimal solution. However, managing strategic tension between the two ITs will require a shared commitment from both the CIO and the COLO to a sense of goodwill, partnership, and institutional mission.

Online Learning Is NOT IT

It is likely that, at some point, every professional working in online learning has had his/her role conflated with that of IT. Whether that is a faculty member complaining about classroom WiFi, a vendor inquiring about identity management, or a staff member seeking desktop support, because the online learning professional's role is so intrinsically tied to the use of computers, there is an erroneous assumption that online learning and IT are synonymous.

Such confusion is natural for those who do not work in the space and the COLO should avoid any sentiments of frustration. Instead, when this type of IT/Online conflation occurs, it can be used as an opportunity to educate and explain the valuable and unique role that digital learning plays at the institution. In many cases, the online learning operation might be better compared to an academic college or the library than an IT department.

It is worth reinforcing that online learning is essentially an academic endeavor, not a technological one. Yes, it uses technology and cannot exist without it, but the learning objectives and instructional outcomes drive the entire enterprise. A traditional F2F course exists in a classroom and uses various technologies such as a projector, computer, microphone, speaker, presentation software, document camera, and a whiteboard (among others). Yet, no one really considers this type of instruction as technology-enabled. Online learning is designed to support the same learning objectives although, instead of a classroom, the course will be contained within an LMS section. A variety of other online tools will also usually be incorporated such as videos, games, discussion threads, collaboration tools, and assessment software (among others). Technology is merely the vehicle used to deliver the instruction online, but just as in the classroom, the instruction is the primary element.

Neither the online learning operation nor the IT department is more important than the other. Each has a critical role to play in achieving institutional objectives. These roles are distinct but complementary, interdependent, and collaborative. At the end of the day, the COLO and the CIO are destined to be partners. An effective COLO will embrace that partnership, cultivate it, and work together with his/her colleague to ensure the maximum impact for both IT and digital learning.

Competency Connection

UPCEA COLO Competency	*COLO Insight*	*Influencing Factors*	*Influencing Factor (COVID-Era)*	*Institutional Risk*
Information and Digital Technology	IT strategy and online strategy must be in synch or progress toward institutional goals will suffer	COLO and CIO must be aligned in both strategy and practice Pressure for the COLO to keep up with peers (e.g., rankings) Comparison to F2F instruction (perception as less than)	Pressures of scale outpaced innovation and resources Rapid procurement and support of new EdTech software/solutions Ensure standards compliance for EdTech tools	Scarce IT resources limit support for online growth and R&D, creating future risk Innovation needs to be a central tenant of new/emerging COLO roles, as well as re-energized in existing COLO roles

References

1EdTech Interoperability Standards. (2023). Retrieved from https://www.1edtech.org/specifications

Hartman, J. L., Dziuban, C., & Brophy-Ellison, J. (2007). Leveraging IT in higher education: A summary of Joel L. Hartman, Charles Dziuban, and James Brophy-Ellison's Educause review. *Educause Review*, 42(5), 62–64.

Simunich, B., Garrett, R., Fredericksen, E. E., McCormack, M., Robert, J., & Ubell, R. (2024). *CHLOE 9: Strategy Shift: Institutions Respond to Sustained Online Demand, The Changing Landscape of Online Education, 2024*. Retrieved from the Quality Matters website: https://qualitymatters.org/qa-resources/resource-center/articles-resources/CHLOE-9-report-2024

Expert Perspectives

- Shawna Dark, University of California Berkeley
- Lev Gonick, Arizona State University
- Adam Fein, University of North Texas

Shawna Dark, Ph.D.

Chief Academic Technology Officer, University of California, Berkeley

As technology has become increasingly ubiquitous, the functional role of technology in higher education has become more specialized and distributed. Because this change has occurred rapidly, there is often a lack of clear delineation between the areas of expertise and technical leadership. As a result, leaders may be asked to make critical decisions without a full view of the decision space. This places an even greater emphasis on strategic partnership between the CIO and COLO as critical thought partners. Ideally, high-level decision-making should be made together, with deference to each other's unique areas of expertise.

The strategies for the COLO to engage the CIO and subsequent strategic success are bound to multiple factors, including the funding models for the two "IT"s (information technology and academic/instructional technology), the organizational placement of the COLO, campus strategic priorities, and the philosophical ideologies of both the COLO and the CIO. Funding models for academic technologies can either exacerbate or reduce the tensions between the two "IT"s. When funding streams are dedicated to each function (or restricted to specific functions), this separation allows for greater autonomy in implementing strategic priorities. Partnership with the CIO then becomes less about dependency and more about coordinating initiatives that add value to strategic priorities.

Campus priorities, both explicit and implicit, are often indicated or even dictated by the campus's organizational structures. COLOs that are organizationally parallel to CIOs reflect campuses that have very clear priorities for learning with technology. Senior leaders might be reluctant to put the CIO and COLO parallel because they're concerned about the proliferation of senior roles or creating a conflict of priorities, but actually the organization is more likely to be successful if learning priorities aren't subject to the logistical management necessary for administrative functions. When the COLO is placed lower organizationally (and subsidiary to the CIO), relationships are extremely important to ensure that the priorities for instruction are weighed equally with administrative priorities.

Finally, the CIO and COLO ideally should be philosophically aligned regarding the management of functions and assignments of personnel to priorities. A great exercise is to spend time with the CIO and ask questions about what it is each leader (and associated teams) does not do. When approached as a mutual exercise between the CIO and COLO, each IT unit can excel in its area of expertise and reduce the tensions between the two ITs. True partnership, respect, and recognition of the growing divergence of expertise are critical for the successful implementation of strategic priorities. Campus leaders also have a responsibility to communicate expectations to the COLO and the CIO that inspire and cultivate strategic partnerships together and with other campus leaders.

There are likely to be other emerging leadership roles as technology continues to reshape how we do our work in higher education. For example, we are now seeing the emergence of the Chief AI Officer and Chief Data Officer. Perhaps one could see the emergence of other roles, such as a position entirely focused on the nexus of student success and technology. These subject matter leaders will need to work together as a team with the CIO and COLO, with each being clear as to what they do and do not do, making space for their peers to be recognized and to excel. This rapidly changing landscape, while confusing and overwhelming at times, is exciting to observe and promising for the future of higher education.

Lev Gonick, Ph.D.

Enterprise Chief Information Officer, Arizona State University

There's an old CIO yarn that goes something like, "God created the universe in six days and was able to rest on the seventh day because God didn't have to deal with legacy organizations." Indeed, the most significant challenges facing enterprise CIOs in higher education are the deeply encrusted legacy environments associated with the norms and practices of universities.

To be clear, the challenges are not just external to the CIO's central organization, but also deeply entrenched mindsets and legacy organizational models that routinely stall most efforts to catalyze digital transformation strategies to advance the institution's aspirations.

At Arizona State University, we're reimagining Enterprise Technology (ET) to be a collective force to advance our digital transformation journey. In this work, EdPlus is ET's strongest ally, led by Phil Regier, ASU's chief online learning architect and leader, Phil's role as CEO of ASU's EdPlus and University Dean for University Initiatives is a central element to ASU's success in our online offerings as well as being an enterprise design feature that allows me to overcome many of the legacy challenges of large central IT organizations.

When I first arrived at ASU, nearly eight years ago, I made what turned out to be a fortuitous decision to spend 20% of my time during the first nine months embedded in the physical facilities at ASU's Skysong campus, home to EdPlus, among other units. I was assigned a desk in Phil's open office space near him and his senior team. My intention was to build some long-overdue trust between the university technology organization and ASU's online unit by dedicating one day per week.

Looking back, this experience enabled – and even empowered – me to rethink my approach to redesigning what has become ASU's ET. I had the opportunity to openly observe the innovative organization and leadership in action. During that journey, I gained key insights through observation, which enabled me to partner with EdPlus to tackle many of the most challenging aspects of a legacy IT organization that is really good but still struggles with overcoming its traditional gatekeeping role and is characterized by teams overwhelmed with tasks from all across ASU. Together, EdPlus and ET are making important progress in helping drive ASU to achieve its highest aspirations.

As EdPlus was designed de novo 15 years ago, it did not have the burden of being a legacy academic unit or added as an appendage to the university. It has leveraged a portfolio of technology systems and platforms to grow student online enrollment to more than 90,000 and leads nearly a dozen strategic digital projects around the globe. However, my first significant insight was that Phil and his leadership had successfully established a values-led culture within an otherwise large and complex research university setting. The organization's aspirations were bold to attract game changers and innovators. And, it has consistently done so.

Second, EdPlus was demonstrably a product-focused organization. It has excelled at product design, A/B testing, user experience, and ongoing assessment of all of its offerings. Next, having been born "whole cloth," EdPlus has harnessed its relative youth, embracing contemporary technical architectures that enable the product focus. Its culture also prioritizes opportunity and belonging, attracting talent genuinely passionate about innovation with new technologies and learning approaches. Inspired by my time at EdPlus, the first senior hire I made as CIO was introducing the role of a new Chief Culture Officer. My goal was to collaborate with this person on an intentional, appreciative-inquiry-oriented organizational journey to rethink and ultimately re-architect our approach to culture.

In a significant shift in mission, ASU's ET has been on a journey from being largely an integration and support services organization to one that is capable of designing and building platforms, applications, and products, as well as integration and services. Finally, pointing to EdPlus as proof positive that it could be done, ET has modernized a significant swath of our technology tools and approaches from the legacy environment to one focused on contemporary architectures.

While the assumption might be that the COLO should engage the CIO to achieve alignment, optimize investment, and drive efficiencies, the CIO should partner with the COLO to overcome the legacy trap, modernize technologies, and help drive business value. Together, EdPlus and ET are accelerating ASU's overall aspiration and drive to be a model of a New American University. At ASU that new model of advancing student success at scale with intentional social consequence is enabled and driven by a commitment to leveraging the full breadth of the technologies, both homegrown and in the marketplace.

This does not mean that EdPlus and ET are fully synchronized across all technology. It also does not mean that ET has the luxury of forsaking the dozens of other key stakeholders across the ASU Public Enterprise who are at different phases of their own digital transformation journeys. We do agree to leverage EdPlus' need to move at the speed of the market as an imperative for the benefit of all of ASU. We have been intentional and agile in evolving ASU's overall IT architecture to support EdPlus and positioning every other business and academic unit on campus to be able to leverage the contemporary services architecture to advance their goals.

It is the responsibility of the COLO to gather market intelligence in order to establish the business plan, the audience, and the total addressable market. With the boundaries of traditional, degree-seeking universities becoming more porous, access and identity management systems are key elements of supporting agility in an evolving customer definition. As a result, the COLO and CIO must work together to ensure students, learners, employees, alumni, and affiliates have access to relevant content and tailored experiences. Our degree and pathway programs are complemented by verifiable digital credentials and certifications that are appropriate for various learning experiences.

EdPlus and ET maintain strong alignment on technical directions, always looking toward the future and designing for social scale. From broad, 10-year-old consensus on SAS and Cloud-first to emergent collaboration to drive adoption of AI-enabled services in all of our enterprise products whether homegrown or procured, there is strong collaboration between the two teams. In order to give online students choice and overall coherence to the ASU experience, digital campaigns, and outreach services for online students are now synchronized with campus immersion students. As a result of this redesign, we are refocusing on helping students from the moment they inquire about ASU, through enrollment in dozens of offerings, and then supporting them throughout their entire relationship with the university. That overall student experience is not only mobile-first, but it is thoughtfully designed and tested with UI/UX teams in both organizations. The rest of the ASU Enterprise has benefited significantly from EdPlus' technology-forward orientation.

Context matters. ASU's entry into the online marketplace and our evolution are unique to our historical journey. Our organization and business models are not easily replicable nor is that necessary. These historical and organizational contexts constrain the choices that COLOs and CIOs have in exploring partnership possibilities. At ASU, there is intrinsic value in the COLO working with the CIO. Here, I have made the case that there is reciprocal value for the CIO to be working with the COLO. The rest is execution.

Adam D. Fein, Ph.D.

Vice President for Digital Strategy and Innovation and Chief Digital Officer, University of North Texas

In the Summer of 2021, the midst of my 24-year journey in higher education, the president of my university asked me to serve 18 months as a "bridge" CIO between the person formerly in the position and our excellent new hire. I already had an immense amount of respect for my CIO colleagues, naturally, and I have an even healthier respect for the job now. CIOs live in a high-risk, low-reward world. Many of the functions they are responsible for, if they fail, can take down large swaths of the campus, if not the entire institution.

Yet, when all is running smoothly, files are able to be accessed quickly, data are secure and safe, and campus servers are chugging along at top speeds, the accolades for this work are limited to a quarterly lunch at the end of the table, if you're lucky. Is it too much to ask of CIOs, who are already responsible for (1) IT infrastructure and operations, (2) application and data analytics, (3) security, risk, and compliance, and (4) telecommunications and Internet access to also ask them to manage the functions most commonly tended to by a COLO: (1) online learning, (2) instructional design and multimedia, (3) faculty development, (4) continuing education/workforce development/corporate partnerships, (5) learning research, and (6) digital accessibility? In a word, yes.

The COLO and the CIO are distinct, but complementary positions. As we speed toward the end of the first quarter of the 21st century, it is more important than ever that these two roles interact and collaborate at a high level and frequently so. Among many other reasons, the federal and state requirements for educational technology and their standards are intricate and overlapping. We can observe this in the emerging potential for generative AI. While CIO divisions are testing campus GenAI solutions for productivity, COLO divisions are working diligently on GenAI applications for teaching and learning. These two areas have synergy but are also distinct.

A good partnership between IT and the digital/online learning units can go a long way toward keeping the university in good standing without sacrificing necessary progress at the boundaries of innovation. Universities must consider effectively and strategically investing in both areas to reduce the risk of falling behind their competitors with respect to the institution's customers – students and faculty – their technological experience, and ability to produce the next great employees and researchers. Conversely, by not investing in digital learning and IT (and not providing some financial room for proactive experimentation) a university is certain to become stagnant and perpetually in a "reactive" state, ultimately restricting students and faculty from the vital 21st-century learning and skill development needed to thrive in today's society.

COLOs and Entrepreneurship: Strategies for Stewarding the Brand

8

Introduction

Alan Kay is famously quoted as originating the phrase, "The best way to predict the future is to invent it." It is a mantra that could also be applied to those occupying the role of a COLO in higher education. COLOs are often faced with challenges that have not previously been encountered by the traditional educational enterprise.

Thus, one of the most important skills that a COLO can learn is the ability to learn new skills. The field of digital learning is rapidly evolving, with constantly emerging new innovations, new technologies, and new practices. Consider just a few of the many seismic EdTech developments that have arisen within the past few years: MOOCs, predictive analytics and early warning systems, adaptive learning, microcredentials, and generative artificial intelligence (not to mention a global pandemic that forced everyone into virtual learning). This continually evolving context requires a digital learning leader to be agile and extremely comfortable with ambiguity.

Yet, within this dynamic professional environment, a sharp-eyed and forward-thinking COLO should also be able to identify hidden opportunities that have the potential to yield positive impacts. When faced with the unexpected, especially in the midst of a crisis, "(u)nprecedented activities, novel processes, and responsive solutions will invariably yield possibilities

DOI: 10.4324/9781003500742-10

that organizations can leverage in the future" (Cavanagh, 2023). Even during the typically full schedule of normal operations, the successful COLO must maintain an entrepreneurial mindset to identify and seize upon promising new opportunities.

Cultivate a Start-up Mentality

Most COLOs will operate within the context of a traditional higher education institution. This context will consistently include established policies, procedures, funding limitations, shared governance, academic culture, organizational politics, regulatory constraints, and myriad other potential obstacles to operational agility and innovation.

Yet, innovation still occurs in many different forms – indeed, it *must* occur. One definition of creativity is solving problems or accomplishing objectives within constraints. To kick-start an untested idea and foster entrepreneurial innovation, an innovative COLO might forge a creative partnership, co-fund a position, run a pilot project, or enlist student interns. There are multiple paths to the same destination. The entrepreneurial COLO needs to be flexible and persistent enough to know when to forge ahead and when to take a step back, pivot, and try another strategy.

While few would describe working within the tradition-bound context of higher education as akin to a start-up company, viewing the COLO role through such a lens can be very useful. Start-up founders continually face all sorts of challenges at least as difficult as those found within a higher education environment (funding, staffing, operational, legal, regulatory, etc.). Cultivating a start-up mentality helps insulate the COLO from being discouraged by obstacles and initial setbacks, keeping focused on the mission, and relentlessly exploring creative workarounds. According to Schlesinger and Kiefer (2014),

> We have come to call these kinds of managers "entrepreneurs inside" because though they work within an established organizational context, like entrepreneurs, they have ideas that upset the status quo. And like entrepreneurs, these entrepreneurs inside face a substantial set of risks—even though organizations are calling for more creativity, more innovation, and more entrepreneurial behavior from employees.

While funding is almost always a challenge, it's a challenge common to all. Keep in mind that to be an internal entrepreneur with a start-up mentality doesn't always require funding. For example, inspired by Atlassian's FedEx

Days, three times a year (fall, spring, and summer) the University of Central Florida's Division of Digital Learning staff are afforded 24 hours to work on whatever projects they want during what is called a Hack Day. These projects can relate to solving a problem or taking on a task that they haven't had time to tackle during the normal course of work. It could be learning something completely new or attempting something that has a high risk of not succeeding.

At the end of the 24 hours, participants (often teams) present their results, findings, failures, and learnings. Voting and prizes follow the presentations. In almost every case, the vast majority of Hack Day projects are immediately implemented into regular operations. These have included innovative EdTech apps, the production of a document style guide, and learning new programming languages. Successful Hack Day projects have also included the administration team organizing the office supply closet and cleaning the shared golf cart. Even those projects that "fail" always result in something useful being learned that can be applied elsewhere.

Convening Hack Days is an inexpensive way to seed innovation and foster an entrepreneurial spirit. COLOs must examine their own particular contexts to identify the opportunities hidden within the everyday work of their units. Opportunities may be undiscovered or they may be known yet unexplored, awaiting for a creative eye to find them and develop them into their full potential.

Benefits and Risks of Being an Internal Entrepreneur

Working as an internal entrepreneur, often called an intrapreneur, can be one of the most effective strategies for keeping your institution relevant. Through innovative pilots and experiments, colleges and universities can mitigate potential risk by probing new technologies, processes, and practices – any one of which could be a disruptor of future competitiveness or relevance. Should the institution face such future risk, perhaps even an existential risk, it's possible that one or more of these pilots can be scaled up as an alternative strategy.

Institutions face questions along these lines every day. Today's digital economy seems to be accelerating the number and impact of possible future risks, making an entrepreneurial COLO that much more important. There are any number of questions that may be confronting colleges and universities today. An entrepreneurial COLO could develop innovative pilots directed at addressing them. For example,

- How will artificial intelligence change teaching and learning?
- Given the forecasted changing demographics of tomorrow's postsecondary learners, how can institutions start pivoting from an over-reliance on traditional high school graduates and cultivate a pipeline of adult, nontraditional learners?
- How can real-time data from the LMS be leveraged to predict student outcomes and improve success for all students?

Of course, the benefits of being an entrepreneurial COLO are far from strictly defensive. By assuming a proactive, curious posture, the COLO intrapreneur can explore new opportunities that could potentially expand enrollment, increase revenue, improve student success, or achieve other strategic institutional goals.

The innovative, entrepreneurial COLO can serve as a key asset in helping to chart an institution's future path. In many cases, the foremost value of an institution's online enterprise is considered by many to be the ability to generate net new revenue. This revenue can be reinvested in other institutional priorities. For example, the new, sprawling campuses of institutions such as Liberty University and Grand Canyon University were funded in large part by online revenue.

However, reducing online learning's sole contribution to revenue generation would be a great disservice to its true potential. Online learning can support any number of the access, enrollment, success, time to graduation, engagement, or other goals that a college or university may have. The exact role that online learning can play and its overall impact are limited only by the imagination and creativity of the COLO.

Of course, not all entrepreneurial bets pay off. All innovation and experimentation come with an element of risk. *To be a successful COLO, you must be comfortable with risk*. Simply put, it is a job requirement. But that doesn't mean you should take unnecessary risks.

When a program doesn't work out, a project loses support, or a technology implementation goes over budget and over schedule, it can damage a COLO's credibility and limit his/her ability to pursue future initiatives. While the occasional failure, in the proper context, shouldn't irreparably damage a COLO's reputation, the successes should far outnumber the failures. That's why a COLO's project portfolio should represent a broad spectrum of risk profiles – much like a financial investment portfolio might. While having a small number of high-risk/high-reward investments can be wise, it only makes sense to balance against a majority profile of more established, less risky projects.

It would be foolish to place any all-or-nothing bets, over-leveraging resources, and risking more than you can afford to lose, whether that means funding, personnel, or credibility (or all three). All risks, whether high or low, should be data-informed (e.g., are there pilot efficacy data that would support enterprise adoption of a new technology or strategy?). In addition, the higher education entrepreneur/intrapreneur must work within a large complex system. That means that the COLO needs to build support from colleagues, faculty, staff, and senior leadership as appropriate to minimize later objections. There is no better method of achieving this than good, old-fashioned conversations. These should preferably be in person (perhaps offer to buy coffee) but can also be accomplished through the increasingly common virtual meeting format. Developing collaborations, partnerships, and coalitions is a time-consuming but critical aspect of managing risk, as discussed in Chapter 6.

Another key element of risk mitigation is understanding the potential roadblocks to success. Developing an entrepreneurial mindset also includes foreseeing the obstacles that stand in the way of progress which must be avoided or overcome. Only by having an objective sense of the challenges to success – and/or a proactive mechanism to identify them when they arise – will the COLO be able to navigate around them and sustain forward momentum.

Where Good Ideas Come From

How can COLOs identify and cultivate entrepreneurial ideas? Since good ideas can come from literally anywhere (faculty, students, staff, alumni, parents, colleagues, other institutions, different industries, etc.), the creative COLO must be vigilant to maintain a receptive posture and an open mind. As renowned chemist Linus Pauling famously said, "If you want to have good ideas you must have many ideas. Most of them will be wrong, and what you have to learn is which ones to throw away" (Crick, 1995).

Note, however, that it is not incumbent on the COLO to be the *source* of entrepreneurial ideas. The COLO does not need to originate all creative ideas. That would be tragically limiting. Rather, COLOs must develop their ability to recognize ideas that have potential. Sometimes, that idea may just be the smallest of concepts, a glowing ember that must be protected and fed but that has the potential to develop into a huge furnace powering impact across the institution. The COLO has the great advantage of leveraging the intelligence and creativity of everyone else. It is not all up to him/her. But the COLO must be able to see possibilities.

This requires COLOs to develop a broad and deep network. The more he/she interacts with others, the bigger the net to capture potential opportunities. In addition, the COLO must have a well-developed "futures literacy." As defined by Larsen, et al. (2020), futures literacy is "the capacity to know how to imagine the future, and why it is necessary." Such an orientation will help a COLO recognize opportunities that others may miss.

Future-oriented COLOs would be wise to also develop futures literacy in their teams. Help those that report to you to recognize undefined opportunities and avoid the trap of tradition and expectation, which limit the possible. Team activities such as a Hack Day can be useful exercises in cultivating a futures literate culture.

Entrepreneurship and the Institutional Brand

An aspect of being an entrepreneurial COLO that cannot be overlooked is its relationship with the institutional brand. Certainly, the online enterprise can support institutional reputation and brand awareness through high rankings in national lists (including online program rankings and larger rankings that online excellence can influence such as most innovative universities). However, chasing rankings is unwise. It is better to align operations to support institutional goals and then execute with excellence. If done well over a consistent period of time, the rankings will eventually catch up.

As COLOs are being increasingly charged with amplifying their institutions' reach through digital means, they must take the responsibility of brand stewardship very seriously. They must adhere to brand guidelines, adopt central marketing messaging, and ensure alignment with broader communications strategies.

Yet the very nature of being an entrepreneurial COLO means that you will be pushing boundaries, challenging the status quo, and experimenting with "what if" scenarios. This entrepreneurial mindset can be in tension with straightforward brand stewardship. How can you help nudge the institution into new, uncharted territory if the paths have already been mapped out? The innovative COLO must be savvy and determine the areas where he/she can push the boundaries of the possible while still maintaining adherence to those areas where compliance is paramount.

Sometimes, depending upon the context, the expansion of online learning can be viewed by some stakeholders as a potential threat to the institutional brand, particularly the academic reputation. Some may consider online learning as less rigorous or serving a lower-performing student population.

There may also be concerns about online cheating or misunderstandings about asynchronous constructivist pedagogy.

In such cases, the COLO will need to build bridges with critics through relationship outreach, as well as leverage data to counter myths or anecdotes. Despite best efforts, some stakeholders may remain skeptical and advocate against the online enterprise. In those situations, having committed executive support will be essential to maintain forward momentum toward achieving strategic goals.

Competency Connection

UPCEA COLO Competency	*COLO Insight*	*Influencing Factors*	*Influencing Factor (COVID-Era)*	*Institutional Risk*
Entrepreneurship, Partnerships and Relationship Building	The entrepreneurial imperative of the COLO role is often unmatched among institutional colleagues, especially considering the dynamic context of today's EdTech	Prior networks of COLOs contribute to institutional success COLOs by definition have to work in partnership and across silos	Leveled the playing field among COLOs, but also created a more collaborative national network Revealed potential new opportunities driven by necessity	Too many unsuccessful projects will undermine COLO's credibility Tension between brand stewardship and innovation

References

Cavanagh, T. B. (2023). Leadership lessons from the pandemic. In B. Bouchey, E. Gratz, & S. Kurland (Eds.), *From grassroots to the highly-orchestrated: Online leaders share their stories of the evolving online organizational landscape in higher ed* (pp. 9–23). United States: Online Learning Consortium.

Crick, F. (1995, February 28). *The impact of Linus Pauling on molecular biology*. Lecture presented at the Linus C. Pauling Day Symposium, Oregon State University, Corvallis, OR. Retrieved from https://scarc.library.oregonstate.edu/events/1995paulingconference/video-s1-2-crick.html

Larsen, N., Mortensen, J. K., & Miller, R. (2020, February 11). What is 'futures literacy' and why is it important? *FARSIGHT*. Retrieved from https://medium.com/farsight/what-is-futures-literacy-and-why-is-it-important-7585e8cd1a7d

Schlesinger, L. A., & Kiefer, C. (2014, July 14). Act like an entrepreneur inside your organization. *Harvard Business Review*. Retrieved from https://hbr.org/2014/07/act-like-an-entrepreneur-inside-your-organization

Expert Perspectives

- Melissa Vito, University of Texas San Antonio
- Nelson Baker, Georgia Institute of Technology
- Vickie Cook, University of Illinois Springfield

Melissa Vito, Ed.D.

Vice Provost for Academic Innovation, University of Texas, San Antonio

As COLOs chart the next chapter of success in online learning for their institutions, an entrepreneurial mindset is an essential leadership quality. The MIT Sloan Global Programs and QUT Business School define an entrepreneurial mindset by three shared traits: solutions-oriented, adaptable, and anti-fragile (Somers, 2022). Another trait of an entrepreneurial mindset I believe is necessary for COLOs to embody is curiosity – a desire to test new models and ideas, quickly learn what works and what doesn't, and inspire quick, continued innovation and implementation of ideas.

But before we examine the role of an entrepreneurial mindset, we must define the online learning landscape. We can view this landscape through the lenses of core elements necessary for leading a successful online program: viable business models and infrastructure, quality course development and faculty engagement, data-driven measures of success for a great student experience, and effective communication.

Now, let's consider a few examples of how COLOs can drive success in online learning by applying an entrepreneurial mindset through these lenses. We will also examine strategies for COLOs to overcome potential pitfalls that emerge when online learning is deemed a threat to the academic brand and highlight opportunities for online programs to provide unique support to institutional goals and help improve institutional processes, programs, and marketing.

Business Models and Infrastructure

Several institutions are examining online business models and making changes, as noted in the 2024 CHLOE 9 report, which found that two-thirds of COLOs either anticipated or were experiencing budget issues (Simunich et al., 2024). Much of what drives this innovation is a desire to explore ways of more fully integrating revenue streams from online programs into the overall revenue of institutions.

Universities today have tighter resources, experiencing lower rates of enrollment coupled with the loss of pandemic financial support. An entrepreneurial approach to address this might be to reevaluate the university's financial models and provide options that can benefit the institution while also ensuring adequate resources for online programs. Offering to take on additional expenses that benefit online students and the institution as a whole

might include marketing that amplifies the institution's brand, which online resources can help fund.

Course Development and Faculty Engagement

Research shows that current students seek more modality choices for their courses, including hybrid, online, and meaningful F2F classes. The quality framework utilized in online course development could be adapted and applied to all course development, including implementing rigorous digital accessibility tools.

In this example, all students receive an elevated learning experience, which benefits the institution's overall stature and increases student success. In addition, online programs frequently support those wanting to finish a degree, seeking advancement or specialization, or moving to a new career. Observing these behaviors can help inform what new academic programs might be emerging in the market, which would benefit the institution as a whole.

Measuring Success

Online student retention is measured over semesters and terms rather than annually, which creates a more urgent and engaged approach to online student support. COLOs partnering with student success and retention units to include a more proactive hands-on approach used by online programs could benefit all students and be easily measurable.

In addition, allowing residential students to move between online and F2F courses can help students stay on track for graduation. As such, these accommodations will require COLOs to lead their institutions toward taking a more flexible or entrepreneurial approach to institutional policies to enable this flexibility.

Embracing an Entrepreneurial Mindset and Ensuring Ongoing Innovation

An entrepreneurial mindset supports a forward-thinking, market-driven, and responsive online program. It creates an energized online work environment where team members feel engaged and see the potential to integrate their ideas. One ironic thing about an entrepreneurial mindset is that it creates an expectation of continual innovation, creativity, resilience, and rapidly evolving ideas. These successes can soon become best practices and traditions.

To fully embrace an entrepreneurial mindset and ensure a culture of ongoing innovation, COLOs must continually monitor the online learning landscape for creative opportunities while assessing all aspects of their own online programs to constantly find areas that can be improved. Piloting approaches to test new ideas is an essential tool for engaging others in change, building partnerships, and finding out what really works.

References

Simunich, B., Garrett, R., Fredericksen, E. E., McCormack, M., Robert, J., & Ubell, R. (2024). *CHLOE 9: Strategy Shift: Institutions Respond to Sustained Online Demand, The Changing Landscape of Online Education, 2024.* Retrieved from the Quality Matters website: https://qualitymatters.org/qa-resources/resource-center/articles-resources/CHLOE-9-report-2024

Somers, M. (2022). 3 traits of an entrepreneurial mindset. *MIT Sloan School of Management.* Cambridge MA.

Nelson C. Baker, Ph.D.

Inaugural Interim Dean, Lifetime Learning, Georgia Institute of Technology

The role of a university's COLO is a wonderful opportunity to lead and shepherd initiatives for a university to reach a cadre of learners who likely cannot participate in an educational journey in any other format. As a public research university, Georgia Tech's strategic plan has six pillars, one of which is to expand access. We take this mantra seriously, for it is at the core of the university's mission, "Progress and Service."

Few items are as important as the university's brand, taking decades to build but easily ruined. The university's reputation attracts faculty and staff to seek to work there. It cultivates the desire for individuals to want to learn there. It upholds the reputation of local, regional, and sometimes farther economies and industries that seek its graduates. The brand for research universities also signals innovation and deep thinking around a variety of important topics. Thus, faculty and university leadership's trust in the COLO with new ideas and concepts takes time to earn; it is not given. The very essence of the quality found in all university endeavors is represented in the brand, and new ideas should undergo scrutiny.

The COLO who has earned trust can have tremendous opportunities within, and beyond, the university ecosystem, increasing and creating new impacts on behalf of the university community, faculty, staff, students, and leadership, and enhancing learning outcomes for collective societal impact. Listening intently, asking questions, and probing for opportunities are some of the key competencies that enable such trust and opportunity. The listening occurs across your organization, across faculty, staff, and leadership, but must extend farther to alumni, industry, and government stakeholders. A good business sense and the ability to identify and manage risk are essential. The ability to communicate ideas and concepts, which are often different from the status quo, is most helpful. The ability to navigate university governance is essential and requires patience, persistence, and sometimes the willingness to pause an idea to gather more data or to decide it isn't the right fit at the time.

Having a team that possesses deep knowledge and understanding of pedagogy and andragogy within learning science is key to successful programs. However, that, in my opinion, is only the beginning of what is needed. The COLO must have a team that also possesses a thorough understanding of technology, including its use, support, and implementation, as well as constantly updating their technical knowledge. The best ideas can flounder or fail due to teams who are not staffed and/or knowledgeable in the proper and efficient use of technology. The effective implementation of the best learning science and technology must then be coupled with policy and business competencies to enable success.

A look at Georgia Tech's journey over the last several decades provides evidence of my perspectives and lessons learned. Georgia Tech started remote-delivered programming in 1977. When MOOCs appeared in the early 2010s, Georgia Tech had been listening. We heard several things such as faculty who wanted to make a difference and individuals seeking classes that looked very much like courses in degree programs but who asked if they could count for degrees – however, they wanted it "free" or at much lower costs than traditionally available. There were impediments from many angles, including from local, state, and national policy to figuring out how scale could assist in achieving lower tuition while maintaining or even improving quality. Our first program, a master's degree in computer science, OMSCS, addressed the question of whether we could offer a degree program with both quality and a low price – could we meet the needs being heard and disrupt ourselves? Now with 12,000 students and 11,000 graduates, the answer appears clear, but we are continuing to listen and learn. We created our second program, OMS-Analytics, to see if we could duplicate that initial success and to understand how one might scale a program's practicum activities, bringing experiential learning into the core of the degree. Lastly, we created OMS-Cybersecurity to see how to scale laboratory environments. Together, these three programs now have nearly 20,000 individuals seeking to earn a master's degree (circa Fall 2023). Each of these programs was founded by listening. They tested how we might learn to scale our educational programs more broadly and the impacts have benefited not just our online programs but our residential ones too.

From these experiences, Georgia Tech is now on another journey, creating a new college within the university, the College of Lifetime Learning. This will be a nexus for research, education, and service in the new, changing, and emerging world of learning across students' entire lives. It is built on the experiences, the listening, and the successes of the past decades of working with a broader population of individuals who seek to learn (https://lifetimelearning.gatech.edu). To reach this point is about trust, relationship building, and confidence that our collective views of the future are correct and worth being pursued by a university.

In my own journey, the combinations of listening, experimenting, looking at the fringes, and the value of relationships inside and outside of the university are all pivotal. Networking with colleagues via professional organizations has been extremely helpful, for ideas emanate from all around you. However, creating a track record of success and building confidence in new ideas are paramount to be successful as a COLO, just as in any career.

Vickie Cook, Ph.D.

Vice Chancellor for Enrollment and Retention Management,
University of Illinois, Springfield

With support from the University of Illinois System office, the University of Illinois Springfield (UIS) innovated learning through its launch of an inaugural online program in 1998. Prior to this launch, faculty had been engaging students with online components in their classrooms through constructivist strategies. The evolving landscape of online learning and its role in amplifying the UIS academic brand became reality.

The UI System office and the leadership at UIS acknowledged the pivotal role that online learning might bring as they considered an ever-growing need for digital strategy. The reputation of UIS has been built on academic excellence, strong connections between faculty and students, innovation, and student access throughout Illinois and beyond. Leaders supported the innovation of new teaching and learning techniques as online learning would amplify the UIS brand.

Online learning at UIS became synonymous with excellence. The Office for Technology Enhanced Learning (OTEL) was the starting point that led to the launch of the Center for Online Learning, Research and Service (COLRS) in 2009. The centralization of COLRS as the branded heart of online learning at UIS has strengthened brand stewardship of online learning and digital strategy. University digital strategy emphasized the importance of aligning online programs with the institution's academic standards and values. Every online program offered provides students with enriched learning experiences and reflects the quality of the UIS brand.

Since its inception, online learning at UIS has had COLOs who have demonstrated strong leadership as entrepreneurs and who have shepherded the digital brand at UIS. Three COLOs have taken on this role in the past 27 years. These intrapreneurial COLOs have been charged with strategic planning to ensure continued engagement with new technologies, supporting faculty, and empowering students while balancing difficult budgets and exploring external funding opportunities.

COLOs at UIS have long advocated for inclusivity, equity, accessibility, and consistency of the digital strategy at UIS. Brand stewardship ensured development of a consistent experience for the online enterprise within the university. COLOs are the guardians of the digital brand. They are the influencers of the online learning collaborative spirit to create advocacy and initiative across the university. It is the responsibility of the COLO to ensure that every aspect of online and digital strategy aligns with the UIS core values and enhances its reputation. COLOs have remained integral in amplifying the UIS brand and empowering UIS learners around the world.

Today's challenges can be summarized in three key areas and are the focus of the continued work of the COLO at the UIS: (1) the impact of artificial intelligence on teaching and learning within the online learning landscape; (2) impacts of enrollment fluctuations within the student profile due to the demographic cliff, continued disparity in digital accessibility, and public perception of the need for higher education; and (3) retention of students within courses, alternative credentials, and degree programs. These challenges will continue to require strong brand stewardship and effective leadership within the online enterprise of the university.

9 Redefining Student Success by Mainstreaming Nontraditional Delivery for Nontraditional Learners

Introduction

Online and digital learning is transforming the academic mission of colleges and universities. The COVID-19 pandemic gave us a real-time look at learner needs through a digital lens. The pandemic also gave all learners – from kindergarten to post-secondary and beyond – an opportunity to experience flexibility across many dimensions of learning.

We owe a debt of gratitude to many COLOs who have worked tirelessly over multiple years to shine a light on learner needs and align those needs with the opportunities that online and digital education affords learners. Learners seek flexibility now more than ever in delivery modality to best suit individual learning styles. The distinctions in adult learning that were first made in the middle of the 20th century remain relevant since today's learner desires autonomy; prefers learning that is self-directed and personalized; and seeks to integrate real-life experiences into the learning process. These principles are particularly germane as we look at the characteristics of today's adult learners who may be income generating, a caregiver, serving in the military, and/or first generation in college, just to name a few. Furthermore, the percentage

DOI: 10.4324/9781003500742-11

of nontraditional students is expected to grow faster than traditional students as we head into the next decade (NPR, 2024). Not only has the evolution in learner profiles evolved, which has impacted modes of instructional delivery, but so too have the types of credentials that learners seek today.

Data as a Tool to Mainstream Nontraditional Learners

Institutional data on learners began being standardized nationally in 1993 with the creation of the Integrated Post-secondary Education Data System (IPEDS) program department within the National Center for Education Statistics (NCES), a part of the Institute for Education Sciences within the United States Department of Education (National Center for Education Statistics n.d.). Over time, these data have generated rigorous insights into learners that inform university initiatives, such as those focused on student success and those that create learning pathways for online students. With more robust digital learning environments, we also increasingly have access to data about learning. Particularly, the recent growth in online and digital learning has contributed to the advancement of learning analytics (the measurement, collection, analysis, and reporting of data about learners and their contexts) for purposes of understanding and optimizing learning and the environments in which it occurs (Long and Siemens, 2011). These analytics enable real-time student data capture for many types of applications across student persistence, success, and wellbeing.

Just as the nontraditional learner continues to evolve toward the centerline of higher education, so too do delivery modalities. Historically, nontraditional delivery modalities included online, hybrid, and distinctions between synchronous and asynchronous delivery. The tireless work of COLOs and the professional organizations supporting COLOs have not only studied the nexus of nontraditional learners with nontraditional delivery modalities, but it has been the data generated by both that substantiate online and digital learning as the best-fit line between these two and increasingly mainstreamed both so that higher education is more inclusive of a diversity of learners equipped with the learning modalities that best support such diversity of learners. Expanding our definitions of adult learners and increasing accessibility by way of innovative educational pathways toward credentials for these learners – inclusive of on-ramps and offramps – has been precisely what has given momentum to the alternative credential movement that COLOs champion.

Nontraditional Learners Defining Online and Digital Learning

So who are our learners today? Recent UPCEA studies in partnership with other national organizations have explored different facets of today's learners in future casting efforts to help higher education institutions best meet learner needs. COLOs in particular are on the front lines of understanding these learners and their needs, as it has been particularly the student vignettes from online and digital learning over the past two decades that have personified today's new adult learner.

Adult learners enrolling at a university to start or finish their degree are growing at a faster rate than traditional-aged learners (18-year-olds) who enroll in a traditional on-campus experience. Furthermore, the percentage of nontraditional students is expected to grow faster than traditional students in the next decade (Berg et al., 2024). Research conducted by UPCEA reveals adult learners' expectations around access to university resources (they want increased access) and the speed and dexterity by which a university meets their needs (they expect immediate and flexible responses). These expectations are ones that COLOs, their teams, and the technologies that they support and/or champion are capable of meeting through strategies that are student centric.

One group of learners that particularly benefits from online and digital learning, and who are increasingly being viewed as a strategic learner population in enrollment growth and management are stop-outs, or those learners who are characterized as having "some credit" and yet "no credential" (SCNC). At the date of this *Guidebook's* publication, that number is more than 36 million nationally (Berg et al., 2024). Online courses and programs that are skills-focused and where industry-aligned courses and/or microcredentials can plug the missing pieces toward a credential of value is one example where higher education institutions are leveraging the data that illustrates a significant problem nationally and uses all that we know about the new adult learner in combination with the flexibility that online and digital learning affords to create a robust solution with learners at the center.

COLOs offer unique contributions in support of higher education's pursuits toward student success. These include:

- *Policy Revisions* – Where institutional, state, or national policies support traditional students, COLOs have been instrumental in expanding the scope of policies to include online learners so that they stand to benefit from student rules, tuition assistance, and successful time to completion, just as any student should.

- *Change Management* – As nontraditional students, nontraditional delivery modalities, and alternative credentials converge on otherwise traditional higher education institutions, COLOs are particularly adept at supporting college/university leadership responsible for managing change and stakeholder expectations through institutional governance processes.
- *Partnerships* – Supporting the new adult learner with diverse instructional modalities as well as an array of credential types necessitates viable partnerships. Chapter 11 goes into further depth on how COLOs foster relationships both internal and external to the institution to further strategies and initiatives in support of online and digital learning.
- *Flexibility* – Learner flexibility has evolved over time to take on various meanings as technology improves, workforce trends shift, and learner responsibilities shift. COLOs are instrumental in continuously defining flexibility in the context of their respective institutions, while also ensuring they keep pace with the realities of learners at any given point in time. How aligned online and digital learning is with learner expectations is a key determinant of success for online and digital learning initiatives at a college/university.
- *Career-Readiness* – Given the way that online and digital learning draws upon labor market data to determine viable program offerings as well as to design skill-based curricula; the engagement COLOs often have with industry partners; and the fact that successfully recruiting an online student today is heavily reliant on a data-driven marketing process, COLOs are among the most knowledgeable to speak to how we can best prepare our learners for the workforce. COLOs are increasingly present in these conversations, yet better institutional alignment between COLOs and the leadership responsible for career-readiness at a college/university could stand to improve this to the benefit of all learners moving forward.
- *Scale of Learning* – As the national debate ensues over the value of a degree (Pew Research Center, 2024), universities are increasingly exploring different scales of learning. The scale of learning trends over the past two decades has spanned from the massive (MOOCs) to the minute (micro-credentials). The majority of these offerings have been online and have leveraged digital technologies. COLOs are uniquely poised to address the myriad considerations that arise as the scale of learning expands or contracts to a size that differs from that of a traditional degree.

Credential Innovations

Many COLOs are seeing their portfolios shift into the alternative credential space. They are the individuals with the competencies to not only lead credential innovations (given their in-depth knowledge of the new adult learner and their propensities toward a more flexible and affordable learning model) but also manage disruptions in a space that has historically been deemed a threat to higher education's product offerings.

We see an abundance of credential innovations emanating from higher education institutions, as the single-sell market of college and university degrees seeks to diversify. Such credential innovations are iterating off activities in the alternative credential space, including certificates, microcredentials, digital badges, and micro certificates. These alternative credentials often signal specific competencies, certification, and sometimes licensure. Many institutions are responding to the need to move quickly by looking at their existing stock of online courses, many of which are credit-bearing classes that have had substantial investments in time and money. Colleges and universities are evaluating their online courses based on industry-aligned skills, and then rebundling content for noncredit offerings. An institution's ability to innovate in the credential space is a product of several factors: careful assessment of readiness; intentional planning to meet workforce and industry needs into the future; and collaboration among multiple stakeholders on-campus, including the University Registrar, Vice President for Enrollment Management, leadership in corporate and/or workforce engagement, the Faculty Senate, and academic partners who serve as subject-matter experts.

Key characteristics of credential innovations include:

Industry-Aligned – Credential innovations that are industry-aligned ensure that students are career-ready and also that employers benefit in the arms race to recruit and retain talent in today's workforce.

Stackable – Credential innovations that are designed for stackability enable more opportunities for continuous learning over time.

Demonstrative – Credential innovations that culminate in a demonstrative qualification or achievement place value on the pursuit of learning, which holds currency for the learner depending on the context the credential is applied.

These characteristics of alternative credentials are leading to credential innovations across a range of inflection points for learners – from those that prepare learners for entry-level jobs where a college degree is not required; to a post-secondary academic experience that becomes á la carte for the learner with alternative on-ramps and affordable entry points made possible through partnerships with employers or third-party content providers; to add-ons to a degree that make learners more employable as they enter the workforce upon successfully completing a degree; alternative credentials at the graduate and professional level; and finally those programs sought throughout the course of a lifetime for personal and/or professional gain.

Competency Connection

UPCEA COLO Competency	*COLO Insight*	*Influencing Factors*	*Influencing Factor (COVID-Era)*	*Institutional Risk*
Supporting and Advocating for Faculty and Students	What No One Really Answered: "Where does the COLO go from here?" Nontraditional learners and delivery methods are becoming more mainstream	Unprecedented rate of change occurring in higher ed Shuffle in the industry due to market pressures/speculation Learners need different types of education at different stages of life and career	Most COLOs worked 2–3x normal hours and many have outgrown the role	COLO competencies are a mechanism to support/advocate for the COLO by recognizing the complexities of the role.

References

Berg, B., Causey, J., Cohen, J., Ibrahim, M., Holsapple, M., & Shapiro, D. (2024). *Some College, No Credential Student Outcomes: Annual Progress Report – Academic Year 2022/23*. National Student Clearinghouse Research Center.

Long, P.L. and Siemens, G. (2011). *Penetrating the Fog: Analytics in Learning and Education. Educause Review*. https://er.educause.edu/articles/2011/9/penetrating-the-fog-analytics-in-learning-and-education

National Center for Education Statistics. (n.d.). *The integrated postsecondary education data system: History of IPEDS data*. https://nces.ed.gov

NPR. (2024, July 8). Walmart and McDonald's announce new college degree benefits for employees. https://www.npr.org/2024/07/08/nx-s1-4758144/walmart-mcdonalds-college-degree

Pew Research Center. (2024, May). *Is College Worth It?*

Expert Perspectives

- Lisa L. Templeton, Oregon State University
- Luke Dowden, Alamo Colleges District
- Bettyjo Bouchey, University of Vermont
- James Fong, UPCEA

Lisa L. Templeton

Vice Provost, Division of Educational Ventures, Oregon State University

Oregon State University recognized the needs of nontraditional learners early on. We understood that not everyone who wanted an education had the ability or time to physically attend classes on a site-based campus. As the state's land grant institution with an access mission, we knew we needed to develop alternative pathways to an OSU education for learners in our state. In 2002, we launched OSU Ecampus, an online education unit, to support our access mission and serve Oregon's nontraditional learners. At that time, we couldn't have anticipated how quickly and significantly this population of learners would grow and how this delivery would shift from a peripheral option to being the preferred delivery method for many students, not just from Oregon, but nationally and internationally.

The types of learners being served through online education units are vast, diverse, and growing. In 2024, OSU had over 15,000 unique learners enrolled in our online programs. These students resided in all 50 states and 60 countries. In Fall 2022, 26% of students nationally, or approximately 4.9 million individuals, were enrolled exclusively online (National Center for Education Statistics, 2023). These online learners are often place bound. They are busy individuals, juggling work commitments at the same time as parenting responsibilities. They are often caring for their aging parents. They are students who are studying while serving in the military. Most online students have previously stopped out and have returned to complete their education, aiming to set an example for their children or to secure their ideal job or a promotion. Coupled with this is an emerging trend of traditionally aged college students who are now also increasingly choosing online or hybrid learning formats.

No matter the reason modern learners are choosing online education, universities that offer online degrees and programs need to ensure they support these learners in achieving their educational objectives. Unfortunately, most universities were not designed for fully online learners. Navigating a university from a distance can be challenging, especially for learners who have been out of school for some time. Additionally, support services and activities at universities are often tailored for on-campus students and available only during standard business hours, making them inaccessible for most online students.

COLOs need to be at the forefront of student success. Universities must support their online students and welcome and integrate them into the university community while providing relevant, comparable, and equitable access to resources and student services. Online students shouldn't feel invisible or like outsiders at their own university. Fostering a sense of belonging in online students has been shown to impact satisfaction and intent to persist (Perez, 2020). Being mindful of language that is inclusive of online learners in communications, providing opportunities to engage with faculty and staff in meaningful ways, and helping students develop an affinity for your institution are all great ways to enhance feelings of belonging to the institution.

Many universities are developing unique services for their online students. At OSU, success coaches work in partnership with online students to improve academic skills, to identify support resources, and to address obstacles to academic success. Online students can participate in many clubs and organizations, access 24/7 tutoring and library resources, engage in undergraduate research, achieve honor roll, gain admissions to our Honors College, and take advantage of study abroad and service-learning opportunities.

It's an exciting time to be involved in online education. The field is rapidly evolving as more universities are recognizing the importance of this delivery modality and viewing online learners as both an enrollment growth strategy and a critical demographic to support. Universities are expanding access to online degrees and pioneering new credentials designed to meet the needs of today's modern learners. Alongside this expansion, universities must create strategies to focus on integrating online students into their communities effectively, ensuring all students receive adequate support to succeed, feel connected, and valued.

References

National Center for Education Statistics. (2023). *Table 311.15: Percentage of first-time, full-time degree-seeking undergraduate students at 4-year degree-granting institutions, by sex and race/ethnicity: Fall 2021*. Digest of Education Statistics. U.S. Department of Education. https://nces.ed.gov/programs/digest/d23/tables/dt23_311.15.asp

Perez, M. L. (2020). *Sense of belonging from a distance: How online students describe, perceive, and experience belonging to the institution* (Doctoral dissertation). Dissertations and Theses. Paper 5463. https://doi.org/10.15760/etd.7335

Luke Dowden, Ed.D.

Chief Online Learning Officer, Alamo Colleges District

A skills-based approach for both credential innovation and hiring is the path forward to social and economic mobility for millions of learners with some college and no degree. Whether it is via credit or noncredit academic or workforce programming, COLOs recognize the need to adapt quickly to not only the demands of business and industry but the evolving needs of today's learners. Skills-based learning models require new forms of credentials, commonly called alternative credentials or microcredentials. These credential innovations are best able to meet specific industry needs and should be situated by both the higher education institution and industry within a skill-based hiring ecosystem. Skills-based hiring has significant potential to illuminate a more complete understanding of a candidate's knowledge, skills, abilities, and personal agility in adapting to an employer's significant workforce needs.

If skills and competencies are the new currency in the future of work, higher education institutions must do more to prepare learners with the understanding of their own skills, to assist each learner in identifying skills gaps, and to provide learning options to close those gaps (Northeastern University, 2023). As an investment in technical and marketable skills, digital badges allow learners to gain confidence in their competitiveness in the job market after completing specific skills assessments. Helping diverse talent pools understand and gain in-demand skills is the first step for institutions of higher education. More robust portfolios of stackable, noncredit certificates may provide the competitive advantage a learner needs to attain a sustainable wage-earning job in a career path. Regardless of gains in equitable practices through digital access to degree programs, skills-based credential offerings (e.g. alternative credentials) can help further level the playing field for those most locked out of opportunity.

New credential options (e.g. micro-certificates, micro-masters, etc.) based on skills taxonomies contextualized by industry alone will not solve the greatest barrier to obtaining a family-sustaining career for millions who have earned credit but no credentials. As leading teaching and learning organizations lean into credential innovations and skills visibility platforms (e.g. comprehensive learner records, skills wallets, learner employability records), interoperability is the greatest need and greatest threat. "Most talent acquisition systems are not yet prepared to accept new types of nondegree credentials or richer skills data: they remain geared around basic educational information and unstructured data such as PDF attachments" (Gallagher et al., 2023). Other key challenges remain to fully operationalize skills-based hiring ecosystems, including: (1) lack of standardized skill taxonomies and frameworks, (2) difficulties in accurately measuring and assessing skills, and (3) potential resistance to change from traditional hiring practices.

Institutions must go beyond unbundling and repacking their curricula and ensure that their stackable certificates facilitate a learner's ability to compete in a skills-based marketplace. COLOs can be the bridge for their institutions and industry partners to close these systems' gaps. Jobs for the Future's *Skills-Based Practices: An Employer Journey Map* offers practical paths forward to make the business case, assess readiness, adopt, and advance skills-based talent practices (Ward et al., 2023). Deeply integrated, interconnected partnerships between employers and talent generators, such as community colleges and universities, are a clear path to realizing the full benefits of a skills-based hiring ecosystem.

By working with willing industry partners, universities and community colleges should re-envision and reimagine current relationship structures and integration strategies. These partnership models are needed to achieve targeted and measurable interventions aimed at improving talent pipelines for the employer and connections to careers with sustainable wages for our learners. These achievements require investments in new ways of collaboration. Partners must commit time, HR, and technical expertise toward integrating talent pipelines generated by teaching and learning organizations into companies' hiring information systems. This work must consider many small to medium-sized employers that have incomplete or no digitized hiring systems. "Establishing an architecture for skills portability and data consistency can benefit all stakeholders" (Northeastern, 2023). Shared investments in skills-based credential offerings and hiring among partners will result in measurable social and economic mobility gains as well as closing pay equity gaps.

References

Gallagher, S. R., Leuba, M., & Houston, C. (2023, March). *Digital Credentials and Talent Acquisition Tech: Closing the Data Gap Between Learning and Hiring*. Center for Public Safety Innovation, Northeastern University. https://cps.northeastern.edu/wp-content/uploads/2023/03/Digital_Credentials_Talent_Acquisition_Tech.pdf

Northeastern University College of Professional Studies. (2023, April). *Understanding the emerging skillstech landscape*. Center for Public Safety Innovation, Northeastern University. https://cps.northeastern.edu/wp-content/uploads/2023/04/SkillsTech_Landscape.pdf

Ward, C., Newsome, D., Jackson, S., & Kaplan, J. (2023). *Skills-Based Practices: An Employer Journey Map*. Jobs for the Future. https://www.jff.org/wp-content/uploads/2023/11/Skills-Based-Talent-Practices-an-Employer-Journey-Map-JFF.pdf

Bettyjo Bouchey, Ed.D.

Chief Officer, Professional and Continuing Education, University of Vermont

Back in 2019, a group of emerging and existing COLOs gathered to kick off research into how online organizations at institutions of higher education were taking shape. While the results of that study, which I was honored to conduct alongside that group of COLOs, showed that the shape and complexion of online education at universities and colleges across the United States can and do take many forms, we had some textured findings related to the support of online students that remain relevant to this day. We designed the research to follow the online student lifecycle, not anticipating that our last interview would fall as the COVID-19 pandemic was shutting down colleges and universities across the globe. We considered waiting, but in the end, those were the most interesting interviews from the entire study.

Our findings revealed that prior to the pandemic it was sometimes very difficult to garner internal support for online students, partly because the residential students represented the majority of the population, but partly because many student affairs professionals lacked experience with supporting students at a distance. COLOs recalled feeling frustrated and defeated, yet still clear in their convictions of the criticality of equitable online student support. Mid- and post-pandemic, however, COLOs were heartened by the infrastructure and acumen that were built to support all students during the shutdowns. Invariably, each COLO ended his/her remarks with high hopes for the future of those systems as well. Fast-forward a few years and many of those study participants have been able to sustain most, if not all, of those structures; I was among them in my last position. In fact, I have grown to firmly believe that designing student systems from an "online first" perspective is a strategic advantage.

Some may read that last sentence and wonder not only what it means, but how it is a strategic advantage, especially if you currently sit within an institution more focused on traditional-aged, residential undergraduate students. But one only needs to look around to notice how many people are currently clicking something on their smartphones to remember that the generations making up our first-time student populations have grown up in an "on-demand" society where they are accustomed to accessing goods and services at the moment they want them and in the way they prefer. This generation of students expects service availability when the need presents itself, and that may be at 3:00 a.m. and/or when they notice the line is too long at the Bursar's office. In short, online student support services provide for flexibility and accessibility to all students, regardless of if they attend most or all of their classes in-person or online.

Institutions that consciously design systems from an "online first" perspective not only serve their existing student population in richer ways whether those students learn online or in-person but also fortify those structures against disruptions that may call for temporary or long-term shutdowns. While designing from an "online first" perspective may be a departure for some, we only need to harken back a few years to see how these designs may have helped some institutions pivot faster during the pandemic. Further, as we all face continued regulatory pressures to produce meaningful online student outcomes, it is now imperative for those wishing to continue to offer online programming to ensure that equitable online student supports are available – and those systems benefit the entire campus community as a residual benefit. As the face of the contemporary post-secondary student continues to evolve, ensuring that access points from the first touchpoint into the institution through to lifelong learning can be accessed in-person, at a distance, or any combination thereof is critical to the long-term viability of higher education and its relevance to its populations served.

James Fong

Chief Research Officer, UPCEA

Dating back to the Morrill Land Grant Acts of 1862 and 1890 (National Archives, 1862), institutions of higher education have sought to be more closely aligned with the needs of the student, employer, and economy. As the economy changed from various industrial revolutions, so did higher education. During the Third Industrial Revolution, higher education provided skilled workers, managers, leaders, and scientists to fuel a mass production economy. Higher education responded during the Fourth Industrial Revolution by contributing to the science, support, and consumer usage of the Internet and wireless communication economies. It now finds itself at the doorstep of the automation and artificial intelligence era of this revolutionary period. Given the speed of technology and rate of change in this era, institutions in the U.S. often find themselves at a disadvantage, being overly dependent on a degree-based model of higher education. While the U.S. is making advances in more modern, industry-aligned higher education alternatives, such as microcredentials; countries such as Ireland, New Zealand (Bruin et al., 2022), China (Martin, 2022), and a number of provinces in Canada have more aggressively pursued transformation.

Shifting demographics, global markets, evolving artificial intelligence technologies, and increased competition have made the nontraditional learner or "the new adult learner" (Fong and Etter, 2022) more important to institutions in the U.S. given their potential to offset lost traditional student enrollments and declining revenues. UPCEA research has also shown that existing college and university systems, processes, and objectives may not be in alignment with serving this new adult learner student in this changing economy (Fong & Etter, 2022).

At the time of this publication, the National Student Clearinghouse (2024) showed that the population labeled as SCNC continues to increase post-pandemic with 36.8 million individuals aged 64 and under in this educational category. There are many theories and hypotheses as to why this trend has not reversed with the adult learner returning to college. Personal economics, such as income, family pressures, and employment factors; and increased tuition costs are factors, among others. UPCEA research (Etter & Sullberg, 2024) has identified that the adult learner population is complex with at least five segments existing, each with different educational needs, preferences, and priorities. Some of these needs and preferences go beyond the degree and into stackability of credentials, as well as noncredit-to-credit transfer and credit for prior learning.

Another UPCEA study (Etter et al., 2023b) sponsored by the education company Collegis shows that employers also want greater input and a more active partnership role regarding educational offerings, including noncredit programming and greater integration of real-world applications. These employers also want improved communication and relationships between the institution and the employer.

The adult learner has cost concerns and seeks value when choosing an institution and credential. UPCEA research (Etter et al., 2023a) has also uncovered that the way the institution markets, communicates, and engages the adult learner in the enrollment process is critical in converting an inquirer to a student. Today's adult learner is often a younger representative of Generation X, typically in their mid-forties in age; a Millennial; or an older representative of Generation Z, usually in their mid-twenties in age. Each generation has different information needs and interacts with colleges and universities differently. UPCEA research (Etter, 2023) has found that many institutions have legacy enrollment practices in place that better serve older adults rather than younger adults.

As can be seen in a UPCEA study (Etter & Sullberg, 2023) with the digital marketing company Search Influence, many institutional websites are not optimized to communicate well with the adult learner or even with search engines. Research has also shown that many institutions have not coordinated their human inquiry responses well with automated or technological responses. These secret shopping efforts have shown long response times. The cause of some of these problems or inefficiencies can also be a result of incorrect staffing or resource allocation toward marketing or enrollment management functions.

Nontraditional learner success depends on many factors, with some stemming from a lack of institutional planning, and others due to not recognizing the needs of the learner and the employer. Institutions must go beyond simply moving a successful classroom-taught degree online, to better support it, resource it, and even design it to be more convenient or stackable to the new adult learner and his/her employer.

References

Bruin, L., Wegewijs, B., Lokhoff, J., Elmers, M., & Bardoel, K. (2022). *The rise and recognition of micro-credentials: Stacking modules and the future of the qualification. NUFFIC.* https://www.nuffic.nl/sites/default/files/2022-03/The%20rise%20and%20recognition%20of%20micro-credentials.pdf

Fong, J., & Etter, B. (2022). *The six personas of the new learner*. UPCEA Research Whitepaper in collaboration with The Thinking Cap Agency.

Martin, S. (2022). *Micro-credentials in the Asia-Pacific*. *FE News*. https://www.fenews.co.uk/exclusive/exclusive-micro-credentials-in-the-asia-pacific/

Etter, B. (2023). *Enrollment process review: Secret shopper analysis*. UPCEA Proprietary Research.

Etter, B., Fong, J., & Sullberg, D. (2023a). *Looking toward the future: Enrollment strategies and evolving expectations of potential inquirers*. UPCEA Research Whitepaper in collaboration with InsideTrack.

Etter, B., Fong, J., Sullberg, D., and Wang, K. (2023b). *Unveiling the Employer's View: An Employer-Centric Approach to Higher Education Partnerships*. UPCEA Research Whitepaper in Collaboration with Collegis Education

Etter, B., & Sullberg, D. (2023). *Slipping through the cracks: Understanding PCO unit SEO capabilities*. UPCEA Research Whitepaper in collaboration with Search Influence.

Etter, B., & Sullberg, D. (2024). *Some College, No Credential Readiness Index*. UPCEA Research Whitepaper in collaboration with Straighterline.

National Archives. (1862). *Act of July 2, 1862 (Morrill Act), Public Law 37-108, which established land grant colleges, 07/02/1862; Enrolled Acts and Resolutions of Congress, 1789–1996; Record Group 11; General Records of the United States Government*. https://search.archives.gov/search.affiliate=national-archives&sort_by=&query=morrill+act+1890

National Student Clearinghouse Research Center. (2024). *Some college, no credential student outcomes: 2024 report for the nation and the states* (5th ed.). https://nscresearchcenter.org/some-college-no-credential/

Section 3

Distinguishing Next-Gen Leaders

This section offers commentary on why UPCEA's eight professional competencies uniquely distinguish COLOs to lead higher education institutions today and into the future. It also includes a discussion on how the field and practice of digital and online education can foster a pipeline of leaders. This section also curates contributions from the leadership of leading and relevant professional organizations who all have a vested interest in formalized competencies for COLOs.

DOI: 10.4324/9781003500742-12

10 What Does the Future of Digital Teaching and Learning Need from COLOs?

Introduction

A theme that has run throughout this book is the undeniable fact that higher education is experiencing a period of rapid change and disruption. Much of this change is due to digital advancements, placing COLOs in the proverbial eye of higher education's disruption storm.

This ever-evolving context requires COLOs to simultaneously straddle both present operational needs and potential future needs, all while balancing a portfolio of activities, research, and projects that will guarantee current requirements are met while also ensuring ongoing long-term relevance. How can a COLO effectively lead in such an environment? The key is to adopt the leadership competencies described in this book and incorporate them into both short-term execution and long-term professional development.

Understanding COLO Leadership

In many respects, COLO leadership is indistinguishable from any other kind of organizational leadership. Taken in isolation, the eight UPCEA competencies of PCO leaders could apply to any industry. All companies, nonprofit organizations, military units, or government entities ask their leaders to demonstrate these very same skills. However, each one of these competencies,

DOI: 10.4324/9781003500742-13

as we have seen throughout this book, must be viewed through the very specific lens of the COLO role. How a COLO applies each will determine his/her success.

Entrepreneurship, Partnerships, and Relationship-Building

All organizations require entrepreneurial activities and investments to remain competitive, as well as the ability to partner and establish win-win relationships.

COLO Connection: Maintain a start-up mindset and continually look for opportunities. Partner with internal colleagues, other institutions, consortia, and commercial vendors. Establish relationships with deans, faculty, students, and senior administration (see Chapter 8).

Resource Management

No organization will be able to survive as a sustained entity if they are unable to generate revenue, manage a budget, and effectively allocate resources.

COLO Connection: Advocate for resources by communicating alignment with the institutional mission and the ROI. Efficiently steward those resources through competent budget oversight and operational management (see Chapter 5).

Supporting and Advocating for Faculty and Students (Stakeholders and Customers)

With its direct reference to "Faculty and Students," this competency is arguably specific to a COLO's higher education context. However, by replacing "Faculty and Students" with "Stakeholders and Customers," it becomes clear how this competency is essential to any organization, drilling down to the organizational mission and its very reason for existing.

COLO Connection: Remain relentlessly student-focused as the "north star" for all activities and decision-making, privileging the faculty's role in the institutional mission (see Chapter 9).

Program Planning

Project planning and management is a core skill for any organization. From product launches to consulting and implementation services to R&D activities, program and project planning is critical.

COLO Connection: Plan and shepherd market-driven online courses and programs from conception to delivery. Ensure that initiatives are led through proven project management practices and leverage data where available (see Chapter 4).

Marketing, Research, and Evaluation

Understanding what is working and why/why not requires research and assessment. Are customers buying the new product line? Did the last deployment have the desired outcomes? By understanding root issues, corrections can be made. Marketing is common to all organizations as it encompasses the strategy and methods that the organization uses to tell its story and make stakeholders aware of its mission.

COLO Connection: Recognize that uncollected data cannot be analyzed. Continually evaluate success/failure to iterate or sunset initiatives. Maintain currency on the latest research in digital learning. Become knowledgeable about marketing strategies for online learning, especially digital marketing (see Chapter 6).

Information and Digital Technology

It would be difficult to find any modern organization that does not require information and digital technology to some degree. Even the smallest businesses use bookkeeping software, email, and likely maintain a website.

COLO Connection: Be fluent in the terminology and infrastructure of basic IT. Understand the technical fundamentals of key software such as the LMS and other EdTech platforms. Establish a productive partnership with the institutional CIO (see Chapter 7).

Critical Thinking and Decision-Making

Any leader at any level in any organization needs to have a well-developed ability to think critically, analyze pros and cons, and make decisions. A deficit in this competency could very easily lead to the failure of the leader's organization/unit/team.

COLO Connection: Make data-informed decisions. Apply critical thinking strategies to all decision-making, especially high-stakes decisions. Recognize that not making a decision *is* a decision (see Chapter 3).

Integrity, Ethics, and Professionalism

The leader sets the example for those he/she leads. Therefore, the leader must exhibit integrity, ethics, and professionalism. Without those attributes, the organization will operate well below its potential and could even be at risk of overall failure.

COLO Connection: Never compromise your integrity or ethics. Be an example for your team to follow and set high ethical standards. Demonstrate professionalism in all aspects of your job. In the midst of stress and chaos, remain calm and be the leader your team can rely on for support (see Chapter 2).

Staying Future-Focused

When it comes to teaching and learning, there are a number of timeless constants. These include foundational premises such as clearly communicating expectations; genuinely caring about the success of students; and ensuring alignment between objectives, activities, and assessments. Of course, these pedagogical principles transcend modality and apply to all teaching formats.

What the COLO must do is leverage digital technologies and techniques to enable best teaching practices in online contexts. This should include not only current practice but a continual striving for new, more effective strategies that will positively impact the student experience and learning outcomes. Given the rapidly evolving state of educational technology and their specific role as the stewards of digital delivery, COLOs are uniquely positioned to spearhead pedagogical/andragogical change within their institutions.

To drive this change, as mentioned in Chapter 8, COLOs must encourage in themselves and their teams a well-developed "futures literacy." They need to be able to imagine future possibilities unrestricted by current or past practice. This may include using technology "off-label" in a way that it wasn't originally intended. For example, one institution conducted a pilot using their LMS's "parent app" designed for parental monitoring of K-12 students to provide proactive insights for college advisors, particularly academic advisors for intercollegiate athletes. An advisor was assigned the members of a team, who were tagged as "children" in the app, allowing deeper real-time monitoring of academic progress. This kind of pilot is the result of viewing possibilities with futures literacy.

These kinds of opportunities exist at every college and university. COLOs should make every effort to keep their fingers on the pulse of the newest technologies (e.g., AI) and practices (e.g., personalized learning) while staying grounded in the quality principles of pedagogy and support. In the pursuit of innovation and efficiency, quality cannot suffer. In fact, none of the three arms of the Iron Triangle should suffer.

According to Immerwahr et al. (2008), the Iron Triangle of higher education consists of three arms: Quality, Cost, and Access. The conventional wisdom is that it is impossible to positively impact any one arm without negatively impacting one or both of the others. For example, if an institution wanted to increase quality, it would result in also increasing costs and possibly even decreasing access. If an institution wanted to decrease cost, it would result in lowered quality. The promise of digital learning viewed through a lens of futures literacy is that COLOs possess the potential to positively disrupt all three arms of the Iron Triangle simultaneously (Kurzweil and Brown, 2015). But to do so requires the online leader to think differently from the conventional wisdom.

No matter what the COLO does (or does not do), the best interests of students should be the North Star of all decision-making. Innovation for innovation's sake and technology for technology's sake, no matter how groundbreaking, are pointless if they are not in the service of students.

The Value of Professional Organizations

One of the most important assets that any COLO can possess in order to stay current and anticipate future needs is an extensive network. The more people you know, the more wisdom and experience you can tap into. As a community we are collectively smarter and more capable than any single individual or institution. Whether you are consulting an associate who has experienced the same (or similar) challenge you are now facing, or you just need to safely talk through future scenarios with a knowledgeable professional outside your own institution, or you simply need an opinion or advice, having a network of trusted colleagues is an enormous benefit to any current or aspiring COLO.

Arguably the best way to develop such a network is by active involvement in one or more (preferably more) professional associations. Organizations such as UPCEA, OLC, WCET, QM, EDUCAUSE, USDLA, 1EdTech, ACHE, and others offer ample opportunities to volunteer, participate in conference activities, and meet colleagues from both the U.S. and abroad. Other groups exist within state college/university systems, athletic conferences (e.g., the Big 10, SEC, and Big 12 all have online/technology groups), and consortia.

In addition to being fertile places to cultivate a professional network, industry associations are also rich sources of resources, including research reports and surveys that help inform future planning. Resources such as UPCEA's Hallmarks of Excellence, QM's course rubrics, WCET's policy analyses, and OLC's Scorecards (plus many more from each and other associations) are critical tools for COLO success. In addition, each organization offers various training opportunities, webinars, and newsletters.

Association conferences and convenings are excellent venues for developing networks and hearing the latest research and practices from colleagues across higher education. Workshops, presentations, keynotes, and panels provide insights into not just the current state of online learning but peeks into the future. As William Gibson has reportedly said, "The future is already here. It's just not evenly distributed yet." Association conference program sessions invariably provide windows into the future, before it becomes more evenly distributed.

References

Kurzweil, M., & Brown, J. (2015, August 26). *Breaking the Iron Triangle at The University of Central Florida*. https://doi.org/10.18665/sr.241922

Immerwahr, J., Johnson, J., & Gasbarra, P. (2008). *The Iron Triangle: College presidents talk about costs, access, and quality*. The National Center for Public Policy and Higher Education and Public Agenda.

Expert Perspectives

- Julie Uranis, UPCEA
- Russ Poulin, WCET – the WICHE Cooperative for Educational Technologies
- Deborah Adair, Quality Matters
- Jennifer Mathes, Online Learning Consortium
- Bethany Simunich, Quality Matters/CHLOE
- Richard Garrett, Eduventures/CHLOE

Julie Uranis, Ph.D.

Senior Vice President of Online and Strategic Initiatives, UPCEA

The future of digital teaching and learning needs COLOs to embrace their roles and act with authority. For too long, COLOs have relied on the permission to lead digital teaching and transformation, when they should be the unequivocal leaders of these efforts. These conditions have been created by the ebb and flow of institutional needs, organizational restructuring, instability in the senior-most roles at institutions, and the transactional granting and revoking of institutional influence.

As we experienced through the COVID-19 pandemic, COLOs were indispensable. Their preparations and past decisions allowed institutions to shift to emergency remote teaching in a matter of hours. As Rovy Branon, Vice Provost for the University of Washington Continuum College, once said, "if you had asked me before the pandemic how long it would take to move all of our courses online, I would have been speaking in semesters or years. We managed to move everyone to emergency remote teaching in a matter of days." What we know is that institutions that had decently resourced online enterprises fared better in those early days of the pandemic. That was not an accident, it was due to the foresight and planning of COLOs.

The specific competencies of entrepreneurship (business acumen), resource management, critical thinking, and decision-making are particularly valuable, as they are not often exemplified in professional development opportunities for academic leaders. COLOs tend to embrace and nurture these competencies in themselves and those they mentor, making them unicorns on their campuses. That's why even the most marginalized COLOs are often called upon when traditionally trained academic leaders cannot comprehend the environment and the work to be done. In those times, COLOs must lead and sustain their influence when their institutions "return to normal."

Once granted "a seat at the table," even if temporary, COLOs must advocate for themselves, their team, their learners, and the online enterprise they lead. COLOs should suggest, if not demand, that online learning be a component of their institution's strategic plan, have a funding model that does not inhibit or constrain growth, and debunk long-held biases and myths that online is inferior. Anything less will doom an online initiative or enterprise to failure. As such, COLOs must also regularly evaluate the conditions and signals that might indicate a changing tide, and identify new employment opportunities and employers that value their skills.

As the great Kenny Rogers imparted, "you have to know when to hold 'em, know when to fold 'em," and this holds true for COLOs. There are bellwether signs that COLOs should be aware of as they assess their work environments. Institutional reorganization, changes in funding models, and academic leaders not known to possess any of the competencies mentioned above promoted into roles with tiles inclusive of "innovation" – these conditions all require inspection and reflection. During these times, COLOs must embrace the unknown and consider new opportunities where the online enterprise and the COLO role are valued. Further, an emerging trend is for COLOs to be tapped as chief enrollment officers, provosts, and even presidents. The career prospects have never been better for COLOs as the skills that make successful COLOs are highly valued – that is, for those who have the courage and fortitude to boldly lead.

Russ Poulin

Executive Director WCET – the WICHE Cooperative for Educational Technologies

There are many sage pieces of advice that leaders receive about looking to the future, such as:

- Understand the needs and emerging needs of those you serve and those you lead
- Set aside time to research and think about the future
- Develop resources and connections that help you identify emerging trends and learn from those on the cutting edge. WCET's "cooperative" nature helps in sharing research on issues that you do not have time to pursue and connections with others faced with the same challenges who can be trusted confidants
- Plan for your future, including contingencies in case something goes awry

In creating that plan for the future, digital learning leaders must exist in a state of "controlled fretfulness." You have to fret about what might go wrong, yet compose yourself so as not to project those worries on those whom you lead and serve. When your plan hits that rock in the middle of the stream (and certainly that will happen), you must project calm leadership in assessing the situation and navigating a path to safety. To control that fretfulness, it is helpful to have imagined contingencies to get you back on track.

A Question That Needs to be Asked

The question "what do you do if something goes wrong" is one that is frequently asked. There is another that is less common but should be asked more often…especially in the realm of digital learning. That question is: "what do you do if you are far more successful than you anticipated?"

My Lesson from Not Anticipating that Question

In my first leadership position, not anticipating this possibility resulted in one of my biggest challenges. Back in the nascent Internet days, I was charged with creating a statewide, two-way instructional video network connecting public institutions across the state.

We were often the pioneers and were the first to implement some new technologies. As you well know, when you are the first in technology, things will go wrong. We had our bumps the first year, but we learned, we solved, and we advanced.

By the end of the second year, we discovered that some on-campus students were choosing our distance courses over the traditional lecture. Why? The faculty had rethought their courses, were more organized, and students enjoyed the interactions with adult learners from non-campus sites.

Our success was the beginning of the problem. More programs wanted to use the network, but our funding and sites were finite. I was called in front of the Board of Higher Education to explain this apparent failure resulting from too much demand. Our "success" led us to be viewed as "failing."

We did our best to develop a complex formula for scheduling priorities. We sought additional funding and institutional support. With the Internet becoming more robust, we encouraged some faculty to use synchronous video when needed and use asynchronous tools to achieve other goals. That sounds trite now, but it was a difficult sell back then. In short, we handled the problems we anticipated but struggled with unanticipated demand.

Modern Day Parallels

We are currently living these same trials with unanticipated success as I faced back then. Some examples include:

- A big fear from the COVID "emergency remote learning" experience was that faculty and students would eschew all digital technologies. At countless colleges and universities, the opposite is true and they are struggling to keep up with the demand for more online, hybrid, and hyflex classes. And we worry about those who plow ahead without realizing that there is an art to quality online instruction.
- Increased demand for digital learning courses from both faculty and students resulted in a community college hosting fewer people on campus. Even though there were not as many faculty or students around, they maxed out the campus WiFi to "crisis" mode. How? For those who remained, the demand for videoconferencing and streaming skyrocketed.
- An overwhelming recent case is the onslaught of artificial intelligence. The uptake of the technology has been at a record pace. It is a success, but it also causes challenges with faculty development, academic integrity, student misuse, and policies that cannot keep up with a service that adds features faster than we can imagine.

It is a worthwhile thought experiment to challenge your team with the question "what do we do if we are more successful than anticipated?" Certainly, it is more fun than thinking about the monsters under the bed who cause us to be fretful.

Deborah Adair, Ph.D.

Chief Executive Officer, Quality Matters

With more than two decades of experience focusing on quality in digital education, working directly with thousands of faculty, instructional designers, and administrators, we at Quality Matters (QM) have seen the importance of expertise and leadership in creating quality learning experiences for students. We've also seen what happens when there is a leadership gap and, as a consequence, the link between the institutional strategy and the operational areas in digital learning is missing or disconnected. This happens too often even at institutions with aspirational growth goals and it results in insurmountable handicaps for digital learning operations. We observe digital learning initiatives that are significantly under-resourced (lacking funding, staffing, or both), aren't aligned to institutional goals, and don't produce positive student outcomes.

Achieving quality takes commitment and resources. As W. Edward Deming, the father of quality management, once commented, "It does not happen all at once. There is no instant pudding." This is where the leadership of COLOs matters the most. They are best positioned to create the ingredients or conditions necessary to achieve quality in digital learning.

COLOs play very specific roles in the institution, directly managing digital learning activity as well as bridging divides between the online learning operation and other parts of the institution. Critically, this includes communicating up the administrative chain to ensure the online enterprise is resourced to meet goals, evaluated with meaningful measures, and fully integrated into institutional assessment plans. This means they not only have to be competent in the work of digital learning but also have to demonstrate the leadership necessary to gain the confidence of the senior decision makers at their institutions. To be effective in their task to link the operational to the strategic, COLOs need to be seen as the digital learning experts who are strategic and goal-oriented, student-centered, and champions of quality. This is where professional organizations in digital learning can often provide the most value for COLOs. Here are just a few ways these organizations, and the professional learning communities developed around them, can help COLOs.

Demonstrate Expertise

Professional organizations in the field of digital learning help COLOs build their expertise in a variety of ways:

- Keep abreast of current issues and news in the field, allowing them to provide informed advice to senior leadership

- Understand and locate the kind of expertise required in a given situation
- Advocate, with data-informed arguments, for the resources necessary to support high-quality digital learning at the institution
- Address misinformation about digital and online learning and support

Make the Case for Strategic Value of Digital Learning

Professional organizations can provide advice and assistance in connecting the operational to the strategic.

- Align digital learning activities to strategic plans and institutional goals
- Create implementation plans for the operational levers that support target strategies
- Position the digital enterprise not just as a fail-safe for future pandemics, or as a competitive tool in the marketplace, but also as a platform for fostering "futures literacy" for the organization where innovation is anticipated and appreciated

Ensure Student-Centered Approaches that Include Online Students

Professional organizations often have repositories of research and practice examples that advance online student support.

- Advocate for inclusiveness across all institutional service units
- Create a profile of the institution's online students in ways that better reveal their support needs and how they can be met
- Ensure data are collected and analyzed in meaningful ways appropriate to the online student profile, supporting continuous improvement as part of institutional assessment

Champion Quality

Professional organizations can partner with COLOs to advance practices that improve digital education and student learning.

- Build internal capacity to achieve well-designed courses, well-prepared instructors, and fully-supported students
- Signal quality to internal and external stakeholders by communicating efforts and showcasing quality recognition
- Create a culture of quality and continuous improvement by communicating pathways, setting expectations, and rewarding achievement

Leaders will create the conditions for success for the human-centered work of baking quality practices into the digital learning enterprise. "There is no instant pudding" in this process. Simply adopting and disseminating quality standards and frameworks is not enough. COLOs have to lead both vertically and horizontally within the institution to implement robust protocols across complex institutional landscapes. Professional organizations like QM are there to help, supporting COLOs as they work to build and sustain quality digital learning.

Jennifer Mathes, Ph.D.

Chief Executive Officer Online Learning, Consortium

Over many years in higher education, I've learned to expect change and be prepared for anything. For COLOs, I have found that this is especially true. After all, these leaders are not only drivers of innovation to support effective digital learning but they are also pivotal to emergency response plans. A crisis (from natural disasters to protests) can happen at any time, forcing an institution to shut down the campus. We saw this happen on a large scale during the COVID-19 pandemic with the rapid shift to emergency remote learning. This is just one example that highlights on a large scale the need for institutions to be perpetually prepared. COLOs are on the front lines in supporting institutional preparedness.

Given the crucial role COLOs play, there are several key strategies they can implement to ensure their institutions are ready for any crisis. It is my belief that by maintaining a focus on these areas, COLOs can significantly enhance their institution's resilience and adaptability.

Be Crisis-Ready with Online Learning Strategies

First and foremost, as noted in the OLC Quality Scorecard for the Administration of Online Programs, online learning should be included in the institution's strategic plan. Rarely do I find an institution that offers no online learning experiences. Even those institutions that are predominantly focused on in-person learning need to address how online and digital learning is incorporated into the student learning experience.

In addition to this, COLOs should be working within their institutions to develop strategies that can be readily implemented for a seamless transition to remote learning during a crisis. This can include how to scale and ensure the reliability of the online learning infrastructure (e.g., the LMS, web conferencing, and other tools).

Provide Access to and Encourage Participation in Professional Development

Over the years, I have attended the OLC Institute for Emerging Leadership in Online Learning (IELOL) many times. I am always amazed by the dedication of these leaders to build their skills and am pleased that they are at institutions that support their professional growth. In my experience, professional development is often only supported by faculty or certain staff (e.g., instructional designers). However, the most successful online programs are found at institutions that prioritize ongoing professional development for their faculty, staff, and leaders, ensuring they are continuously prepared rather than scrambling to provide quick training only in the face of a crisis.

Create a Culture of Flexibility and Innovation

While there is already so much that they do, COLOs are in a unique position to support and encourage faculty and staff to experiment with new technologies and teaching methodologies. Encouraging this environment can help an institution shift more quickly to remote learning during a crisis, but also do so in a way that maintains the quality of the student learning experience.

Ensure the Accessibility and Inclusivity of the Learning Experience

Providing a quality experience for students starts by making sure that it is accessible to all students. COLOs have the responsibility of making sure that the programming offered at their institutions includes the appropriate support mechanisms to meet the needs of their learners. This preparation can also help the institution maintain educational equity during a crisis.

Leverage Partnerships and Networks

In my opinion this can be one of the most important lifelines for COLOs. These partnerships can be with other institutions, EdTech providers, or organizations like the Online Learning Consortium, but can be useful to share resources and best practices. Leaders don't have to wait for a crisis to leverage these relationships, but they can definitely be invaluable in these situations. One thing to remember here is that we can reach out to our networks to find solutions to common problems we are experiencing as well as learn from one another.

COLOs play a critical role in their institutions. They not only lead ongoing online and digital learning initiatives, but they also play a pivotal role in preparing their institutions to navigate potential crises, all while keeping pace with emerging technologies and trends. As the higher education landscape continues to evolve, I envision the role of COLOs not only growing in importance but becoming indispensable to the long-term success and sustainability of colleges and universities.

Bethany Simunich, Ph.D. and

Vice President, Innovation and Research Quality Matters
Co-Director of the Changing Landscape of Online Education (CHLOE) with Eduventures and EDUCAUSE

Richard Garrett

Eduventures Chief Research Officer at Encoura Co-Director of the Changing Landscape of Online Education (CHLOE) with Quality Matters and EDUCAUSE

The CHLOE Project, founded by QM and Eduventures (and now with EDUCAUSE as a partner), has tracked COLO sentiments, perspectives, and actions since 2016. CHLOE reports capture the pre-pandemic online learning landscape in U.S. higher education, as well as mid- and post-pandemic trends.

In Spring 2020, institutions made a rapid, pandemic-driven shift to remote learning, enabling greater exposure and future opportunities for online modalities. Most COLOs reported that additional resources were made available for foundational investments, including relevant staffing and technologies. Many institutions heavily relied on external organizations with online-specific expertise; about half reported working with QM and 40% with the Online Learning Consortium.

As student interest in online options began to grow, the COLO role became even more pivotal. In the CHLOE 6 Report (concerning Fall 2020), nearly 60% of COLOs reported that the pandemic prompted a strategy re-evaluation, positioning COLOs at the forefront of institutional conversations about modality, growth, and operations.

In CHLOE 7, reflecting Fall 2021, most COLOs reported greatly increased interest in online across all student groups and projected that most students would have a "balanced modality" experience by 2025, with few studying exclusively on campus or online. COLOs focused more deeply on resource management for growing online offerings, including an average 20% growth in instructional designers (along with concerns that ID staffing was still insufficient for future needs).

The CHLOE 8 Report (Fall 2022) underscored the dominance of 100% asynchronous delivery in online courses and programs, regardless of student type, with synchronous and hybrid modalities much less common. Only 7% of COLOs from graduate-serving institutions said that hybrid graduate programs were "widely used"; the response was even lower for adult undergraduate and traditional-age undergraduate programs.

However, COLOs may benefit from modality innovation beyond the 100% asynchronous norm. Eduventures' longstanding Adult Prospect Survey has consistently found that about half of prospective adult learners, both undergraduate and graduate, say they prefer a form of hybrid learning. Another possibility is that practicalities outweigh preference. Prospects may say they prefer hybrid, but in reality, most opt for maximum convenience. This may explain why few COLOs report significant hybrid or synchronous programming or enrollment.

The latest CHLOE Report, CHLOE 9 (concerning Fall 2023) showed a more strategic approach to online – about half of institutions have now fully incorporated online goals into institutional strategy, whether institution-wide or targeting select student groups. Most COLOs think the future is (still) local, however, and report a regional enrollment focus. The typical institution is fundamentally place-based, suggesting that COLOs need to craft a strategy that combines campus and online rather than doubling down on campus for one audience and online for another. Few institutions can thrive in the national fully online market.

Future-oriented COLOs would do well to frame digital teaching and learning deliberations in whole-institution terms. Superior student outcomes, market alignment, and long-term institutional sustainability will stem from creative combinations of campus and online, physical and digital. The "superpower" of the typical institution may turn out to be taking advantage of the physical-digital intersection, developing student experiences that fully online schools, however large and well-resourced, cannot match.

COLOs must lead by balancing present operational capacity with future enrollment targets, as well as weigh traditional mission and culture against student demand for flexible, accessible, online options. In the coming years, COLOs should remain focused on relationship-building with internal stakeholders, including ongoing dialogue with faculty and developing online staff and student support structures. Scaling online learning forces COLOs to reckon with tensions that have been brewing for some time (e.g., faculty autonomy, mission).

Future-focused COLOs need a structured, systematic plan for implementing and supporting high-quality online courses and programs, including a deep knowledge of online staffing, and leadership for the associated processes, policies, and support resources. Focusing on stakeholder buy-in, clear and consistent communication, and an effective change management approach that ensures collaboration and minimizes disruption is key. Additionally, COLOs must continue to lead the way in strategic decisions and initiatives that are grounded in business-focused practicalities, including market research for in-demand degrees, new considerations for alternative and flexible online pathways, and smart marketing that reflects the unique needs of online programs.

Now in its tenth year, CHLOE will continue to follow the trends that matter to COLOs, helping individual online leaders benchmark against peer and national data. Thank you to CHLOE sponsors (particularly long-time supporters of iDesign and Archer Education) and the online leaders who are members of the CHLOE Advisory Panel.

Fostering a Pipeline for COLOs 11

Introduction

UPCEA's Competency and Attribute Statements for PCO Practitioners (UPCEA, 2023) define eight competencies that distinguish COLOs from other leaders in the academic C-Suite at universities and beyond. What happens when we look to the future? Will these competencies continue to be relevant to distinguishing the COLO role and also creating a clearly delineated pathway for new and aspiring COLOs? This chapter looks at emerging competencies that we predict will influence the COLO role and thus the competencies necessary for the next generation of leadership in online and digital learning. This chapter will also explore some of the professional activities that aspiring COLOs typically engage with in preparation for becoming a COLO, as well as the spheres of influence that are available to all career levels that intersect with online and digital learning.

New and Emerging Competencies to Distinguish Next-Gen COLOs

Just as online and digital learning continues to evolve, so will the essential knowledge, skills, and dispositions required of COLOs. Today's COLOs cite publications, events, organizations, and peers as their most valuable resources for staying informed about online learning; and they list artificial intelligence, financial management, working with faculty, legal and regulatory issues, and marketing/enrollment as key areas for professional development (Fredericksen, et al., 2024). Below are four critical areas through

DOI: 10.4324/9781003500742-14

which current and aspiring COLOs are encouraged to continuously seek to acquire the new knowledge, skills, and expertise that tomorrow will require. As we look to a future iteration of the competencies necessary for a successful COLO, we anticipate that they will evolve to include dimensions of the domains listed below.

Artificial Intelligence – Artificial intelligence is transforming the job market and the skills and competencies needed to be competitive today and into the future. It is incumbent upon all industry leaders to reskill themselves for generative AI. From a business perspective, COLOs in particular will see several facets of their role and associated portfolios be transformed by AI. On the teaching and learning side, just as COLOs were on the front lines of issues with academic integrity and online proctoring during the COVID-19 pandemic, so too are COLOs as colleges and universities grapple with the ethical dimensions of artificial intelligence in teaching and learning. COLOs are also championing many of the tools and innovations that are transforming teaching and learning to be more personalized. With AI's tremendous impacts on the creative and design industries, intelligent tools are being increasingly leveraged to generate content for online courses where the staff to support such activities can be expensive to recruit and/or challenging to retain. Additionally, COLOs are among the most uniquely positioned to inform emerging Chief Artificial Intelligence Officers, with a few universities in the U.S. and Canada already hiring for this role. COLOs will no doubt be expected to be thought leaders and experts across the many domains (technical, ethical, pedagogical, curricular, and financial to name a few) at the inflection point of artificial intelligence on higher education today and into the future.

Engendering Trust across Diverse Stakeholders – As the organizational structure of higher education institutions continues to evolve, managing up and down will be a key competency of COLOs. COLOs will be faced with onboarding their leadership, as the average tenure of presidents and provosts continues to decline (Pritchard et al., 2020). Change management and effective interpersonal communication are already core competencies of a successful COLO. These combined leadership characteristics engender trust across diverse stakeholders. COLOs found themselves amid an unprecedented reality during the COVID-19 pandemic. Many of the COLOs who contribute their expert perspectives to this *Guidebook* garnered trust among their leadership, peers, faculty, students, and staff based on their abilities to mobilize and sustain a response to the COVID-19 pandemic. COLOs into the future will step into roles with this expectation. How effectively aspiring COLOs engender trust among their leadership, peers, and others will be a key determinant of their success.

Leadership Development – As COLO roles continue to ascend into the academic C-Suite, it will be important that COLOs continue to hone their leadership development skills. Higher education's complexities will necessitate multi-dimensional leaders who possess not only the technical expertise and experience to lead in online and digital learning but also the leadership domains that all academic leaders are thrust into today. This is compounded by the growing expectations related to revenue generation amidst enrollment declines; and the unknown impacts that artificial intelligence has yet to have on higher education will demand a great deal of COLOs moving forward. Aspiring COLOs should consider their leadership potential as leadership competencies continue to evolve in the face of motivating a workforce; fostering strong relationships; and making informed decisions; all while navigating, driving, and inspiring others toward change.

Futures Literacy – As our future horizon continues to shift, COLOs will need to develop new competencies to navigate a multitude of future possibilities with heightened foresight. Futures literacy is the competency that allows people to better understand the role of the future in what they see and do, as we explored in Chapter 10. Rooted in the discipline of anticipation, futures literacy can improve our capacity to shape policies and systems that withstand shocks and create long-term resilience (Miller, 2018). This will be a core competency that stands to distinguish COLOs from their C-Suite peers.

Professional Networks and Activities

Another area of competency development that COLOs will be expected to have in the future will be an established public reputation. With the various outlets available to aspiring leaders today, those in leadership positions at colleges and universities will increasingly rely on their own networks to vet candidates. An aspiring COLO can leverage the tools, outlets, and opportunities explored below to build upon his/her public reputation.

Participate in State and National Professional Associations – Professional associations are an excellent vehicle through which to start and grow your network. There are several dimensions to networking that these organizations provide. They create an entrée for those early in their careers; a platform to share impacts and successes once work commences in earnest; and leadership pathways for those looking for additional involvement. These venues also create spaces for informal mentoring at all levels.

Contribute to Podcasts and Blogs – In addition to more traditional presentation and publication outlets, podcasts and blogs are a great way to showcase impact in a forum that allows you to contribute more of your own personality and perspective on any given topic. This may also offer a chance to step away from your day-to-day work to demonstrate your thought leadership. There are a number of established podcasts that have either been developed by COLOs – including the popular TOPcast by the co-author of the *Guidebook* (Cavanagh & Thompson, n.d.) – or that regularly engage COLOs. We encourage aspiring COLOs to subscribe to these as yet another point of access to thought leadership in the COLO space.

Pursue Teaching and Learning Grants at Your University – Colleges and universities will often make funds available to support the exploration and application of pedagogical and technological innovations in online and digital learning that target improvements to student learning outcomes. These grant programs can be an excellent way for aspiring COLOs to quickly demonstrate impact on academic leadership, as these grant programs are often administered by units that COLOs support. Pursuing such grants can help establish a reputation for being innovative and in alignment with trends and best practices for online and digital learning. The communities of practice that are often stewarded by grant administrators can also offer aspiring COLOs access to a new-found interdisciplinary peer group that may not otherwise be available within an academic department.

Seek out Academic Leaders and Understand Organizational Structure and Associated Politics – Informal mentoring and networking with academic leaders who are in COLO or adjacent leadership roles can be an excellent way to gain an understanding of organizational structures within a university and their associated politics. Having insights into this dimension of the COLO role will contribute a layer of savvy to aspiring COLOs and will serve those well in the interview process and beyond.

Become a Public Intellectual – LinkedIn has become the gold standard for professional networking and learning. Additionally, prospective employers leverage LinkedIn in the hiring process to learn more about job candidates. The LinkedIn sphere for COLOs and aspiring COLOs is quite robust. It is a useful tool to help aspiring COLOs research new roles and prospective teams; connect with peers and sitting COLOs to expand professional reach; foster professional growth through engagement with groups; explore industry best practices and news from a curated network of COLOs; and establish a professional reputation by sewing the seeds of the activities listed above through posts that highlight career updates and accomplishments. LinkedIn also has a learning component to it. As COLOs acquire new skills (e.g. in artificial intelligence), LinkedIn allows you to amplify those by posting badges on your LinkedIn profile. This is a great way to participate in the online and digital learning ecosystem while promoting your professional brand (Coursera, n.d.).

Spheres of Influence Along the COLO Pathway

As evidenced in the biographies of each of the more than 50 expert contributors to this *Guidebook*, there is no one path to becoming a COLO. While there are fewer opportunities available for growth beyond the COLO, COLOs are increasingly transitioning into positions with broader scope and impact at universities, with some ascending to university president and provost roles (as well as those choosing to work outside of an institutional context), as we explore in Chapter 12. It is anticipated that there will continue to be interesting and fulfilling roles for COLOs as the future of learning and working evolves in parallel (see Epilogue). For aspiring COLOs, the sections below highlight some of the more common spheres of influence that may deliver one into a COLO role. While no one career pathway defines the COLO role, inevitably it is these spheres of influence that distinguish successful COLOs from those who may fall short of securing the role.

Influence among Faculty and Staff Circles – Aspiring COLOs may begin to influence online and digital learning as early as their time as students. There are a number of examples of undergraduate students who sought to pay it forward by starting companies that improve student tutoring, proctoring, or gradebook experiences, just to name a few. Graduate and doctoral students occupy unique roles in that they may carry a teaching load as part of their assistantships, often facilitating online courses, and thereby exposing them to the many facets of online and digital learning from both an administrative and student perspective. Many of these graduate students are also taking their own online courses, so their perspectives are often the most dynamic in an academic department. On the faculty and staff side, an aspiring COLO's spheres of influence may include, for staff: IT, student success, or enrollment management units; for faculty, those who teach and/or then transition to leading online programs; either of these groups who work in the noncredit space; as well as in areas such as global education that often has adjacencies to online learning.

Influence among Professional Organizations and in the Policy Realm – Not necessarily mutually exclusive from the spheres listed above, this particular grouping may be its own career trajectory for some aspiring COLOs, as well as serving as an arena for professional growth for those who move beyond the COLO role. There are a wide range of non-profit organizations that influence online and digital learning within the academy, as well as in the state and national policy arena. Individuals who have influence in these circles will transition into COLO roles with certain advantages compared to those who ascend from within a university. These individuals often have a diverse and national/international network that serves them well in a COLO role at a college/university.

Influence as COLO – COLOs increasingly wield extensive influence within their roles. This influence has implications for the particular institution the COLO serves, as well as far beyond. As we have explored across this *Guidebook*, the COLO's domain is extensive and necessitates collaboration at nearly every level to achieve the desired impacts. Now more than ever COLOs are impacting a college/university's academic mission and associated operations as higher education institutions continue to evolve into hybrid-serving and hybrid-functioning entities.

Influence Beyond the COLO Role – While some COLOs run up against limitations to their spheres of influence as a COLO, particularly when university leadership may typecast the COLO, there are several instances where the COLO role evolves and expands. Such scenarios include: success in online enrollment growth that transitions into influence over the university's enrollment management or marketing strategies; effectiveness at growing online programs segues into leadership of a broader domain of academic programming; or the COLO role grows from supporting online and digital learning at one university to stewarding COLOs across a university system. Chapter 12 will highlight the careers of several prominent COLOs who have gone on to become leaders in higher education both in the policy realm, as well as from the position as university president.

References

Coursera. (n.d.). *How to Use LinkedIn*. Retrieved September 23, 2024, from https://www.coursera.org/in/articles/how-to-use-linkedin

Fredericksen, E., Simunich, B. & Uranus, J. (2024) *COLO Profile Study 2024 – A National Research Project about Chief Online Learning Officers.* Presented at OLC Accelerate 2024, Orlando, FL. https://olc.secure-platform.com/accelerate/gallery/rounds/82030/schedule/items/17650

Miller, R. (Ed.). (2018). *Transforming the Future: Anticipation in the 21st Century*. Routledge.

Pritchard, A., Nadel-Hawthorne, S., Schmidt, A., Fuesting, M., & Bichel, J. (2020). *Administrators in higher education annual report: Key Findings, Trends, and Comprehensive Tables for the 2019-2020 Academic Year* (Research report). Available from https://www.cupahr.org/surveys/pricing-and-ordering/

Cavanagh, T., and Thompson, K. (n.d.). *TOPcast: Teaching Online Podcast*. Retrieved September 23, 2024, from https://cdl.ucf.edu/teach/resources/topcast/

UPCEA. (2023). *Competency and Attribute Statements for Professional, Continuing, and Online Practitioners*. Retrieved from https://upcea.edu/competency-and-attribute-statements-for-professional-continuing-and-online-practitioners/

Expert Perspectives

- Ray Schroeder, UPCEA and University of Illinois Springfield–Emeritus
- Katie Linder, University of Colorado Denver
- Tonya Amankwatia, North Carolina Agricultural and Technical State University
- Amrit Ahluwalia, Western University

Ray Schroeder

UPCEA Senior Fellow and University of Illinois Springfield
Professor Emeritus, UPCEA and University of Illinois Springfield

The COLO post is rapidly becoming one of the most important roles in higher education. Certainly "traditional" online learning programs are expanding, but the newcomer to the online field, Generative AI, represents the single greatest and most rapidly changing advance in modes and methods of teaching and learning since the internet. It marks the advent of the Fourth Industrial Revolution. AI application to teaching and learning fits squarely in the domain of the COLO.

I became a COLO a quarter century ago as a full professor in the area of communication technology. The specialization was new and emerging technologies, which included tracking and visioning the developments in AI, VR, and associated fields. The communication academic discipline spanned the use of technologies and societal impact across business, industry, government, and education. So, I was well versed in the technologies of the field. The prior 25 years on the faculty gave me a deep understanding of Academic Affairs and the pedagogies, policies, procedures, and practices in that part of the university.

My years as COLO were marked with expansion of the online learning program I initiated. With the help of my faculty colleagues, I pursued grants from private foundations as well as federal entities. National awards flowed to the campus for quality and innovation, based in large part on the enthusiastic engagement of faculty members.

I brought to the position the credibility and support of my faculty colleagues. I will note that I am aware of circumstances at other institutions in which COLOs who come to the position from outside the faculty are viewed with initial distrust until they are able to demonstrate that they can effectively represent the best interests of the faculty in online administration and expansion.

Given the faculty-centric nature of higher education, COLOs who come from the faculty where they have enjoyed good collegial relationships have a distinct advantage in gaining the trust of colleagues. However, that is not the only viable path for a leader of the Online Learning initiative.

Many COLOs may come from Instructional Technology departments where they have gained experience in the relevant technologies as well as student and faculty support. The background from this track addresses the deep understanding of the technologies and their applications.

Other COLOs may come from outside academia. It is incumbent on these newcomers to immediately address and fully demonstrate their commitment to the faculty at large.

Given the diverse skills and knowledge needed in the position, the creation of a kind of apprenticeship – in the form of Assistant or Associate COLO – has numerous advantages, including providing applied experience and recognition while cultivating the needed experiences and qualities in an individual who is preparing to step into the position when the COLO leaves. They will have had the opportunity to engage fully in the operation and working relationships with colleagues. They will have had the opportunity to build a positive reputation both internally and externally. This kind of seamless transition is the most desirable for this important position of COLO. It is the approach I pursued in the development of my successor who is one of the expert contributors of this book.

Katie Linder, Ph.D.

Associate Vice Chancellor for Academic Innovation and Strategy
Interim Vice Chancellor for Strategic Enrollment and Student Success, University of Colorado Denver

When I think about the competencies that have most influenced my development as a leader in digital strategy and online teaching and learning, change management is at the top of the list. Early in my career, I had no idea what change management was. I didn't know that it was a field and discipline with its own literature, practices, and approaches. I also had no idea that there was a relationship between effective change management and effective project management, or a relationship between change management and being an effective leader. Over multiple leadership roles across different institutional types, I quickly started to see how other leaders were engaging in change management practices that led to the success of their projects and initiatives.

A couple of years ago, I chose to earn the Prosci credential to become a Certified Change Practitioner (CCP) since I wanted to better understand the fundamental components and tools that help change managers be effective. When I posted the information about this credential to my LinkedIn page, I immediately had colleagues reach out to learn more about the credential, what I learned, and whether they should also pursue professional development in this area. Clearly, other leaders are also seeing the benefits of studying the field of change management and are becoming curious about its potential positive impacts. For any higher education leader who is engaging in change initiatives, and especially those of us trying to keep pace with the speed of technology changes in our industry, I can attest that training and education in change management will make your job easier and more efficient and that the challenges you might face with leading change initiatives will make a lot more sense.

Change management theories and approaches not only help you to understand the fundamental role that communication plays in the success of change initiatives but also provide concrete strategies and tools for how to foster both buy-in and trust with the diverse members of our institutional communities. The complex change projects that COLOs often undertake frequently require broad community engagement, education and training, and word-of-mouth testimonials from peers. Without knowledge of change management, these initiatives will be less successful and may even fail. Thus, COLOs must learn how to be excellent communicators, including how to create communication plans with strategies that engage community members across a variety of mediums from project websites, to campus-wide emails, to meetings with shared governance bodies, and more.

Although technologies will come and go, change is the constant in a COLO's work. Another key area of change management that helped me to think differently about my work as a higher education leader and COLO is the focus on the "how" of engaging in change initiatives. Early in my career, my focus was much more on the "what" of my own knowledge. In various places and spaces, I needed to show up as a content expert. However, the more leadership experience I gained, the more I shifted from focusing on the "what" of my own knowledge to the "how" of the work I needed to do. Because of the way change management theories and approaches can be broadly applied, the practice of managing change keeps you focused on the most effective approaches to engagement with your community. You become a practitioner of building relationships and trust, rather than an expert who is lauded for what you know.

Although successful project outcomes are always important, it is also the process along the way that is often where the learning, growth, and evolution of my own leadership skills happen. As higher education continues to experience the turbulence of constant change, I have found that change management principles and approaches have helped me to effectively lead a wide range of projects and initiatives with confidence, clear direction, and an eye toward what I can learn from each experience to do better next time.

Tonya B. Amankwatia, Ph.D.

Assistant Vice Provost, Distance Education and Extended Learning, North Carolina Agricultural and Technical State University

Constructing Mentorships to Develop New Competencies

Next-generation and current COLOs must be introspective when faced with novel opportunities and the evolution of the role; and thus, become adept at constructing mentorships to gain new competencies (Grogan & Crow, 2004). This strategic approach to professional growth involves cultivating relationships with mentors from diverse fields to receive tailored guidance for professional development.

Constructed mentorship begins with assessing strengths and setting task performance goals. COLOs must identify areas where they can make significant contributions and where mentorship can enhance their performance on a novel undertaking (Méndez-Morse, 2004). The goal guides the selection of mentors whose expertise aligns with the mentee's career trajectory. One effective strategy is engaging recent retirees for specific, time-bound tasks. Retirees often have the availability and wealth of experience to tackle complex challenges (Mertz, 2004). This approach allows COLOs to benefit from their insights while addressing pressing needs. In my experience, constructing mentorships with recognized retirees has proven beneficial for assistance with university-wide deliverables. For instance, I collaborated with Gary Miller on strategic planning, Badrul Kahn on modernizing e-learning, and Stephen Ehrmann on ensuring academic quality. Each mentor not only helped with a timely task but also joined scholarly contributions to the academy via global technology and training conferences, campus retreats, or publications. These experiences enriched my leadership skills and understanding to perform and share with others.

Moreover, constructed mentorships do not have to be restricted to higher education alone. I have learned invaluable business skills related to alliance building and institutional transformation from professionals provided by the Partnership for Education Advancement, Thurgood Marshall College Fund, and United Negro College Fund. These experiences highlight the importance of seeking mentorship across diverse sectors, broadening the scope of learning, and enhancing the ability to drive institutional change.

Table 11.1 Assessment Instruments and Resources

Resource	*Description*	*Link*
Authentic Leadership Questionnaire	Measures self-awareness and transparency in leadership	https://www.mindgarden.com/69-authentic-leadership-questionnaire
Center for Creative Leadership	Provides a range of leadership assessments for development	https://www.mindgarden.com/69-authentic-leadership-questionnaire
Entrepreneurial Potential Assessment	Assesses entrepreneurial skills and mindset	https://www.bdc.ca/en/articles-tools/entrepreneur-toolkit/business-assessments/entrepreneurial-potential-self-assessment
Gallup StrengthsFinder	Identifies strengths and talents for personal and professional development	https://store.gallup.com/c/en-us/1/cliftonstrengths
Leadership Orientations Inventory	Evaluates leadership style and orientation in organizational settings	https://leebolman.com/wp-content/uploads/2021/02/Leadership-Orientations-2012.pdf
Myers-Briggs Type Indicator (MBTI)	Assesses personality types to understand leadership preferences and interactions	https://nexalearning.com/the-myers-briggs-leader-16-different-leadership-types/

Before constructing a mentorship, aspiring COLOs can begin their growth journey by utilizing various assessment instruments and resources to identify their strengths and competency areas for growth (Table 11.1).

Influence with External Innovation Partners

For COLOs, building strong relationships with external innovation partners is essential for student success and future-proofing educational offerings. Throughout my career, I have prioritized connecting with the R&D teams of technology companies to stay informed about product development and programming priorities. This connection enables me to advocate for ethical approaches, inclusive excellence, and learner empowerment features to ensure that technology aligns with institutional goals.

Enterprise software for online learning is a prime example where these partnerships are crucial. I joined Anthology's Adaptive Learning Advisory

Board to influence the implementation of AI tools that enhance the online learning experience. By engaging with these companies at conferences, COLOs can ensure that their institutions are aware of pilots, grants, and the technology roadmap to meet students' evolving needs.

Additionally, organizations aligned with the future of work and learning play a pivotal role in shaping educational strategies. I serve on the advisory council for Credential Engine and have been involved with the T3 Innovation Network since its inception. These collaborations are vital to fostering curricular innovation and ensuring that academic programs remain relevant in a rapidly changing landscape.

Representation matters, and technology partners value input from diverse educational leaders. My background in the EdTech industry and my extensive network allow me to contribute effectively to new product development. The LinkedIn HBCU Digital Leadership Network, which I founded, provides an opportunity for constructed mentorships that did not exist when I started my career. Engaging with external partners including technology companies is crucial for COLOs aiming to lead their institutions effectively. These relationships provide insights into emerging trends and technologies, enabling COLOs to prioritize strategic initiatives that align with institutional priorities. By fostering these connections, COLOs can position their institutions at the forefront of educational innovation, ensuring they remain competitive and responsive to the needs of diverse learners.

References

Grogan, M., & Crow, G. (2004). Mentoring in the context of educational leadership preparation and development—Old wine in new bottles? Introduction to a special issue. *Educational Administration Quarterly*, 40(4), 463–467. https://doi.org/10.1177/0013161X04267107

Méndez-Morse, S. (2004). Constructing mentors: Latina educational leaders' role models and mentors. *Educational Administration Quarterly*, 40(4), 561–590. https://doi.org/10.1177/0013161X04267112

Mertz, N. T. (2004). What's a mentor, anyway? *Educational Administration Quarterly*, 40(4), 541–560. https://doi.org/10.1177/0013161X04267110

Amrit Ahluwalia

Executive Director of Continuing Studies, Western University

The COLO – and all leaders helping to build access for diverse audiences across postsecondary institutions – plays a critical role in the future-proofing of colleges and universities.

Institutions that historically served a "traditional-age" learner with a two- or four-year, on-campus experience have been forced to pivot in recent years. Addressing both moral and financial realities, colleges and universities (but especially universities!) have had to diversify their student audiences – serving a wider range of learners with a wider range of programming leading to a wider range of credentials and supporting a wider range of outcomes.

And in expanding scope and reach, many institutions have realized that diversification requires more than saying "we're accessible!" It requires commitment, focus, and a clear strategic purpose. Enter the COLO. This individual is charged with extending the reach of the institution to serve those diverse demographics with highly accessible offerings.

The mental image we use here at Western University is to think of ourselves as the prism in Pink Floyd's seminal *Dark Side of the Moon* album cover. Where the university has historically served a very specific learner with very specific programming and services, we exist to reach a more diverse audience of learners with learning solutions tailored to meet their needs.

To that end, there's a range of competencies and a mindset the COLO must bring that differs massively from the traditional image of the university leader. And it all starts with a service mindset. A service mindset is a commitment to contributing positively to the well-being and satisfaction of others, and a focus on fostering relationships that are built on trust, respect, and mutual benefit. Importantly, it's about going beyond providing assistance to create meaningful and lasting value.

Consider emerging core competencies that will be critical for success as a COLO as we head into the future: Understanding of AI, Engendering Trust across Diverse Stakeholders, Leadership Development, and Futures Literacy. It may even be worth adding additional competencies, including Clarity of Strategic Vision. To be successful, each of these competencies requires a component of the service mindset.

A COLO sits at the institutional hub, facilitating transformation and growth for colleagues across the institution. It is essential for these individuals to understand the needs of learners, and to collaborate with diverse stakeholders to ensure the institution is positioned to respond to those needs.

In many cases, this work must also happen efficiently, effectively, and without creating too much of a cost burden.

To be able to thread this needle, COLOs must keep the service mindset front and center – service to the learners and service to their colleagues. Simultaneously teaching and guiding, simultaneously supporting and leading…often with a thick skin and a quick smile!

Adopting a service mindset positions the COLO to be the professional that institutions in transition require to drive their success and achieve viable growth.

12 Safeguarding Higher Education's Relevance

Introduction

Higher education in the U.S. is entering a challenging time. Forecasts predict fewer high school graduates in the coming years. Populations are shrinking in parts of the North and East, where there is a higher concentration of colleges and universities – especially smaller, tuition-dependent private schools. It seems that every week the news reports the closure or merger of another college or university. General societal distrust of higher education, particularly along political lines, is contributing to more and more students opting to delay or forego college altogether. The overall trend of fewer men choosing postsecondary education continues and may even be accelerating.

It is within this difficult context that institutions must chart their paths forward, relying on solid execution with the right strategy. Business as usual or the status quo will no longer be sufficient. Only the most unique of institutions have a chance to continue with unchanged strategies (e.g., military service academies, top of the Ivies, performing arts institutions, seminaries). The vast majority of higher education will need to diversify their strategies to remain relevant and competitive in a world being changed daily by technological developments.

Given the innovative and technology-focused nature of the position, the COLO finds him/herself uniquely positioned to play an outsized role in ensuring the long-term relevance of their institutions. Doing so will require forward-thinking institutional leadership that recognizes the urgency of the moment and proactively includes the COLO in key discussions and decision-making. However, as addressed in Chapter 1 of this book, this can only happen if the COLO is "in the room where it happens." Omitting the COLO's

DOI: 10.4324/9781003500742-15

expertise (or, worse, not having a COLO at all) certainly puts the modern postsecondary institution at risk.

Beyond addressing online, blended, and digital learning strategies, the COLO can add specific value across a range of strategic areas. One of these areas of high need is workforce development. With the number of high school graduates forecasted to decrease, it only makes sense that institutions cultivate and grow their pipelines of nontraditional learners now so that it is healthy and robust when it will be most needed.

According to the Postsecondary National Policy Institute (PNPI), "(i)n fall 2019, post-traditional students made up 33.4% of all postsecondary enrollment" and "(p)ost-traditional students are much more likely to enroll in online courses than traditionally aged students." PNPI defines a post-traditional student as:

> over the age of 24 when they enter higher education...In general, post-traditional students have one or more of the following characteristics: they delayed enrollment in college after high school, they attend part-time for at least part of an academic year, they work full-time while also enrolled in school, they are financially independent, or they have dependents (spouse and/or children).
>
> (PNPI, 2023)

However, truly serving the needs of adult learners includes much more than delivering online academic programs, as critical as they are. Today's modern worker is facing the same rapidly evolving technological context as those working in higher education. AI is disrupting all sectors from healthcare to financial services to manufacturing. These workers also need to stay current and relevant. The COLO position, arguably better than almost any other role at a college or university, is ideally suited to supporting the institution's workforce development strategy and helping to further cultivate the pipeline of nontraditional learners.

Upskilling/Reskilling

The terms upskilling and reskilling typically refer to the concept of a worker making him/herself more valuable to an employer. In the case of upskilling, an employee is provided training that moves him/her to a higher level of competence or knowledge. With reskilling, on the other hand, training is targeted more at learning an entirely new skill, often due to automation threatening their long-term employment or in service of a career change.

In both cases, online learning plays a necessary role in providing access to education for busy, employed workers. These students don't have the time or ability to attend traditional, F2F classes during normal work hours. Family and other commitments make it difficult for them to attend class after hours or on weekends. Only online learning, particularly asynchronous online learning, can offer them the flexibility they require to pursue the upskilling or reskilling they will need to remain professionally competitive.

These kinds of workforce-oriented programs are typically the domain of an institution's Continuing Education (CE) department. CE units can exist under a variety of names (Professional Education, Lifelong Learning, etc.), and their position within the broader institutional organizational structure can vary widely. They may exist as their own stand-alone department/school/college, as part of an Extension School, under a community outreach umbrella, or some other positioning. However, increasingly, it seems that more and more CE departments are falling under the responsibility of the institution's COLO, leading to the widely used PCO education label.

If the CE unit falls under the COLO, it becomes much easier to deploy best practices in online education toward workforce development upskilling and reskilling needs. The COLO will need to deploy expertise and allocate resources accordingly, based on mission, market demand, and ROI.

However, if the CE department does not fall under the jurisdiction of the COLO, it is critical that the COLO establish a productive working collaboration. The COLO will need to cultivate a partnership with CE leadership to define roles, responsibilities, and revenue. Doing so will enable both units to serve the institutional mission. Some of the COLOs serving as expert contributors to this book either have purview over CE or serve in a leadership capacity over CE and work in collaboration with their institution's COLO. There are too many workforce needs and too many opportunities for professional upskilling/reskilling for any institution not to have an intentional strategy in this area.

Microcredentials

Looking ahead, one of the primary means by which upskilling and reskilling programs will be delivered is through microcredential programs. These are short, often noncredit (but not always) programs typically oriented toward practical workforce needs. Completion of a microcredential may be accompanied by an industry certification; and job placement may even be a component of some microcredential programs, such as many coding boot camps.

Microcredentials are developed for and targeted to learners who are uninterested in or unable to participate in traditional academic programs. Such learners may not be able to commit to completing a long-term academic credential. Or they may only need a particular, specific skill and view general education or other subjects as superfluous. Or they may already possess an academic degree and only require a skill refresh on the latest developments in their professional field.

These short, focused programs often come with a certificate or digital badge, allowing the completer to share his/her new skill on social media and on a resume. These public recognitions of skills and abilities carry inherent workplace currency, making the learner a more valuable employee or recruit. When microcredentials come with academic credit, they offer the added advantage of stackability. With stackable credentials, the earned credit becomes portable and can be applied toward larger credentials, up to and including full degrees. The most intentional degree programs consist of a series of smaller, stackable microcredentials.

Given the nontraditional nature of these programs, they are typically offered in online modalities, bringing them under the purview of the COLO. Further, the entire concept of microcredentials and stackability is an innovation that is consistent with the entrepreneurial culture of the online learning department. COLOs will need to monitor this trend and start experimenting now.

Employer Partnerships

The hegemony of the academic degree is cracking as more and more employers (both corporate and government) are eliminating the requirement of a bachelor's degree as the minimum credential for hiring. The American Opportunity Index (2024) has developed a list that identifies the 50 best large companies for those with high school degrees to start their careers. The top quartile of these companies are 4.3 times more likely to hire people right out of high school than other big companies. Instead of requiring a bachelor's degree, an increasing number of employers are willing to hire for skills and competence, making the concept of microcredentials not just relevant but essential as COLOs look to support their institutions going forward.

As employers evolve their requirements for entry to a job, they will continue to need skilled and knowledgeable workers. Colleges and universities are ideal partners for employers to provide the knowledge and skills to keep their workforces competitive. Such partnerships should include both credit-bearing and noncredit offerings, full degrees, certificates, and microcredentials. In a recent survey by UPCEA and Collegis Education, 7 out of 10 employers want to be approached by colleges or universities to develop non degree credentials to benefit their workforce (UPCEA & Collegis Education, 2023).

The COLO can serve as a central point of contact for these employer relationships, perhaps working with a central institutional partnership office. Online learning is ideally suited for supporting already employed learners – and a necessary modality for those who require flexibility such as shift workers and those with family caretaking responsibilities.

Employer partnerships will grow increasingly critical for higher education institutions as demographic changes reduce the number of traditional students attending college. These demographic changes, combined with the elimination of degree requirements for initial hiring, and societal trends away from college enrollment, will challenge higher education to find other ways to remain relevant. When the primary value proposition being offered is a degree but the degree is no longer required to enter the workforce, there is the potential of an existential threat to higher education.

However, colleges and universities still have much to offer – including the degree. Beyond the aforementioned skills-based microcredentials, many employers still recognize the value of the bachelor's degree. They just may not require it for initial hire. More and more companies are now offering college tuition as an employment benefit. Whether managed internally through a HR department or outsourced to one of a growing number of Tuition-as-a-Benefit enabler organizations, these programs are serving several purposes.

First, they are educating their workforces in business-critical disciplines, making them more valuable employees. Often, tuition programs require a certain period of continued service at the company, helping to reduce turnover. Employees are happier, appreciating that their employer is investing in them. Finally, employers can use these programs as a recruiting tool, touting the program to potential employees.

There may even come a time where high school graduates treat initial employment akin to military service, where a motivating factor for many enlistees is military tuition assistance or the G.I. Bill. Military recruiters often extoll the benefit of a free college education being available as part of enlistment. Similarly, high school graduates may select employers based upon whether or not they offer tuition benefit programs. For some graduates, especially the economically challenged, the traditional sequence of college then career may become reversed as they instead choose to enter the workforce first and then pursue company-funded postsecondary education.

The COLO is ideally situated to support such employers and students. Whether through short microcredentials, stackable certificates, or full degrees, these students will need the flexibility of online learning. And the employers will need a reliable partner who can evolve with them to best meet their workforce development needs.

Lifelong Learning

All the strategies described in this chapter for maintaining relevance fall under the broader umbrella of lifelong learning. Ultimately, the ability of postsecondary institutions to maintain relevance and continue to have impact may hinge on their commitment to serving the lifelong learning needs of their students.

In what some have described as the 60-year curriculum (Dede and Richards, 2020), students will continually move in and out of education throughout their lives and careers. Driven by specific requirements at specific points in time, learners may need a microcredential to pursue a particular job, a bachelor's degree for a promotion, a short course for upskilling, a test prep program for a licensure exam, a master's or professional degree for advanced knowledge, and another microcredential to reskill or change careers. These and many other circumstances will vary by the individual and will extend even into retirement, with many senior citizens now participating in educational offerings and lifestyle learning.

Again, arguably the most important position within a college or university for meeting the needs of the 60-year curriculum is the COLO's. Lifelong learners will require the enhanced flexibility of online education. With forethought and intentionality, the COLO will be able to position his/her organization to serve this population. In so doing, institutions won't simply be hedging against the demographic changes of traditional age students. Rather than simply offering a four-year experience, institutions will be establishing and cultivating a lifetime relationship with students.

References

American Opportunity Index. (2024). *Insights: 3*. Retrieved August 6, 2024, from https://www.americanopportunityindex.org/insights/3

Dede, C., & Richards, J. (Eds.). (2020). *The 60-year curriculum: New models for lifelong learning in the digital economy*. Routledge.

Postsecondary National Policy Institute. (2023, March). *Post-traditional students in higher education* [Fact sheet]. https://pnpi.org/wp-content/uploads/2023/03/PostTraditional_FactSheet_Mar2023.pdf

UPCEA & Collegis Education. (2023, February). *The effect of employer understanding and engagement on non-degree credentials*. https://core.upcea.edu/viewdocument/the-effect-of-employer-understandin-1?1?CommunityKey=82a51688-4da7-42af-9cee-7de58d6f6eef&tab=librarydocuments

Expert Perspectives

- Robert Wagner, Idaho State University
- Gregory Fowler, University of Maryland Global Campus
- Mark David Milliron, National University
- Karen Vignare, Association of Public and Land Grant Universities

Robert W. Wagner, Ph.D.

President, Idaho State University

Speedboats, Tugboats, and Harbor Pilots

I like to teach with analogies, especially those where I can demonstrate my rudimentary drawing skills on a white board (typically showing why I was not an art major). Since serving as a COLO I have used an analogy that has evolved over time, which in retrospect demonstrates how COLOs can help their institutions stay relevant in a variety of ways.

In the first years as my institution's COLO, I felt like I was on a speedboat, moving through the waters of the institution's in-state and out-of-state market with speed, agility, and unfettered control. These were the early days of online education when it took an entrepreneurial spirit to build online programs, market them, and build revenue-sharing models that invigorated our institutional partners. We did everything, from student services such as registration and financial aid to recruiting, tutoring, and advising. We built programs based on our community's needs and market demand. The institution's senior leadership was aware of the speedboat zipping ahead and even used it occasionally to demonstrate institutional innovation and "being relevant" in a changing landscape. Our students were traditional, nontraditional, full-time, and part-time. We worked hard and enjoyed the ride.

As online education became ubiquitous in higher education, eventually institutional leadership recognized the speedboat needed to integrate more with the mainstream institution. Things like duplication of services, equitable tuition and revenue models, and meeting students' growing demand for flexibility brought me, as the COLO, to the table with academic affairs, student affairs, institutional marketing and communication, and the President's Office. I found myself no longer moving in a speedboat out ahead of the institution, but rather captaining a tugboat that was now helping move the institution in directions it needed to go to compete and be sustainable. Things moved slower, as the institutional freightliner required new skills from the COLO such as compromise; the ability to work in a shared governance model; budget modeling and integration; and a focus on institutional values, mission, and strategic priority. However, together our institution embraced new opportunities. We worked hard while enjoying greater recognition and institutional relevance.

The global COVID-19 pandemic and its impact on higher education brought on the third phase of the analogy. I still remember the moment in the president's conference room when university leadership gathered around the table and they looked to me, as the COLO, to lead our very abrupt transition to fully online delivery. The talented and extremely hard-working online team was no longer serving on the tugboat, pushing, pulling, and maneuvering the institutional freightliner; we had now been given the wheel, like a harbor pilot. Although the task was daunting, the team was ready to navigate the shoals, tides, and breakers of the pandemic. Together, with outstanding faculty and staff who stepped up to the deck, the institution managed to eventually dock the ship in a post-pandemic harbor.

So, where does the analogy leave COLOs today? Some of us might find ourselves in the roles of speedboat, tugboat, or even harbor pilots. However, we have proven our validity, impact, and potential to higher education. Whatever our role, we can help our institutions adapt to new types of students, innovative credentials, and important partnerships that provide a sustainable future. That is what all three phases of the analogy have in common: COLOs help move our institutions forward.

Gregory W. Fowler, Ph.D.

President, University of Maryland Global Campus

The COLO and The Karate Kid*: Parallels in Teaching and Learning*

In my mind, the COLO serves as the architect of both the environment and the experience of acquiring new skills. As experts in postsecondary learning delve deeper into where and how learning happens – seeking to optimize those experiences across populations and at scale – it becomes clear that it does not happen by accident. Success involves the intentional design and creation of an experience with outcomes that can be articulated explicitly by learners or employers.

As president of the University of Maryland Global Campus (UMGC), I enjoy a unique vantage point on this evolution, and I often reflect on my formative experiences as a teenager working at a Six Flags theme park. There, I was reminded every day of the power of a coordinated team, of understanding the user experience, and of treating customers as guests.

In education, designing a learning environment must be just as intentional. The infrastructure is important, but so too is the way it makes users feel, how it aligns with their motivations, and how it responds to their needs. This argues in favor of making the COLO an integral part of the conversation – an equal partner with the Chief Academic Officer, Chief Technology Officer, and other peers.

As a movie buff, *The Karate Kid* offers one of my favorite metaphors for educators. As you likely recall, an aging handyman – Mr. Miyagi – mentors a young Daniel LaRusso, who lacks confidence and resources, by teaching him the fundamentals of karate through challenging and seemingly unrelated tasks – waxing a car, painting a fence, driving nails, etc. While this is very different from the traditional dojo experience of Daniel's adversary, Johnny Lawrence, both paths lead to a common goal – karate mastery in a tournament environment.

In education, many types of learning experiences may ultimately bring learners to the same place in terms of skills. But not all are lucky enough to know Mr. Miyagi. The COLO takes on the challenge of considering the student, resources, and environment and crafting a framework that leads to success.

At UMGC, this has meant replacing a legacy Digital Teaching and Learning unit with a dedicated Integrative Learning Design unit that manages the entirety of the learning environment, ensuring that it responds to workforce needs that are evolving faster than most institutions can respond. The role of the COLO is critical, akin to a general contractor overseeing a project while framers, roofers, electricians, and plumbers do their respective jobs – each different, but each critical to the integrity of the structure.

As president, I focus on establishing the institution's health, vision, and strategy, while the Chief Academic Officer deploys content experts to verify outcomes and mentor students and the COLO focuses on building the environment in which learning happens. This may require a paradigm shift, particularly in traditional institutions where faculty are often assumed to be masters of all trades. It is unrealistic to expect them to be equally skilled at designing a course, building it, delivering content, and mentoring students. In fact, studies have shown that expertise can present challenges when guiding novices.

I equate this with guiding someone to my house without the benefit of a GPS. What seems simple to me – because I am familiar with the route – might be daunting to someone else. Ultimately, the platinum rule trumps the golden rule: It's not about how I see the path, but how my visitor needs me to lay out the path for them to succeed.

When I first entered the college classroom as a professor, I had content expertise, but in hindsight, I marvel at how little I knew about pedagogy, andragogy, and the factors that determine student success. This is why the role of the COLO – along with other nonacademic roles – is so critical, especially for diverse learner populations.

At UMGC, I am excited by our increasing ability to create different learning environments to meet the needs of different types of students. The COLO role is key, whether we are creating a livestream, hybrid, or field study course that immerses a learner in a historic site or city.

Since the end of World War II, UMGC has accepted the challenge of designing learning environments on seven continents, on beaches, in jungles, and deserts, even in active battle zones. We craft learning experiences of different lengths, all providing the same skill mastery.

Different learners find success with certain modalities. As we delve deeper into the nature of learning, I believe the COLO role will only increase in importance, with the COLO functioning as an equal partner in the learning journey and an advocate for students, helping ensure that institutions continue to deliver a ROI and that students get what they came for. Informed by a deep understanding of the learner populations they serve and the desired outcomes, COLOs can leverage their expertise to ensure success for students and institutions alike.

Mark David Milliron, Ph.D.

President and Chief Executive Officer, National University

With contributions from Angela Baldasare, Deputy Chief of Staff and Vice President of Strategic Institutional Research & Planning and Errin Heyman, Associate Vice President, Learning Experience

National University, one of the largest private non-profit universities in the U.S., has a 50+ year history of innovative learning and support models for nontraditional, working, and military students with on-ground, online, hybrid, VR-fueled, four- and eight-week classes, and one-on-one personalized models. Having recently merged 3 universities, we have nearly 240,000 diverse, successful graduates in the field making a positive impact on their communities and society at large. However, our focus is not on getting bigger, it's on getting better. Our mission and collective focus is, we believe, the essence of staying relevant – "to deliver accessible world-class student experiences by providing quality programs and services that ensure student success through meaningful learning."

Our vision is "to be an inclusive and innovative university serving lifelong learners who contribute to the positive transformation of society." Our theory of change aimed at achieving our mission, vision, and the related core outcomes – e.g., more credentials, improved persistence and graduation rates, increased engagement, closing equity gaps, and more – makes the case that we will adopt Next-Generation Education, wrap that in Whole Human Education™, and then aim that at value-rich education. As we succeed in executing this plan, we will improve student success, enhance the educational experience, and create an environment where students realize deep value in market-recognized credentials, personal and professional connections, and transformative experiences.

To bring this mission, vision, and theory of change to life, learning design at NU relies on a systematic approach that draws in education research and neuro-connected frameworks that engage students not only with content but with the faculty, peers, and other affinity groups at the university. The course development process relies on strategy, execution, and engagement for faculty and students alike.

Our learning pathways provide students with an educational experience stacked with value from start to finish. We curate connections, ensuring opportunities for students to connect to peers, faculty, mentors, and experts in the field. The experience-rich aspect has us building rich learning experiences for the students including project-based learning, internships, mentorships, and clinical and civic engagements.

Courses are designed with our three pillars in mind: (1) we use appropriate technology to engage students and infuse support (next-gen); (2) we offer lifelong learning to current student and to alumni (whole human); (3) we seek to offer on and off-ramps and credential density in programs (value-rich). Ultimately, we rally around a theory of change to make good on the promise of education. Making good on that promise also requires that we are grounded and effective in the use of data.

Two systems integral to the effective use of data, and critical to the safeguarding of higher education are systems of accountability and systems of care. Systems of accountability in our regulatory environment mandate external compliance reporting but offer little institutional self-awareness. Internal systems of accountability, however, are essential to performance and financial sustainability. At NU, quarterly and monthly operating reviews provide a drumbeat of accountability for every functional unit. Student success metrics, division/unit strategic-plan progress, and financials anchor our conversations in these reviews, all aligning to our strategic-plan goals and, hence, our delivery of value-rich education. Our systems of accountability internally safeguard our institution by ensuring that we review progress each month and identify emergent areas of opportunity or concern in real time.

These internal systems of accountability have, in turn, supported and sharpened our focus on the equally essential systems of care. Systems of care employ data to provide personalized support for our students. Aligned with our Whole Human™ pillar, our prioritization of student success science applies our mixed-methods research to systematically improve student success. Actionable analytics and insights identify the right supports for the right students at the right time, and we rigorously measure the impact of our interventions so we can strategically invest. Weaving together systems of accountability and our systems of care, we create a virtuous cycle doing the right things for our students and our institution.

With over 80% of NU's instruction and service delivered online, in many ways all NU leaders are COLOs. We must take this work seriously and tackle it strategically. We cascade our innovative work from a strategic plan anchored in who we serve, and a theory of change aimed at achieving our mission, vision, and strategic outcomes for those learners. Put simply, for a COLO to be successful, the tools, technologies, policies, and practices championed must be grounded in purpose, guided by data, and deeply connected to a global community of practice committed to making a difference.

Karen Vignare, Ph.D.

Vice President, Digital Transformation for Student Success
Association of Public and Land Grant Universities

The world of higher education in the U.S. has changed. While we hear those words often, the combination of less traditional-aged students, post-COVID demand for flexible learning, and more adults who either need to reskill or have not finished their undergraduate degree, means that institutions that expect students to show up on a campus are likely to experience negative growth and negative financial impacts. Including the COLO in innovation is necessary to help the institution continue to thrive.

While most states in the U.S. do feel the pain of the enrollment decline of students aged 18–25, those data also underestimate the impact since many males are also choosing not to attend college. There is likely some opportunity to reach these students online as they are digital natives. It would require the kind of specific outreach and programming that COLOs have led for years. There is no doubt that the younger students who do attend higher education could benefit from a community of learners. However, if the choice is between creating online programs or not having students enroll at all, then institutions need to explore flexible learning environments where students can easily move from online classes to F2F classes and possibly to online programs as critical pathways to engaging more students.

The IPEDS data very clearly reveal that post-COVID, while many institutions have returned to a primarily campus orientation, few are offering only F2F options. The institutions most successful at bringing students back to campus have thriving learning and student communities, where students want to be co-located with other students. Yet even some of those students still demand flexibility in their schedules – a willingness to be on campus but a need to take some online courses to make their schedules work.

The national data from IPEDS including the 2022–23 collection, show that for 12-month enrollment, 36% of all students attend through exclusively distance education and another 32% enroll in some distance education. Remarkably, these data show that more students are choosing some distance ed than the previous year. While your institution may not reflect national data, the trend is clear: more than half of our students want the flexibility afforded by online learning options.

The COLO operation has invested in instructional technologies, learning science, and instructional design. These skillsets mean they are increasingly focused on the design of learning that meets students' needs. Creating a digital learning environment that supports multiple modalities is critical to the digital transformation of higher education. Building a flexible learning environment also supports the exploratory and innovative demands of a changing workforce. Whether designing microcredentials or a series of open courses to support the upskilling and reskilling needs of employees and employers, these learning experiences must be created online and then customized for learners. Higher education leaders must include the COLO in supporting institution-wide learning initiatives.

The digital transformation of learning within higher education can no longer rest on the creativity and ingenuity of an individual. There is a need to have the learning enterprise (especially instructional delivery) organized and transformed. The transformation allows for learning experiences to be customized to different student populations who might be at different life stages and want different credentials depending on their various life stages.

Higher education only maintains its relevance if it ensures that it can meet the varied needs and expectations of its many stakeholders. The COLO's operations are not only currently serving 36% of all currently enrolled students with fully online distance education programs, but they are supporting another 32% with some online learning. The magnitude of this change has happened in 25 years, which is a relatively short timeframe for higher education. In addition to this substantial shift in the delivery of programs is the fact that online operations are now also inclusive of critical student services, as well as marketing and retention activities. Higher education is crucial to our continued success as a nation, but we need to make it relevant and available to all learners. Including the COLO in the transformation of higher education will be essential to developing a new vision for higher education.

13 Epilogue: Other Duties as Assigned: Is There Life Outside of the Academy for COLOs?

Introduction

In the Foreword of this book, Bob Hansen posited that the 2020s ushered in the decade of the COLO. Accelerated by the remote learning of the COVID-19 pandemic, postsecondary institutions have come to recognize that online learning is both critical and strategic for them to serve the 21st-century learner. However, the need for digital learning leadership is not limited to colleges and universities.

A useful comparison, once again, is the ascendancy of the CIO. As the CIO role grew in stature and strategic importance in colleges and universities over the last two or three decades, the same role also rose in corporate, nonprofit, and government spaces. Likewise, a number of organizations outside academe have recognized the importance of digital learning and have established key leadership positions to lead these efforts.

In some cases, the non-academic COLO may focus on serving external constituents, such as through an online program management (OPM) company or an EdTech content/platform provider. Leaders in such roles often serve as key partners for the academic COLOs with whom they work. In other cases, the COLO may be internally focused, concentrating instead on training and workforce development of a specific employee population. They may have

DOI: 10.4324/9781003500742-16

titles such as Chief Learning Officer, Chief Academic Officer, Chief Content Officer, Vice President of Instruction, or some other organization-specific title. In each case, the person in the role has broad senior leadership responsibilities over a portfolio of digital learning programs and products.

Common Competencies

If they didn't already have a deep understanding of the complexities of a college/university, the COVID-19 pandemic provided higher education COLOs with a crash course. Higher education COLOs work in complicated, often decentralized organizations layered under policies, regulations, compliance, politics, tradition, and culture. COLOs who were faced with responding to the learning needs that the COVID-19 pandemic necessitated were forced to consider how all facets of the university could and/or did function online during a time of extreme stress. In the midst of this, they needed to respond, act, and lead.

Yet, the same complexities and dynamics exist in many organizations outside of higher education (consider healthcare, financial services, telecommunications, government, and insurance as just a few examples). In addition, all organizations are now facing the same post-COVID tectonic pressures such as a remote/hybrid workforce, employee retention, resource limitations, increased customer/student expectations, bandwidth challenges, and an assumption that everything can now be done online.

The UPCEA competencies that have been used as a framework for this book are equally applicable to the competencies required for success in comparable positions outside of higher education. As discussed in Chapter 10, in many ways the UPCEA PCO competencies can be more broadly considered in the context of general (digital operations) leadership. Leaning on these competencies, COLOs in all organizations will be able to navigate the ambiguity of the modern workplace and leverage the rapid change being wrought by digital transformation.

Emerging Opportunities

So what does this mean for those leaders who possess COLO competencies but prefer to work outside of higher education? They are as uniquely positioned to drive organizational change as their academic counterparts. Organizational leaders will look to these positions for guidance and counsel, recognizing that continuous learning is as critical a skill for the modern workforce as it is for the students served by colleges and universities.

The remote-first imperative of the COVID-19 pandemic accelerated many organizations' digital transformation. The goal of digital transformation is to continuously deploy technology at scale to improve both the experience for the customer and lower costs for the organization (McKinsey & Company, 2023). According to McKinsey, there are six capabilities critical for successful digital transformation. These capabilities (both individually and collectively) are directly relevant to the work that COLO (and COLO-adjacent) roles can play within an organization. The six capabilities are:

- The ability to craft a clear strategy focused on business value
- A strong talent bench with in-house developers/engineers
- An operating model that can scale
- Distributed technology that allows teams to innovate independently
- Access to data that teams can use as needed
- Strong adoption and change management

COLOs achieve impact by championing and leading organizations to possess a culture of learning. With this essential portfolio, they are key contributors to their organizations' missions and objectives. When the work of the organization is explicitly learning related (such as with an EdTech company or an OPM), the impact of the role becomes high profile. However, even in other organizations with various missions and objectives, the impact of training/learning can be made visible, such as through Kirkpatrick's (n.d.) fourth level of evaluation: Results, or "the degree to which targeted organizational outcomes occur as a result of the training initiative."

Leaders in these non-academic positions face the same challenges as academic COLOs, which are to explain and prove the value of online and digital learning and the resources and talent needed to scaffold such a value proposition. Yet, as in higher education, corporate chief learning officers (CLOs) are increasingly able to drive impact through digital learning innovation. As described by Lundberg and Westerman (2020), forward-looking CLOs within receptive organizations are

> embracing a more powerful role in which they reshape capabilities and organizational culture. We call this new type of leader the *transformer CLO*. Transformer CLOs are strong senior managers whose mission is to help their companies and their employees thrive, even as technologies, business practices, and whole industries undergo rapid change.

Transformer CLOs (or COLOs) recognize that workforces must evolve and that digital learning strategies must be central to their strategies. "These CLOs are personalizing, digitizing, and atomizing learning. They are shifting their attention from specific courses to the whole learning experience" (Lundberg and Westerman, 2020). They are using artificial intelligence to help manage curricula and are leveraging training for upskilling, reskilling, and stewarding a competitive advantage, as well as integrating learning into the flow of work. As an added bonus, when employees see that organizations are investing in them by providing training and even education as a benefit (Lurie, 2020), turnover decreases and retention increases, which further contributes to the CLO's impact.

Mounting Pressures That Are Necessitating the Transformer CLO

If the COVID-19 pandemic did not drive non-academic institutions to invest in a CLO, corporate and government sectors are increasingly feeling the urgency of needing a learning strategy and the infrastructure to support learning at scale. AI's impact on work and its future, as well as national trends in the labor market, are validating that COLO competencies will lead institutions in the age of these mounting pressures.

Open AI's Impacts on Work – Enterprise adoption of AI is key as companies and government agencies develop, optimize, and deploy AI applications. We are amid an era where AI is creating opportunities for corporate and government sectors to re-calibrate processes and operations, explore new ways of working, and scale AI solutions to accelerate continuous improvement. A key determinant of corporate and government success will be how AI nests within a corporate learning strategy. There is no better role to devise this strategy than the CLO.

National Trends in the Labor Market – Higher education institutions have leveraged labor market data to inform credential offerings by knowing industry-aligned skills gaps and to identify targeted student populations as a way of creating more robust industry-aligned talent pipelines. Non-academic sectors have historically relied on university partnerships for this information and the subsequent learning strategy brought to life by way of university-produced learning products. Increasingly, corporate and government sectors are becoming more savvy with national trends in the labor market and more sophisticated with their own

> internal workforce data to know and even predict workforce gaps into the future (Lightcast, 2024). Linking these data with a targeted learning strategy will ultimately yield the best outcomes when a CLO is at the helm. As the CLO strives for a seat at the leadership table, as in the case of the academic COLO, he/she must align his/her unit's activities to the strategic plan, execute effectively, and then ensure that leadership is aware of online learning's broader link to workforce outcomes.

Learners and workers alike are navigating the changing world of work. Many of the same data sources, methodologies, technologies, and interventions being developed and/or leveraged by COLOs and their teams in the college/university context to address AI and related trends in the labor market are informing CLO priorities on the non-academic side. The roles of COLO and CLO are instrumental to the health and vitality of our national workforce into the future. The handoff between learners being career-ready and workers pursuing continuous and lifelong learning won't happen by accident.

Looking Forward

Some of the most effective leaders today recognize the role that learning plays in the life and vitality of their organizations. The ways in which COLOs have transformed academic institutions is something that is increasingly manifesting in industry, the government, and the military. This trend will likely continue to evolve and stands to have positive impacts on our national workforce, in many of the same ways that COLOs have championed student success.

Research by Fredericksen, et al. (2024) found that the biggest challenges listed by COLOs at their institution are issues with institutional leaders, faculty issues, financial and budgeting issues, organizational structure and operations, and online priorities not being aligned with leadership. These issues will likely remain key challenges for both COLOs and CLOs well into the future (substitute departmental politics for faculty issues in a non-academic context). Yet, the competencies discussed in this book will serve those in COLO roles well as they face these challenges and others in the years ahead.

As described by Bob Hansen in the Foreword, while the COLO role has been growing in prominence and impact over the past quarter century or more, the digital learning requirements brought by the COVID-19 pandemic ushered in the "decade of the COLO." During that time, and even more so since, both academic and non-academic organizations have acknowledged the strategic importance of having a senior leadership role focused on integrating the strategies that leverage digital learning as a key lever for institutional culture change to enable institutions to achieve goals and ultimately fulfill their missions. Both the number of positions needed across higher education / industry and the scope of the COLO role will only expand; with 1 in 7 current COLOs declaring that their next career step is retirement (Fredericksen, et al., 2024), the need for the next generation of online learning leadership is even more urgent now than it was during the COVID-19 pandemic.

There will soon come a time when the thought of an institution not having a COLO will be as unimaginable as not having a CIO. It will be considered irresponsible in the face of an increasingly digital 21st-century learner. The competencies, perspectives, insights, and advice contained in this book will help current and aspiring COLOs to not just serve in these emerging roles but to thrive.

References

Fredericksen, E., Simunich, B. & Uranus, J. (2024) *COLO Profile Study 2024 – A National Research Project about Chief Online Learning Officers.* Presented at OLC Accelerate 2024, Orlando, FL. https://olc.secure-platform.com/accelerate/gallery/rounds/82030/schedule/items/17650

Kirkpatrick Partners. (n.d.). *The Kirkpatrick model.* Retrieved August 4, 2024, from https://www.kirkpatrickpartners.com/the-kirkpatrick-model/

Lightcast (2024). The Rising Storm: Building a future-ready workforce to withstand the looming labor shortage. Retrieved from https://lightcast.io/rising-storm download?submissionGuid=1bf8101b-8edb-4538-b4a5-fa084131ce0b

Lundberg, A., & Westerman, G. (2020, January). The transformer CLO. *Harvard Business Review.* Retrieved from https://hbr.org/2020/01/the-transformer-clo

Lurie, H. (2020). *A new "guilded" age? Education-as-a-benefit arrives.* Encoura. Retrieved from https://www.encoura.org/resources/wake-up-call/a-new-guilded-age-education-as-a-benefit-arrives/

McKinsey & Company. (2023). *Rewired: A McKinsey Guide to Outcompeting in the Age of Digital and AI.* Wiley. Retrieved from https://www.mckinsey.com/featured-insights/mckinsey-explainers/what-is-digital-transformation

Expert Perspectives

- Melissa Loble, Instructure
- Jenn Stringer, J. Paul Getty Trust
- Cristi Ford, D2L

Melissa Loble

Chief Academic Officer Instructure

As strategic online learning practices grow in both importance and value within education organizations, educational technology ("EdTech") providers are investing throughout their organizations to best serve these practices. An output of this investment is the rise of a Chief Academic Officer ("CAO") or "CLO" executive role aimed at leading and evangelizing the impact technologies have on online learning strategic success. While a more recent phenomenon, these roles are a hybrid of the more traditional CAO role within education organizations and the CLO role within corporate organizations. These executive roles, and their subsequent teams, often report into the CEO of the technology provider. They also appear in a diversity of organizations, from large to small, from public to private, and from early stage to more substantially funded.

The remit of the CAO or CLO within an EdTech organization generally includes five key areas of focus. Some organizations will lean more directionally in a subset of these areas; however, these are largely the areas of impact of the executive leaders.

- *Thought Leadership*: CAOs/CLOs gather education thought leadership around the challenges, disruptors, and opportunities for education in the short and medium term. They summarize, curate, and expand on this thought leadership to share both externally to education organizations and internally to inform educational technology strategy. They also act as a convener of education leaders to discuss critical issues facing the broader education industry and workforce development.
- *Product Roadmap Advisory*: Sourced from the thought leadership work they conduct, CAOs/CLOs work closely with product leadership within the EdTech organization to ensure roadmaps best serve academic and online learning opportunities in education.
- *Community Development & Research*: CAOs/CLOs lead the development of resources for the broader education community, often in the form of whitepapers, conference presentations, e-books, podcasts, and other formats valuable for leaders of online learning. They may also sit on various industry governing boards or engage in external collaborations to drive online learning success. Alongside this, the CAO/CLO may lead an academic research team that is focused on conducting unique research in the education field or partnering with academic institutions on their research agendas.

- *Stakeholder Enablement*: As an extension of the thought leadership and research work conducted, CAO/CLOs may lead the professional development programs internally within their organization to expand the breadth and depth of understanding around online learning, teaching, research, and other academic areas. In concert with this, the CAO/CLO may also be responsible for ensuring the organization is a "learning organization" where its daily practice reflects continuous improvement and ongoing equitable access to professional growth.
- *Government Collaboration*: Post-pandemic, EdTech organizations are becoming more involved in government policy and research, with the CAO/CLO acting largely in an advisory capacity to this work. More traditional lobbying activities typically fall outside the CAO/CLO role (and instead live within a revenue organization); however, actively engaging in cross-organization federal alliances and workforce development initiatives is growing in importance for this EdTech leader.

Outside of the academic institution, COLO skills are incredibly valuable to EdTech organizations and broader technology providers with education agendas. To successfully lead an academic or online learning agenda as a CAO/CLO, the COLO brings both strong discipline and leadership skills that complement an overall organizational strategy focused on societal impact through equitable access to lifelong learning.

Jenn Stringer, M.L.I.S

Vice President and Chief Digital Officer, J. Paul Getty Trust

> The only thing that you absolutely have to know is the location of the library.
>
> (Albert Einstein, Theoretical Physicist, 1879–1955)

This quote from Albert Einstein has always been one of my favorites. It feels even more true now as you can find "the library" on your phone or your computer and access resources that I would not have been able to imagine in 1989 when my career began. I started my career as an academic librarian at Stanford University just as the Internet was birthed – yes, I was there when Mosaic, created by the NCSA, began being used in academic libraries as a resource. I knew that I would end up at the intersection of education and technology. My career choices, always at the core, connected teaching, research, and technology. I was the director of academic technology at New York University and then the Chief Academic Technology Officer at UC Berkeley, and finally the CIO for the campus. I would not have ever expected to leave the academy. Then the J. Paul Getty Trust knocked on my door and had a job that pulled together my love of libraries, learning, research, history, architecture, and art. Who could say no?

In my current role as the Vice President and Chief Digital Officer of the J Paul Getty Trust (Getty), I haven't drifted too far afield from my roots. My team is responsible for Getty's digital presence, web, scholarship, research collections, library systems, as well as the more traditional IT functions like HR and payroll systems. Getty, not affiliated with Getty Images, is much more than the two museums that people are most familiar with. It houses the Getty Research Institute that is home to one of the most comprehensive libraries for art history, as well as an amazing archive. It also develops and supports the Getty Vocabularies which are structured resources for the visual arts domain that provide authoritative information for catalogers, researchers, and data providers. They are freely and openly available for use under the Open Data Commons Attribution License (ODC-By) 1.0. Getty also houses the Getty Conservation Institute, which creates new scholarship around the conservation of cultural heritage and has chemists, material scientists, archaeologists, and other researchers as a part of the organization.

All of the skills that I learned in the academic technology and online learning space have positioned me for my current role. I work with scholars, researchers, conservators, and curators to help translate Getty's collections, research, and scholarship to a broader audience. I have a seat at the table reporting directly to the CEO and president of the trust and actively participate in conversations directly related to the mission of the organization. The UPCEA competencies outlined in Chapter 10 and expanded upon in Chapter 11 are skills that are the foundation for how I operated at work and have transferred seamlessly to the cultural heritage space.

If I were to point to one competency that I would advocate for everyone to spend more time on, it is "futures literacy." This has been key to my current work. For example, Getty is currently working on sustainability efforts that will inform the future of cultural heritage conservation across the world taking into account climate change. Part of that effort is bringing together conservation scientists, climatologists, and policymakers to understand how we bring the current research together and work to make recommendations across the field. This includes how we use current conservation science data in new ways to help inform policymaking.

In the ever-evolving landscape of technology and education, the ability to adapt and grow is paramount. My journey from the halls of academia to the digital corridors of the J. Paul Getty Trust has been a testament to the power of a strong professional foundation in the academic technology space.

Cristi Ford, Ph.D.

Vice President of Academic Affairs, D2L

> The journey is not linear. It is a spiral, with each turn bringing us closer to our destination, but also taking us back to where we started, so that we can see it with new eyes.
>
> (Jeanette Winterson, Author, 1959–present)

This quote encapsulates the unexpected twists and turns of my career trajectory. While the transition from academia to a non-academic role in 2019 might have seemed unconventional to some, my background in distance education had already positioned me as an outlier within traditional faculty ranks. A focus on impactful work has always driven my career, and the opportunity to make a significant difference in the lives of others proved to be an irresistible force.

The full weight of this decision became apparent just three days before the onset of the COVID-19 pandemic. Suddenly, as a newly appointed CLO at a nonprofit, I was tasked with developing nationwide training programs to address the burgeoning housing crisis and homelessness epidemic, all while navigating the uncharted waters of a global pandemic. With a staff of 60 and an organization deeply rooted in traditional F2F training, the challenge was immense. We had to pivot rapidly, transforming our operations to deliver essential online training to thousands of housing counselors in record time.

This crisis accelerated my entrepreneurial spirit, forcing me to forge new partnerships, develop innovative revenue streams, and master the art of change management. With limited online resources and a predominantly in-person curriculum, we faced a steep learning curve. However, within six months, we launched a groundbreaking online event that generated a million dollars in new revenue.

This experience underscored the critical role of COLOs in driving organizational success during times of upheaval. To thrive in such dynamic environments, we must possess a keen understanding of resource management and financial modeling while simultaneously cultivating the ability to generate new revenue streams. As the pandemic demonstrated, COLOs are often called upon to be strategic visionaries, capable of leading their organizations through uncharted territory.

Building upon this foundation of rapid adaptation and innovation, my career trajectory took another turn when I assumed the role of Chief Academic and Leadership of Academic Affairs at a learning organization. This position presented an opportunity to leverage my leadership and academic expertise to enhance the student and faculty experience on a broader scale. I focused on improving the learning experience by collaborating with internal colleagues on product development and by partnering with institutions to implement best practices in teaching and learning. This role demanded extensive networking, both internally and externally, which aligned with my strengths as a connector. The chance to continually learn, forge new relationships, and contribute to the advancement of the field of learning has been immensely rewarding. Witnessing the transformative power of education remains a constant source of inspiration.

Transitioning from academia into the broader education landscape requires a unique blend of intellectual curiosity and entrepreneurial spirit. One must possess the ability to anticipate future trends and create new opportunities. Moreover, a willingness to challenge the status quo and embrace personal growth is essential for success. The dynamic nature of the education industry, with its diverse perspectives and global reach, offers a rich tapestry of experiences that can significantly enhance one's contributions to the field.

For those contemplating if there is a career beyond academia, the answer is a resounding yes. The expertise honed in an institutional setting can be seamlessly translated to a variety of roles within the broader educational ecosystem. By aligning skillsets and competencies with mission-driven work in different industries, COLOs and other higher education professionals can unlock new opportunities and make a substantial impact.

Michelle Wiese's concept of "long-life learning," as outlined in her book, aptly describes the future of work (Weise, 2020). The traditional model of learn-earn-rest is evolving into a cyclical process of continuous learning, earning, and reskilling. COLOs who venture outside of academia are at the forefront of this transformation. Their ability to upskill and adapt will be instrumental in shaping the future of learning and development across various sectors.

Reference

Weise, M. (2020). *Long life learning: Preparing for jobs that don't even exist yet*. Wiley.

Expert Contributors' Biographies

Deborah Adair, Ph.D. is the Chief Executive Officer of Quality Matters (QM), a global organization with a widely adopted quality assurance framework and capacity-building resources for online and innovative digital teaching and learning environments. QM recognizes and certifies quality at the course, program, and institutional levels in online education and currently serves over 1,300 institutions across education sectors in more than 30 countries in support of its mission to improve online and digital education. Under Dr. Adair's leadership, Quality Matters has helped focus the education community on the practical application of quality standards to online and blended courses and programs and has worked to improve student outcomes through a focus on continuous quality improvement. Dr. Adair has more than 30 years of experience in higher education, faculty, and administration, as well as nonprofit leadership. She has served QM in a leadership role since 2007.

Amrit Ahluwalia is the Executive Director of Continuing Studies at Western University, overseeing post-degree professional programming, professional development and corporate programming, and the Western English Language Centre. Ahluwalia joined Western in 2024 after founding and serving as Editor-in-Chief of The EvoLLLution, the online newspaper developed by Modern Campus to create a conversation hub focused on nontraditional higher education and the transforming postsecondary marketplace. He also served as Senior Director for Marketing at Modern Campus, ensuring thought leadership assets align with industry trends. He regularly speaks on topics related to the changing higher education environment at conferences across Canada and the U.S. and hosts the EdUp

PCO podcast focused on innovation and transformation in Professional, Continuing & Online Education. Ahluwalia earned his B.A. (Honors) in Political Studies from Queen's University and his M.A. in International Politics from McMaster University. He and his family live in London, Ontario.

Asim Ali, Ph.D. is the Executive Director of the Biggio Center at Auburn University where he advances professional development programs and resources to enhance instructional innovation and support scholarly and creative activities. Prior to this role, he served as Founding Director of Auburn Online, helping launch the institution's first undergraduate online programs. Asim earned a bachelor's in software engineering, a master's in information systems management, and doctorate in adult education, all from Auburn. Asim leads work on artificial intelligence literacy, and he has modeled implementation of generative AI in the introduction to information systems management course he teaches for the Harbert College of Business. Asim also co-leads innovative initiatives for micro-credentials, augmented and virtual reality, and skills articulation. He is active in several professional organizations, including serving as an executive board member of UPCEA. He has been an invited speaker at conferences and universities nationally and internationally.

Tonya B. Amankwatia, Ph.D., is a leader in digital learning and educational innovation, with over 15 years of leading university-wide distance education units. She holds a Ph.D. in Learning Sciences and Technology from Lehigh University and has served as the founding digital teaching and online administrator at three institutions, including private universities and the largest public land-grant HBCU. Tonya has taught credit and non credit courses, earning the rank of associate professor, and holds microcredentials in enterprise design thinking, AI, and academic program evaluation. She currently serves as North Carolina A&T State University's Assistant Vice Provost of Extended Campus. Over the years, her leadership in AECT, Anthology, UPCEA, and Credential Engine's Data Currency for Quality Advisory Group, along with facilitating mentorship opportunities for graduate instructional design students through a NATO partnership and founding the HBCU Digital Leadership Network, underscores her commitment to curricular innovation, professional development, and impactful research-to-practice initiatives in digital education.

Nelson C. Baker, Ph.D., is the inaugural Interim Dean of the Lifetime Learning Division and professor in the School of Civil and Environmental Engineering at the Georgia Institute of Technology. As dean, Dr. Baker leads a multifaceted enterprise that interacts with Georgia Tech faculty to create and deploy Georgia Tech's research, educational programs, activities, and services for the ongoing learning needs of both individuals and employer workforce demands throughout a lifetime. This new division, formed in 2023 under Dr. Baker's leadership, touched more than 250,000 K-12 teachers, students, and working professionals last year from nearly half the world's countries, providing them new knowledge and skills for tomorrow's world. Prior to this role, Dr. Baker served as the dean of professional education for the last decade.

M.J. Bishop, Ed.D., is Vice President for Integrative Learning Design at the University of Maryland Global Campus (UMGC), where she leads the evidence-based design and development of learning experiences across disciplines, delivery modalities, and global boundaries. Prior to UMGC, she was Associate Vice Chancellor and inaugural director of the University System of Maryland's (USM) William E. Kirwan Center for Academic Innovation, where she led major statewide initiatives in the areas of open educational resources, online education, comprehensive learner records, alternative credentials, and adaptive learning. Prior to USM, Dr. Bishop was Associate Professor and Director of Lehigh University's Teaching, Learning, and Technology Program, where she led the institution's graduate programs in instructional design and technology, taught graduate-level courses, and mentored master's and doctoral students. M.J.'s research interests include understanding the psychology behind instructional media to discover their pedagogical capabilities and devise more effective ways to design instructional technologies to enhance learning.

Bettyjo Bouchey, Ed.D., is the Chief Professional & Continuing Education (PACE) Officer at the University of Vermont. As one of the longest-standing PACE units in higher education, the team serves the institution by offering high-quality online and hybrid nondegree and degree offerings in collaboration with the university's academic units and institutes, workforce development, and lifelong learning opportunities to Vermont residents and beyond. Dr. Bouchey holds a B.A. in Psychology from the University of Albany, an M.B.A. in Entrepreneurship from Rensselaer Polytechnic Institute, and a Doctorate in Education from Northeastern University. Her research interests include the nature and future of organizational structures of online units in institutions of higher education, as well as inventive and high-impact pedagogical practice in online teaching, inclusive of artificial intelligence and machine learning. Dr. Bouchey writes and is widely quoted in the academic and popular press; her articles and curriculum vitae can be accessed here: www.drbouchey.com.

Robert Bruce, Ph.D., has served as Rice University's Adjunct Professor of Humanities and Dean of the Susanne M. Glasscock School of Continuing Studies since 2017. Prior to joining Rice University, he led online, continuing, and professional studies departments at the University of North Carolina at Chapel Hill and the University of Texas at Austin. Bruce earned a B.A. in English from UT Austin and an M.A. and Ph.D. in English from Texas A&M University. His teaching interests include American satire, banned books, and 19th- and 20th-century dark humor. He is the 2025 President-Elect for the 15,000-member UPCEA. He is also a member of the Inprint Houston Advisory Council, the Center for Houston's Future Advisory Council, and the Greater Houston Partnership.

Carmin Chan, Ph.D., currently serves as the Vice Provost for NAU Online at Northern Arizona University. Before joining NAU, she served as the Senior Director of Online Student Success Initiatives at the University of Arizona, where she spearheaded student engagement and retention efforts within Arizona Online. Dr. Chan earned her Ph.D. in Higher Education from the University of Arizona, where her research focuses on Military Funds of Knowledge brought by college student veterans and the impact they have as change agents within higher education. She currently serves on the Council for Chief Online Learning Officers (C-COLO) and previously served as the Chair of the Online Administration (OA) network within UPCEA. Throughout her education career, Carmin has been a staunch advocate for increasing access and promoting institutional changes necessary to make higher education more inclusive of the needs of post-traditional student populations including online learners, transfer students, and student veterans.

Amy Collier, Ph.D., is the Associate Provost for Digital Learning at Middlebury College, where she provides strategic vision and leadership to create and sustain a global learning community through the effective use of digital pedagogies and technologies. Working closely with the provost and senior academic leaders, Amy identifies and pursues opportunities for Middlebury to create online and hybrid/blended courses and programs that build on Middlebury's pedagogical values, leverage its intellectual and pedagogical resources, connect diverse programs with each other, and enrich the experience of current and potential Middlebury learners. Amy received her doctorate from Texas Woman's University in 2008. Through her graduate studies in social sciences and more than 20 years working in faculty development, Amy has been an advocate for learners and teachers across a variety of educational institutions, from community-based service organizations to large public broad-access universities. She frequently presents at universities and conferences, sharing her passion for topics such as student privacy, critical instructional design, design justice, and complexity in education.

Vickie Cook, Ph.D., is Vice Chancellor for Enrollment and Retention Management and a Research Professor in the College of Education at the University of Illinois Springfield. Dr. Cook has been actively engaged in providing consulting and faculty development with educational leaders across the U.S., Canada, and Mexico seeking to expand or evaluate their online learning programs and leadership. Cook has published multiple journal articles and book chapters, and she serves as a peer reviewer for six of the top journals in the field of Online Learning. She is a co-author of the UPCEA Hallmarks of Excellence in Online Leadership and UPCEA Hallmarks of Excellence in Alternative Credentials. Dr. Cook was named a 2017 University of Illinois President's Executive Leadership Fellow; 2017 Online Learning Consortium (OLC) Fellow; 2020 University Professional and Continuing Education Outstanding Leader, and 2024 Mildred B. and Charles A. Wedemeyer Award for Outstanding Writer / Scholar in Distance Education.

Shawna Dark, Ph.D., has worked in higher education for over 20 years as a tenured faculty member, Department Chair, and now in administration. For the past 10 years, she served in leadership roles with oversight of instructional and research technologies. In her current role as the Assistant Vice Provost for Undergraduate Education and Chief Academic Technology Officer at UC Berkeley, she oversees Research, Teaching, and Learning (RTL), which includes academic technology, research IT, and other technologies related to student success. As part of the Division of Undergraduate Education, RTL partners with the campus to inspire, enrich, and innovate Berkeley's collective practice and pursuit of inclusive teaching and research excellence.

Luke Dowden, Ed.D., is the Chief Online Learning Officer for the Alamo Colleges District and a member of the Chancellor's Strategic Leadership Team. Through Dowden's leadership, the five community colleges in the district are actively engaged in microcredentialing from marketable skills digital badges to healthcare skills micro-courses to professional certificates. Dr. Dowden is a frequent speaker on the topic of digital credentials and microcredentials having served as a panelist at numerous events.

Dr. Dowden was honored by the Online Learning Consortium as a member of its distinguished Class of Fellows in 2022. He was recognized in 2023 by 1EdTech with a Leadership Award in Digital Credentials. Dr. Dowden earned a bachelor's in History and a master's degree in Adult Education from Northwestern State University before earning his Doctorate of Education in higher education administration in 2009 from Nova Southeastern University.

Adam D. Fein, Ph.D., is the Vice President for Digital Strategy and Innovation and Chief Digital Officer (CDO) at the University of North Texas. As the head of UNT's online and digital strategies, he leads the charge to identify new directions and opportunities to improve the academic quality, reach, and performance of the university in the online and global education markets as well as with corporate, state, and federal partnerships in workforce development. Prior to joining UNT, Dr. Fein served the University of Illinois at Urbana-Champaign for 17 years in numerous roles, including as Assistant Provost for Educational Innovation, where he was responsible for overseeing the campus efforts in online learning. Dr. Fein has published book chapters and numerous professional papers and was featured in the Wall Street Journal and Forbes for his work in helping the Dallas Cowboys coaching staff use digital learning with great success during the COVID-19 pandemic.

James Fong is the Chief Research Officer at UPCEA. Prior to joining UPCEA, Mr. Fong was the Director of Marketing, Research, and Planning for Penn State University Outreach. In this role, he was responsible for marketing and enrollment management teams and research-driven initiatives for program development for Penn State World Campus and professional programs. Mr. Fong has published a number of papers on marketing online education. He holds an M.B.A., M.S., and B.S. from the University of Vermont.

Cristi Ford, Ph.D., is Vice President of Academic Affairs at D2L, leveraging over two decades of educational experience. She leads D2L's academic affairs unit, focusing on thought leadership in teaching and learning. Her career spans secondary and higher education, with a focus on quality online learning in the U.S. and Africa. Recognized as an OLC Fellow and recipient of the 2024 Wedemeyer Award, Ford is a passionate advocate for faculty development and instructional design. She has guided institutions in expanding online programs. Ford holds a Ph.D. in Educational Leadership and degrees in Psychology.

Gregory W. Fowler, Ph.D., is President of the University of Maryland Global Campus (UMGC), Maryland's largest provider of postsecondary education and the country's most transfer-friendly university. The premier learning partner of the U.S. military, UMGC has more than 175 classroom or service locations in 22 countries and territories. Dr. Fowler – a nationally recognized leader in developing innovative learning models and experiences for adult and underserved populations – is leading a transformation at UMGC that aligns the entire learning journey with the needs and expectations of learners and the global workforce. Prior to joining UMGC, he served as president of Southern New Hampshire Global Campus and before that on the senior leadership team of Western Governors University. A two-time Fulbright Senior Scholar and graduate of Morehouse College, Dr. Fowler holds master's degrees from George Mason University and Western Governors University and a Ph.D. from the State University of New York at Buffalo.

Eric E. Fredericksen, Ed.D., is the Associate Vice President for Online Learning and Professor in Educational Leadership at the University of Rochester. Eric has almost 30 years of leadership experience in online education in positions at the University of Rochester, Cornell University, and the State University of New York System Office. His research includes studies of the student and faculty experience in online courses, and more recently Leadership for Online Learning in HE through the national CHLOE project. Eric served on the Board for the Online Learning Consortium, was President 2018–2019, and was honored as a Sloan-C Fellow.

Richard Garrett is Eduventures Chief Research Officer at Encoura, a higher education enrollment services and data science company. He has almost 30 years of experience in higher education, specializing in online learning, nontraditional students, innovative program and institutional models, market research, and internationalization. Richard has also worked at the Observatory on Borderless Higher Education, i-graduate, the Association of Commonwealth Universities, the University of Surrey (UK), and the Quality Assurance Agency for Higher Education (UK). Richard is co-founder and co-director of the CHLOE (Changing Landscape of Online Education) project with Quality Matters and EDUCAUSE.

Lev Gonick, Ph.D., is the Enterprise Chief Information Officer at Arizona State University. He leads the design and agile management of all enterprise infrastructure, applications, products, services, and analytics at the nation's largest and most innovative university. Dr. Gonick has over 30 years of experience in education, technology, and smart city architecture. He is passionate about enabling and celebrating innovation, collaboration, and productivity through the broadest possible access and utilization of next-generation technologies in the service of learner success.

Asher Haines is UNC Charlotte's Associate Provost of the School of Professional Studies. In this role, he directs the school and leads the university's strategies related to supporting adult learners, partnering with companies and organizations to develop their employees through education and training, and collaborating with the university's academic colleges to develop and deliver programs for adult learners while also supporting overall excellence in teaching and learning for the university.

Deborah Keyek-Franssen, Ph.D., is Associate Vice President and Dean of University Connected Learning (UCL) and works with a talented team at the University of Utah to provide a full range of online education opportunities and services and a rich set of professional education, workforce alignment, and personal enrichment programs. As AVP for Digital Education at the University of Colorado, she advanced online education initiatives, including MOOCs, and directed the Colorado Learning and Teaching with Technology (COLTT) Conference. At CU Boulder, she was the Director of Academic Technology, overseeing strategy and research in educational technologies. Deborah has served on various advisory boards, including NASH Institute, Colorado OER Council, and Coursera Advisory Council, and was Faculty Director of the EDUCAUSE Management Institute. A Dartmouth College graduate, she holds a Ph.D. in German Literature and a master's in Higher Education Administration from the University of Michigan. She received the EDUCAUSE 2020 DEI Leadership Award.

Joshua Kim, Ph.D., is the Assistant Provost for Online Learning Strategy at Dartmouth College and a Senior Fellow at Georgetown University. Josh has a Ph.D. in sociology and demography from Brown University. He started his career on the faculty at West Virginia University, helped start Britannica.com's education division in San Francisco, and was one of the original founders of Quinnipiac University Online. He has taught both on-ground and online courses in sociology, marketing, and higher education leadership. With Eddie Maloney, Josh published *Learning Innovation and the Future of Higher Education* and *The Low-Density University: 15 Scenarios for Higher Education*. Both books are from Johns Hopkins University (JHU)

Press, and both came out in 2020. His latest co-authored JHU book, *Recentering Learning: Complexity, Resilience, and Adaptability in Higher Education*, was published in December of 2024. Josh is best known for his Learning Innovation blog on InsideHigherEd.com, a website that receives over 2.3 million unique monthly visitors.

Katie Linder, Ph.D., has a passion for helping others engage in and create meaningful change. Currently, she serves as the Interim Vice Chancellor for Strategic Enrollment and Student Success and the Associate Vice Chancellor for Academic Innovation and Strategy at the University of Colorado Denver. Katie is also a credentialed project manager through PMI, a credentialed coach through the International Coaching Federation, and a Certified Change Practitioner through ProSci.

Melissa Loble serves as Chief Academic Officer for Instructure, where she oversees thought leadership and academic strategy to drive educational industry advancements, stakeholder partnerships, and company efforts to both influence and respond to legislation in the EdTech space as well as advance employee development. Melissa has spent 25+ years in the educational technology world, working for a number of technology suppliers and educational institutions in a variety of teaching and learning leadership capacities. Melissa earned her B.A. in political science from the University of California, Los Angeles, her M.A. in educational policy from Teachers' College, Columbia University, and an M.B.A. in leadership from the Columbia Business School.

Jennifer Mathes, Ph.D., serves as the Chief Executive Officer of the Online Learning Consortium (OLC). In her role, she sets the strategic direction for the organization and spearheads the development of key projects and programs to benefit OLC members. She began her academic journey as a faculty member, eventually ascending to the role of Chief Academic Officer. Dr. Mathes has also served as a consultant, advising educational institutions on implementing best practices in online, blended, and digital education. Her recent work has involved collaborating with higher education associations and institutions internationally to support the global adoption of best practices in online learning. Dr. Mathes earned her Doctor of Philosophy in Education from the University of Illinois at Urbana-Champaign. She also holds a Master of Science in Business Education and a Bachelor of Science in Mass Communications, both from Illinois State University.

Deb Miller, Ed.D., is Assistant Vice President for Digital Learning and Innovation at the University of North Florida. In this role, she provides leadership for digital learning policy, practice, and strategy. She provides oversight for UNF's Center for Instruction and Research Technology (CIRT) and UNF Online, as well as digital badging and textbook affordability initiatives. Deb also works with campus stakeholders to investigate new digital learning technologies and facilitate the adoption of appropriate tools. Her research interests include alternative credentialing, the role of relationships in organizational decision-making, and the influence of institutional and individual factors in faculty decisions to engage in innovative teaching practices.

Mark David Milliron, Ph.D., is an award-winning leader, author, speaker, and consultant who works with universities, community colleges, K-12 schools, foundations, corporations, associations, and government agencies across the country and around the world. He serves as President and CEO of National University (NU), one of the largest private, nonprofit universities in the U.S. NU is designated as a Hispanic-Serving Institution (HSI) and has a 50-year history of innovating around the needs of military, working, and nontraditional students. In addition to his work with NU, Dr. Milliron helps catalyze positive change in education through his service on the boards and advisory councils of leading-edge education organizations, including the Trellis Foundation; Bennett College; the Global Online Academy; Civitas Learning; the Mastery Transcript Consortium; and ISKME/Open Education Resource Commons. He also holds an appointment as a Professor of Practice in the College of Education at the University of Texas at Austin. Regardless of his activities and accomplishments, he will quickly tell you that the most important job and the greatest blessing in his life is serving as Julia's husband and father to Alexandra, Richard, Marcus, and Max.

Cheryl Murphy, Ed.D., is the Vice Provost for Distance Education at the University of Arkansas and oversees the Global Campus. Her areas of expertise include online learning in higher education, the use of technology to enhance learning, and accreditation. She is a full professor with numerous publications and presentations to her credit and has assumed a variety of administrative positions including Program Coordinator, Department Head, Director of Distance Learning, and Co-Director of the Teaching and Faculty Support Center in addition to her current Vice Provost position. Dr. Murphy has served in leadership roles for numerous higher education organizations including positions within UPCEA on the Council for Credential Innovation, Diversity and Inclusive Excellence Committee, Council for Chief Online Learning Officers, and Board of Directors. She has also served as a Peer Consultant Reviewer, Team Chair, and currently sits on the Institutional Actions Council for the Higher Learning Commission.

Todd Nicolet, Ph.D., serves as Vice Provost for Digital and Lifelong Learning at UNC-Chapel Hill. In this role, Dr. Nicolet provides leadership and direction for all the University's digital, flexible, and lifelong learning programming as well as administration of summer sessions and management of the university's conference center. He has held administrative leadership positions at the UNC Gillings School of Public Health and the UNC School of Government, where he served as director of MPA@UNC, guided the development of MPH@UNC, and helped establish a joint MPH with UNC Asheville. Dr. Nicolet also had direct oversight over several functional units within each school, such as finance, IT, human resources, research support, library, publications, and strategic analysis. He holds a doctorate in higher education administration from UNC-Greensboro, a Master of Arts in English from UNC-Chapel Hill, and an undergraduate degree in literature from Eckerd College.

John O'Brien, Ph.D., serves as the president and CEO of EDUCAUSE, a nonprofit organization seeking to inspire the transformation of higher education in service to the greater good. EDUCAUSE serves over 2,000 member colleges, universities, and organizations from 41 countries that collectively serve over 14 million students. He speaks and writes on a variety of topics related to higher education, technology, and the crucial intersection where the two meet. Throughout his career in higher education, John has served as an academic, technology, and institutional leader. He was a faculty leader in instructional technology, a statewide IT project leader, and associate vice chancellor/deputy CIO at the system level. He has been a college provost and president in the Minnesota State Colleges and Universities system. Immediately prior to his appointment at EDUCAUSE, he served as the system's senior vice chancellor of academic and student affairs. John is the former president of North Hennepin Community College, a minority-serving institution (MSI) in his home state of Minnesota, and he serves as vice chair of the board of regents of Augsburg University. He was recently appointed to the board of the American Council on Education (ACE) and the board of Achieving the Dream. John holds a bachelor's degree in English from Augustana University, a master's degree in Anglo-Irish Literature from Trinity College Dublin, and a doctorate in English from the University of Minnesota.

Karen L. Pedersen, Ph.D., is a consultant with Summit Search Solutions in addition to various professional organizations. Her career in higher education included serving in online learning leadership roles for both public and private institutions, most recently as Dean of Global Campus and then Associate Vice Provost of Academic Innovation at Kansas State University. Her experience in higher education included leading award-winning adult-serving academic/operational units, initiating a university-wide microcredentialing initiative, serving on the launch team for a competency-based education program, engaging a system-wide enrollment management transformation, and building academic collaborations internationally. Pedersen holds a B.S. and M.S. from the University of Nebraska-Lincoln and a Ph.D. from Oklahoma State University. As a lifelong learner, Karen is a PROSCI-certified change management practitioner and an ROI Institute-certified ROI professional, and she has completed courses through IDEOU.

Russ Poulin is the Executive Director for WCET – the WICHE Cooperative for Educational Technologies, which has member institutions in every U.S. state. WCET also includes the State Authorization Network (focused on interstate distance education compliance) and Every Learner Everywhere (focused on the intersection of digital learning and equity). He guides a talented team in supporting effective practices and policies for the post-secondary use of digital learning. He is a sought-after expert and leader regarding federal and state policies and emerging policy uses of educational technologies. Russ was honored to have represented the distance education community on federally negotiated rulemaking committees and subcommittees. He has received recognition for his contributions from the Online Learning Consortium, the Presidents' Forum, Excelsior College, and the National University Technology Network. One of his staff called him the "Forest Gump of distance education."

Joseph Riquelme served as the first Vice Provost and Chief Online Officer at American University. Over the last 17 years, he has significantly contributed to the success of two esteemed universities: Florida International University (FIU) and American University. With a passion for creating opportunities and access to education through high-quality learning experiences, he has been a transformative leader in the field. During a 14-year tenure at FIU, Joseph led FIU Online, the distance education team, through a period of remarkable growth. This growth was accompanied by the expansion of new services, improved infrastructure, and the development of over 100 high-quality degree programs that consistently receive numerous awards, recognition, and rankings annually. Additionally, Joseph championed the implementation of innovative technologies and built teams that were essential to enhancing services for students, faculty, and staff.

Susan D. Seal, Ph.D., is currently the Dean of the College of Professional and Continuing Studies at Mississippi State University and was instrumental in the planning and approval processes associated with its inception. Prior to her current role, she was the Executive Director of the Center for Distance Education, moving from a faculty position in International Agricultural Education. She has served on the Robert Holland Faculty Senate, Associate Dean's Council, Dean's Council, and many other councils, committees, and task forces providing her with a broad higher education perspective. Susan had also spent 10 years with the Mississippi State Extension Service as the Distance Education Coordinator. Although she had been in administration in the private sector, this was the beginning of her academic career in distance and online education, which now spans over 20 years.

Ray Schroeder is a nationally respected leader in higher education online learning. He is the Professor Emeritus of Communication at the University of Illinois Springfield (UIS) and a Senior Fellow at UPCEA, the Online and Professional Education Association. With a career as faculty and administrator in higher education spanning more than five decades, Ray has been a trailblazer in the integration of Online Learning. He has received numerous awards, including in 2023, an Honorary Doctorate of Humane Letters and the inaugural UPCEA Leadership Award for the Advancement of Digital Learning. His work has made a significant contribution to the field of online learning in education, inspiring discussions on how distance education can revolutionize teaching and learning and improve lives through enhanced access to information and insight. Ray Schroeder's expertise and influence continue to shape the future of education, particularly in the context of emerging technologies.

Kevin N. Shriner, Ed.D., is the inaugural Assistant Vice Chancellor of Digital and Online Learning at the University of Nebraska-Lincoln. Kevin's role at UNL is to provide an overall strategy for online degree and nondegree programs. As a first-generation college student and Pell grant recipient, he is deeply committed to the opportunity of a college credential to a diverse population regardless of socioeconomic status. His passion stems from over 30 years of strategy development, consulting, thought leadership, commercial growth, and team leadership experience within higher education and education companies. In 2004, Kevin became involved in online learning and has continued to make an impact in this area. He has assisted over 800 institutions in applying enrollment strategies, marketing insights, and market data on developing, launching, and strategically planning academic programs to meet the educational requirements of students and provide pathways to workforce outcomes.

Kim L. Siegenthaler, Ph.D., is the Associate Vice Chancellor for Academic Innovation at the City University of New York, where she leads strategic initiatives for transformative pedagogy, academic technology, and online education. Before CUNY, Dr. Siegenthaler served as the inaugural associate provost for Online Strategies at Georgia State University, responsible for developing and implementing the university's online education enterprise, and as the director of Mizzou Online, responsible for leading the University of Missouri toward a strategic vision for distance education. She has held faculty and/or administrator positions at Baptist Theological Seminary at Richmond, Appalachian State University, and Texas State University. Dr. Siegenthaler earned degrees from the University of New Mexico, the University of Oklahoma, Baptist Theological Seminary at Richmond, and Baylor University. She serves as the 2024–2025 UPCEA Board President.

Bethany Simunich, Ph.D., has held faculty roles for both in-person and online teaching, as well as educational technology, instructional design, and faculty development for online learning over the past 20+ years. As an online learning administrator, she has created and managed instructional design processes and teams; led faculty development for online teaching; and served in leadership and consulting roles for institutional, state, and national efforts for online quality assurance and online learning administration. Dr. Simunich is also co-Director of the CHLOE Project (Changing Landscape of Online Education), which reports the unique perspective of senior leaders in online learning from U.S. higher education institutions, and co-author of High Impact Design for Online Courses (HIDOC), which presents an instructional design model purpose-built for the unique considerations of online learning modalities.

Christopher P. Steele, Ph.D., is Vice Provost for Professional and Extended Studies at the University of Maryland Baltimore County, where he leads high-impact workforce development and community-engaged programs in the Division of Professional Studies and the Shriver Center. He and his colleagues place partnership and stewardship as the cornerstones of their work to enhance economic prosperity, social mobility, and social justice.

For nearly 25 years, he has collaborated with virtually every academic and administrative unit at UMBC to develop innovative approaches to reaching new student audiences through new and / or enhanced programs. Steele has been an instrumental leader in: the development of UMBC's institutional presence at the Universities at Shady Grove; the development of more than a dozen in-person and online applied master's programs; and the founding and development of UMBC's Institute of Extended Learning (IXL).

Josh Steele, Ph.D., serves as Associate Vice Dean of Digital Learning at the University of Tennessee, Knoxville, joining the university in 2021 when it created its inaugural COLO position. He has over 15 years of higher education experience, starting as an academic adviser, which inspired his drive to make higher education more accessible and inclusive for post-traditional students. He is particularly passionate about the role that public land-grant universities must play in developing online pathways to truly achieve their land-grant mission in the 21st century. He holds a B.S. in Psychology, an M.A. in History, and a Ph.D. in Geography, all from the University of Arizona.

Jenn Stringer, M.L.I.S., is the Vice President and Chief Digital Officer at the J. Paul Getty Trust, where she leads strategic digital initiatives across the Trust. Her oversight includes digital collections, cultural heritage data, and the Getty Library archives. With a rich background in IT and libraries, Jenn has served at Stanford University and New York University, and she was the Associate Vice Chancellor for IT and CIO at UC Berkeley. A leader, technologist, and librarian passionate about technology and access to information as strategic enablers to support public institutions, she believes technology can and should be a force for good in the world. Jenn holds degrees from UC Santa Cruz and San Jose State University. Her leadership extends to being a Frye Institute Fellow, a former EDUCAUSE faculty member, an EDUCAUSE Review editor, and a current member of the CNI Steering Committee.

Lisa L. Templeton serves as the Vice Provost of Oregon State University's Division of Educational Ventures. In this role she strategically leads a dynamic team focused on growing OSU's national and international work as an innovator in the delivery of education. Lisa and the division work in partnership with colleges across campus to offer in-demand academic programs and alternative credentials. Under Lisa's leadership since 2008,

Oregon State Ecampus, a part of the Division of Educational Ventures, has positioned OSU as a recognized national leader in the field of online education. OSU ECampus offers over 1,750 courses and more than 100 degree and certificate programs to over 15,000 learners in all 50 states and 60 countries. Lisa is active nationally in the field of online and continuing education, workforce development, regularly presents at conferences, and has served in numerous national leadership roles, most recently as President of UPCEA.

Sasha Thackaberry-Voinovich, Ph.D., serves as the President of SkillsWave, having led Wave and D2L for Business at D2L. Previous roles include: Vice President for Student and Partner Services at Pearson, Vice President for Online and Continuing Education at Louisiana State University, AVP for Academic Technology, Course Production, and New Learning Models at Southern New Hampshire University, and Director for eLearning Technologies at Cuyahoga Community College. She has consulted for Fortune 500 companies, colleges, and K-12 districts. She serves on the Quality Matters Board, and former committee involvement includes CHLOE, WCET, and COLOs for UPCEA. Sasha authored a book released by Routledge in February of 2025 entitled "How to Grow Enrollment in Online Higher Education: Strategies for Marketing and Recruitment." She has published articles in Inside Higher Ed, EDUCAUSE Review, Distance Learning, e-Literate, WCET, evoLLLution, and more. Sasha holds a Ph.D. in higher education administration, an MAT, and a BFA.

Julie J. Thalman, Ed.D., is the Vice Provost for the University of Cincinnati, where she oversees UC's online programs, focusing on degree development and strategic higher education initiatives. She leads a team in enrollment and retention services, marketing, and instructional design, collaborating with deans and senior leaders to create in-demand online programs. Previously, Thalman was Assistant Provost for Online and Continuing Professional Education at West Virginia University, where she launched numerous online support programs over 16 years. She is a member of UPCEA's leadership team for the Council for Chief Online Learning Officers and served as the Chair for the Mid-Atlantic region. Thalman holds a bachelor's degree in psychology and a master's in integrated marketing communications from West Virginia University, and an M.B.A. with a project management emphasis from Boise State University. She earned an Ed.D. in applied learning sciences from the University of Miami.

Kelvin Thompson, Ed.D., works to make online and blended learning even better a little bit every day while serving at the University of Louisville as Vice Provost for Online Strategy and Teaching Innovation. Kelvin writes, speaks, and consults within the U.S. higher education community. During his 24+ years at UCF, he created a number of resources for use by the broader online community (e.g., the Teaching Online Pedagogical Repository; the Faculty Seminars in Online Teaching; and the BlendKit Course). He also co-hosts the popular "TOPcast: The Teaching Online Podcast" and is co-editor of the SAGE Handbook of Online Higher Education. Dr. Thompson has held leadership roles within the work of EDUCAUSE, the Online Learning Consortium, and WCET. In 2020, Kelvin was selected as a Fellow of the Online Learning Consortium.

Julie Uranis, Ph.D., serves as the Sr. Vice President for Online and Strategic Initiatives at UPCEA. In this capacity she is the Managing Director of the National Council for Online Education and leads the planning efforts for the Summit for Online Leadership, the Council of Chief Online Learning Officers, and the Council for Credential Innovation. Prior to joining UPCEA she led the distance learning and continuing and professional development teams at Western Kentucky University as the Director of Distance Learning and Innovation. She began her career at Eastern Michigan University (EMU), where she held both teaching and administrative positions. Uranis has a Ph.D. in Educational Leadership, a Master of Science in Technology Studies, and a Graduate Certificate in Community College Leadership from EMU. She completed a Bachelor of Arts degree in History from the University of Michigan-Dearborn.

Karen Vignare, Ph.D., is a strategic innovator leveraging emerging technologies to improve access, success, and flexibility within higher education. As Vice President of Digital Transformation for Student Success and Executive Director for the Personalized Learning Consortium (PLC) at the Association of Public and Land-Grant Universities, Karen manages a U.S. network of public research universities committed to improving student success focused on enhancing teaching and learning. The PLC is committed to the effective use of technology to scale improved learning. She also oversees several million-dollar adaptive courseware grants providing leadership and support to multiple public four-year universities. Karen previously served as a Vice Provost at the University of Maryland University College, the largest online public open-access institution, where she led innovations in adaptive learning, OER, student success and analytics. She has published extensively on online learning, analytics, and open educational resources.

Melissa Vito, Ed.D., has over 35 years of experience in public higher education. As Vice Provost for Academic Innovation at the University of Texas San Antonio (UTSA), Melissa has transformed teaching and learning at UTSA, grown an infrastructure for fully online programs and created dynamic learning environments that prepare students to thrive in a world, where digital literacy and fluency are required. Under her leadership, UTSA Online, a fully online university experience, climbed to the top 20% of all online U.S. News and World Report's Best Online Programs list in 2024. Melissa was instrumental in uniting UTSA and Adobe Creative Campus and creating a research project to measure the impact of curricular use of Adobe tools on student learning. At the University of Arizona, she earned a bachelor's degree in Journalism and English and a master's degree in Higher Education and Counseling. She has a Doctorate in Educational Leadership from Northern Arizona University.

Robert W. Wagner, Ph.D., began serving as Idaho State University's 14th President in January 2024. Before coming to ISU, he was the Executive Vice President and Chief Operating Officer at Utah State University (USU). He also previously served as the Vice President for Academic and Instructional Services, a unique organizational blend of student, faculty, operational, innovation, and academic programming responsibilities. While in various leadership capacities in the Provost Office and President's Office at USU he served as USU's chief online learning officer.

Craig Wilson, J.D., Ph.D., is Vice Provost for Outreach, Distance, and Continuing Education, and Professor of Practice at the University of Arizona. He strives to broaden access to quality education programs for learners around the world. Dr. Wilson led education enterprises that spanned multiple campuses and online. His background in online education started in the 1990s, and he has been actively involved in each growth phase. He has served in multiple capacities including as an instructional designer, faculty, and executive administrator in university and K-12 settings. His current research covers AI and the metaverse in relation to higher education resulting in his Metaversity Framework (#metaversityframework), and his development of the Offline Campus to bring online learning to students without internet access.

Author Biographies

Jocelyn Widmer, Ph.D., serves as the Dean for Weapons Learning Transformation at Los Alamos National Laboratory, USA. She has worked in digital and online education for more than 15 years in various faculty and leadership roles within academic colleges and as the Chief Online Learning Officer of Texas A&M University. Prior to her role at TAMU, Widmer held joint faculty appointments in the Colleges of Architecture and Public Health at both the University of Florida and Virginia Tech where she developed, administered, and taught in online and face-to-face undergraduate and graduate programs, including leading the first and only professionally accredited online master's of urban and regional planning (University of Florida) through the accreditation process.

Widmer has been invited to serve on several national boards, including Zoom's Higher Education Advisory Board, UPCEA's Council for Chief Online Learning Officers, and Inside Higher Ed's Student Success Advisory Board. She has consulted for the National Academies of Sciences, Engineering, and Medicine; UNICEF, USAID, and various R1 universities on digital and online education. With global field experience across 18 countries, Widmer is also recognized for her teaching and research that integrate technology to build digital literacy capacity in low-resource communities around the world.

Widmer holds a Ph.D. in Urban and Regional Planning (University of Florida), a Master's in Public Health (University of Florida) and Landscape Architecture (Texas A&M University), and a Bachelor of Arts in English and Art History (Southwestern University).

Thomas B. Cavanagh, Ph.D., is Vice Provost for Digital Learning at the University of Central Florida, USA. In this role, he oversees the distance learning strategy, policies, and practices of one of the nation's largest universities. Prior to UCF, he led online course design and production for Embry-Riddle Aeronautical University and had a long career in corporate e-learning and film/television. He has been recognized with a number of leading industry awards, including the Richard Jonsen Award (WCET's highest career recognition), USDLA's Leadership Award, and the 1EdTech Community Leadership Award. He has also been named a Fellow of the Online Learning Consortium.

His experience has earned him positions on a number of state and national online learning boards including as Chair of the EDUCAUSE Learning Initiative advisory board, Secretary of the 1EdTech Board of Directors, service on the WCET Steering Committee, service on the EDUCAUSE Leading Academic Transformation advisory board, twice serving as a coach for the EDUCAUSE Breakthrough Models Academy, Chair of UPCEA's Council of Chief Online Learning Officers, and Chair of the Florida Distance Learning Consortium's Distance Learning and Student Services council, among others. He has presented both domestically and internationally on online and blended learning and is a frequent presenter at industry conferences. He has been interviewed as an online learning expert by numerous print and broadcast outlets. He has keynoted numerous events and often consults for higher education institutions regarding online strategy.

Cavanagh holds a Ph.D. in Texts & Technology (University of Central Florida), an MBA in Technology Management (University of Phoenix), and a Bachelor of Science in Communications (University of Miami). He is also the co-host of a popular podcast on online learning, TOPcast: The Teaching Online Podcast, and is an award-winning author of several mystery novels.

Index

Pages in **bold** refer to tables.

Made in United States
Troutdale, OR
07/27/2025